ROUTLEDGE LIBRARY EDITIONS:
ORGANIZATIONS: THEORY & BEHAVIOUR

MANAGEMENT, ORGANISATION AND EMPLOYMENT STRATEGY

MANAGEMENT, ORGANISATION AND EMPLOYMENT STRATEGY
New directions in theory and practice

TONY J. WATSON

Volume 30

Routledge
Taylor & Francis Group

LONDON AND NEW YORK

First published in 1986

This edition first published in 2013
by Routledge
2 Park Square, Milton Park, Abingdon, Oxfordshire OX14 4RN

Simultaneously published in the USA and Canada
by Routledge
711 Third Avenue, New York, NY 10017

First issued in paperback 2015

Routledge is an imprint of the Taylor & Francis Group, an informa business

British Library Cataloguing in Publication Data
A catalogue record for this book is available from the British Library

ISBN: 978-0-415-65793-8 (Set)
ISBN 13: 978-1-138-98030-3 (pbk)
ISBN 13: 978-0-415-82505-4 (hbk) (Volume 30)

Publisher's Note
The publisher has gone to great lengths to ensure the quality of this reprint but points out that some imperfections in the original copies may be apparent.

Disclaimer
The publisher has made every effort to trace copyright holders and would welcome correspondence from those they have been unable to trace.

Management, organisation and employment strategy

New directions in theory and practice

Tony J. Watson

ROUTLEDGE & KEGAN PAUL
London and New York

First published in 1986
by Routledge & Kegan Paul plc

11 New Fetter Lane, London EC4P 4EE

Published in the USA by
Routledge & Kegan Paul Inc.
in association with Methuen Inc.
29 West 35th Street, New York, NY 10001

Set in 10/12 Monophoto Plantin
and printed in Great Britain
by Butler & Tanner Ltd, Frome and London

Library of Congress Cataloging in Publication Data
Watson, Tony J.
    Management, organisation, and employment strategy.

    Bibliography: p.
    Includes index.
    1. Management.   2. Personnel management.   I. Title.
HD31.W355 1986   658.3   85-25643

British Library CIP data also available
ISBN 0-7102-0638-0
ISBN 0-7102-0863-4 (pbk.)

Contents

Figures

Introduction

The main purpose of this book is to provide those interested in management, organisation and business studies with a broad overview of thinking in the behavioural and employment aspects of the managing of work organisations.

It pulls together and relates to questions of practice those various ideas normally parcelled up in separate packages like management studies, organisation theory, personnel management, motivation theory, organisational behaviour, industrial relations and 'work and society'. This conventional division of effort and material is seen more as a matter of educational convenience and the self-interested desire of practitioners and theorists alike to carve out specialist domains than it is one of caring about how we can assist those who have to cope in practice with organising and managing productive work.

To achieve the required degree of integration of thinking across these areas, a number of devices are used. The first of these is the presenting of a clearer conception of *what managerial work is* than those which have previously been offered. Managing is seen as synonymous with organising and it is argued that ideas on motivation, leadership, job design and the rest, have to be closely related to ideas about organisational structures, cultures and strategies if they are going to help towards an understanding of how organisational and managerial effectiveness can be achieved in practice.

The development of a clear concept of *organisational and managerial effectiveness* itself provides a second integrative device. Recent theoretical developments have provided a much more useful concept of the terms in which the performance of any kind of organisation - and its managers - can be evaluated than has existed before. And this leads on to a third device: an attempt to consider how the newer directions in theory appear to be parallel-ing *new directions in organisational practice*. A much more explicit concern with what constitutes and leads to organisational effec-tiveness has been a significant feature of theoretical and practical thinking alike. In the final chapter I try to show that emerging concepts and research can throw a lot of light on important issues like those of how organisations and their workforces will be struc-tured in the future, how people will be employed and how the new technologies will be implemented and used.

A fourth device is the use of a simple model of *waves* of thought which is applied to both the more structural traditions of organ-isation theory and the more 'behavioural' emphasis. A trend is noted, in both of these areas, away from the early view of organ-isations as machines or of employees as living robots towards a view of the organisation as a set of social, economic, political and cultural processes and of the employee as involved in mental and social processes which underlie their expectations and behaviour. In the structural area, however, there was an intervening wave in which organisations were looked at as adaptive systems or organ-isms and, on the behavioural side, there was a second wave in which employee attitudes and behaviour were considered in terms of certain universal (human) needs. The overall direction has been from mechanical to *processual ways of seeing organisations and or-ganisational behaviour*, with emphases on organisational systems and human needs coming in between.

The importance of the waves analogy is that it is used as an alternative to what I see as a wretched and all-too-common practice in the teaching and writing about organisation and man-agement theory. This is the presenting of ideas as belonging to successive 'schools', each of which 'comes along' to discredit or replace what went before. Whilst the 'schools of thought' device has some value as a provider of useful headings and whilst we must recognise that newer ideas do attempt to replace existing ones, it is very important to see that the older ideas in manage-ment and organisational thought still have a major impact on actual practices. And they still contain valuable insights which contribute to newer understandings. Hence the use of the waves analogy. New ideas, like new waves, do arrive and appear to cover up those which came before them. In reality, however, they merge with what came before as well as clashing with them. And their impact on the shore is one which comes from this combined clashing and intermingling.

Old and new ideas, then, are all grist to the mill. We revisit – and reinterpret – old favourites like the Hawthorne experiments and that astonishingly popular idea of a 'hierarchy of needs'. We even go back to Adam Smith and we reconsider Max Weber's notion of the 'ideal type' of bureaucracy. But we also give full weight to the recently highly influential thinking about organisational cultures and we attend to the extensive discussion which has taken place about trends in the management of the 'labour process' in capitalist organisations. Considerable emphasis is put on the newer views of managerial work which recognise that it is as much about manipulating symbols, making meanings and engaging in politics as it is about setting up and maintaining a system. The idea that managerial work involves art, politicking and even magic is shown to be much more than simply a joke!

The fifth integrative device which is used is the centrally important concept of *employment strategy*. Although both theorists and practitioners are increasingly using this concept, it is much more fully developed here than is usually the case. It is put forward as a notion which can bring together, for theorists and practitioners alike, all of the structural, behavioural and employment 'bits and pieces' which are often thought about as separate matters. An organisation's employment strategy – which may be more or less consciously planned or explicitly stated – is seen as the overall direction which an organisation takes in how it recruits, motivates, rewards, and negotiates with employees and organises them into jobs, groups, departments and divisions. It equally involves matters of technique, structure and procedure as it does issues of culture and managerial philosophy. Moreover, it valuably relates employment and behavioural issues in the organisation to questions of market, technology, finance and so on. The employment strategy – alongside marketing, technological and financial strategies – is just one aspect of the overall direction, or strategy, being followed by the organisation as a whole in its struggle to cope with a changing and often threatening environment.

The final device which is used to achieve some integration in how we can understand organisational and managerial behaviour is a conception of the organisational social sciences themselves and how they relate to practice. The book both begins and closes with a view of social or 'behavioural' science which some will see as cheeky, others will see as iconoclastic and yet others might condemn as naive and simplistic. But I hope that it is a view which many will welcome as a healthy piece of demystification. It is a view which suggests that there is nothing terribly special about the social science perspective and that behavioural scientists themselves often fall badly short in terms of their own ideals of scientific endeavour.

In the end, it is suggested, both good theory and good practice come down to the application of *critical commonsense* mixed with a healthy dose of *constructive scepticism* about existing ideas and practices. This does not mean, however, that what follows is going to make simple all the complexities, ambiguities and contradictions which are involved both in the academic materials being considered and the organisational world which they attempt to understand. Nobody expects to find the study of economics, of medicine, of computing or of engineering simple. We should expect even less to find the study of human behaviour and the management of complex organisations a simple matter. All we can do is to work at developing concepts, frameworks and knowledge which can make all this complexity just a little bit more manageable. I devote what follows to this end.

Chapter 1

Theory, practice and commonsense

Work for people in all ages and in all societies has been much more than a matter of simply providing the material requirements of life. It has also played a major part in giving meaning to people's lives and has helped them achieve a sense of identity. This means that problems of work and work organisation are ones which go to the heart of the problems of 'being human'. Upon the choices we make about organising work will depend whether we struggle or prosper, whether we are hungry or well-fed or even whether we live or die. But, in addition to this, these work arrangements will also contribute to our feelings of being important or unimportant, of being valued or of being despised, and of being fulfilled or unfulfilled.

Problems such as these arise for people generally, regardless of their culture or time in history. But there are certain social and historical situations in which we can expect all of these problems to become particularly significant. This is likely, for example, when we have a social order like that of today in which there is a very considerable division of labour: one in which the prevailing technology and culture lead to there being a wide variety of occupations, jobs, professions and responsibilities. With a large degree of specialisation we can expect there to be considerable problems of control and coordination. And the difficulties of satisfying the large number of interests and expectations which arise are no less considerable.

It is hard to imagine a period of human history when the problems of organising work have been more complex than they are in the late twentieth century in those economies which utilise complicated and ever-changing technologies within large and complex corporations. The degree of change made likely by

developments in electronic and electronically controlled technologies is, in itself, enormous. But if these changes are put alongside
the kind of economic, social and personal expectations which the
citizens of modern societies have come to hold, the challenge can
seem to become almost overwhelming. How can we find ways of
organising work tasks which help meet the increasingly tough
competitive challenges which the international economy is imposing and which at the same time ensure that both meaningful
productive activity and material welfare are distributed in ways
which are perceived to be fair and just? Emerging technologies
have the potential not only to transform workplaces but to alter
radically the whole pattern of society.

So complex are the problems of managing work in this period
in such a way that we meet both the material wants of people
and their need for meaning that we cannot rely totally on an
unsystematic muddling-through philosophy. The practice of
organising and managing work needs some kind of underlying
principles, some kind of intellectual framework, some kind of
theory. And this theory needs to be able to relate organisational
activity to the wider pattern of society and to people's lives as a
whole.

The relationship between theory and practice in the area of
work organisation has always been a difficult one. But, to many
people, it was believed to be a matter of time before the social or
behavioural sciences reached a degree of maturity whereby they
would be accepted as offering a clear and objective knowledge-
base for managerial practice in this area. Once the researchers got
the theory right and the practitioners learned how to apply these
ideas, then the management of work would become a much more
rational and effective practice. Although there is sense in this
approach, it is in large part mistaken. A new direction has to be
followed if a more successful relationship between theory and
practice is to be achieved.

What is needed is a recognition that there will never be a full
and generally acceptable body of organisational or managerial
theory. Instead, there will continue to be a variety of perspectives
and approaches which often compete if not actually conflict with
each other. These approaches will vary in the values which inspire
them, the facets of work behaviour upon which they focus and
the level at which they are directed. And the relevance of this

multiplicity of theoretical materials to practice will be dependent
on the ability of the practitioners to understand the range of ideas
and on their ability to select and apply insights and suggestions
from them which are appropriate to the particular practical problems which they face at a particular time.

The main purpose of this book is to help practitioners – or
potential practitioners – to make sense of the bewildering variety
of theoretical and research ideas which are available and which
may inform practice. Although it is the case that some theories or
models are more useful than others, the view that is taken here is
that most of them have something to offer by way of insight. To
see things clearly in a three-dimensional world, it often helps to
light them first from one angle and then from another. This is
very much the case in the social sciences and how they throw
light on the social world. If we change the metaphor, we might
say that in the same way that a comprehensive atlas will use one
type of map to bring out one aspect of the geography of a country
and a different map or projection to bring out another aspect, so
we can use one theoretical approach to bring out, say, the human
tendency to cooperate and another to bring out the ever-present
likelihood of conflict. Having said this, however, let us recognise
that the development of an approach which would do justice to
both aspects of life is still something worth working towards. But
it is most successfully worked towards, I would argue, if we work
through existing attempts to model and explain, learning from all
of these as we go along. For this reason, this book will pay attention – if often rather critical attention – to older as well as newer
ideas.

It is no simple matter to come to terms with the bewildering
array of ideas which exist. Therefore I am concerned that this
book should, as one of its prime purposes, provide the reader
with what will prove to be a usable map of the jungle of both
conventional and newer thinking. Yet, at the same time, I intend
to point out some general directions which are currently being
taken in the thinking of theorists and practitioners alike. And,
among these, there are certain lines along which I hope to nudge
my readers. The synthesis which will eventually be attempted
will itself be partial in the emphasis it will give to particular issues
which are taken to be of key contemporary relevance. Nevertheless, this partiality, it is hoped, will be a less problematic one than

some of the hidden partialities to be found in certain of the existing approaches.

An important new direction is that of a currently growing willingness among practitioners and theorists alike to take more seriously questions about what makes work organisations *effective*. The economic pressures towards better levels of performance on the part of business organisations coping with growing international competition have had a corresponding effect on the non-business organisations which have to live in the same economic environment. The felt need to be seen to organise more effectively in the practical world has been reflected in the theorists' increased attention to the idea of effectiveness. And this has meant trying to develop more sophisticated understandings of just what 'effectiveness' might mean.

It is increasingly being recognised that work organisations are not, and never can be, like big machines or meticulously planned computer systems set up to meet clear-cut and uncontestable 'goals'. It is being more clearly recognised that, to make an organisation effective, it is necessary to see the organisation as a combination of various social, political and economic *processes*. Within organisations, people not only cooperate, they also compete and conflict, define and redefine the meaning of what they are doing, negotiate and renegotiate the nature and the outcomes of their activities. Effectiveness is ultimately a matter of successfully coming to terms with the range of interests, both internal and external to the organisation, to which the leaders of the organisation must look if their organisation is to continue to exist. Management is not a matter of setting up the right system and then simply persuading people to operate it. Management is about dealing with differences, with ambiguities, with politics as well as with money, technology and organisational structures.

The qualitative dimension of organisational functioning is coming increasingly to the fore in our understanding of the human aspects of work management. For an organisation to operate to any extent as a coordinated whole it is being more generally accepted that issues in the 'human' sphere cannot be totally delegated to or dumped upon technical specialists in personnel management or employee relations departments. Specialists are indeed seen as necessary, but for their expertise to have a significant effect it has to infuse the whole of the management. Only then can a coherent organisational culture develop in which people feel it worthwhile to contribute at more than a grudging level to overall organisational purposes or policies. But that culture cannot exist totally separately from the history, culture, priorities and, indeed, politics of the society in which it is located. This too is an issue being given greater attention by practitioners and theorists alike and it is one which will be stressed at various points in this book.

The new directions being suggested here are ones which will become clearer as our review of older and newer ideas proceeds. The present concern, however, is to develop more fully a general approach to the relevance of social or 'behavioural' science thinking to organisational practice. To this end I shall attempt in the rest of this chapter to argue four things. First, I shall suggest that there is far less of a difference between the activities of the social scientist and those of the organisational practitioner than is often supposed or claimed. At their best, both activities involve the application of *critical commonsense*. Second, I shall argue that behavioural science ideas need to be treated with *scepticism*, albeit in an informed and constructive spirit. Third, I shall examine the extent to which practitioners and theorists tend to live in separate worlds and I shall argue that there is a problem here in our culture which needs urgent attention. And, fourth, I shall suggest some of the basic ways in which we need to change the manner in which we look at work organisations.

Critical commonsense

To help sell their wares and to give themselves extra credibility, social or behavioural scientists often distinguish between their own allegedly scientific thinking and the type of 'commonsense' explanations used by non-specialists. To some extent, they have a point here. Very frequently people offer woefully simplistic generalisations like 'people only go to work for the money'. And typically added to this comes the comment, 'it's commonsense isn't it?'. This is indeed a type of commonsense thinking. We might call it Commonsense I. It is a commonsense based on easy unthought-out, taken-for-granted assumptions. We all make these kind of assumptions about the way the world is. It makes life simpler. But these assumptions are often dangerous guides to action on matters of any importance. Here we need to turn to the other version of what is called commonsense.

Commonsense II or *critical commonsense* is that kind of thinking which involves being basically logical or rational about things in the way which is common to all human beings when they are alertly and critically putting their mind to whatever matter is in hand. This is the kind of commonsense which we can more reliably use as a guide to action. It is something we can indeed celebrate. And it is an activity of the same order as that in which the scientist engages. Science, in this view, is simply a formalised version of critical commonsense. Scientific thinking – in principle if not always in practice – is the more formal, systematic and painstakingly analytical application of Commonsense II.

Commonsense II analysis inevitably starts from a consideration of the most obvious or likely explanation of what is going on. But it then goes on to ask whether things are really as they at first seem. Possible alternative explanations are considered and attention is paid to available evidence in judging these rival

Commonsense I	*Commonsense II*
Uses unthought-out, taken-for-granted, easy, everyday assumptions	Uses the basic logic and rationality to be found in human beings whenever they alertly and critically put their minds to an issue
e.g.	e.g.
'Obviously, if you pay workers in proportion to their output they will produce more than if they get the same wage whatever they turn out. They will clearly work better with an incentive payment system.'	'Paying workers in proportion to their output may well be more productive than paying them a basic rate. On the other hand, if you think about it, the workers may well prefer the comfort of a steady work rate and the security of a steady wage and may resent the pressures of a bonus system. We have to examine the range of factors applying in a specific situation when choosing a payment system.'

Fig. 1.1 Two kinds of commonsense thinking

explanations. Extra evidence may be sought to help with this. And the thinker will carefully consider whether they are perhaps being pushed down the line of thinking which they are following by any prejudice or preference which may colour their view.

Commonsense II thinking in the area of human behaviour will also tend to operate with a relatively complex view of the nature of human motivation and behaviour. It would not assume, for example, that there is a direct and obvious connection between people's attitudes and their behaviour. We find cases of people whose talk reveals strong racial prejudices, for instance, but who, when they find themselves working with people of a race which they appear to deprecate, act in a perfectly friendly and normal way. Commonsense I thinking might lead to quite different work allocation practices in an ethnically mixed organisation, for example, than would this more subtle Commonsense II form of thinking, regardless of the important ethical issues which arise in this area.

Another facet of the greater subtlety of Commonsense II in the behavioural sphere is that it recognises that the outcomes of actions are not always the ones we might most obviously expect. An example of this would be in the area of applying budgetary controls within a work organisation. The intended and, at first sight, expected outcome of allocating budgets to departments is to keep expenditure below the level which it might otherwise be. Yet the application of critical commonsense thinking here would warn us of other, perhaps contrary, effects. Reference to evidence which we might have – or could obtain – about how people use budgets in practice and some thought about how human beings generally tend to react to controls applied to them would point out what the social scientist would call an 'unintended consequence' of budgets. This is the effect whereby people spend *more* than they otherwise would in order to use up all of their budget for the current period. The point of this is to avoid the departmental budget's being lowered in the next period, with the consequent reducing of the department's freedom of manoeuvre.

A manager who made budgetary or budgeting policy decisions on the basis of Commonsense II thinking would not necessarily avoid the use of budgets because of an awareness of their possible unintended consequences. But the actual decisions made are likely to be of a higher quality as a result, we might say, of their being much better *informed*. And the greater ability of this particular manager could be the result of their being personally adept at critical commonsense thinking in the area of human behaviour. Alternatively, it could be the result of that individual's having studied the social sciences and learned how to think and analyse in this more sophisticated mode.

We can find a simple but useful illustration of the difference between Commonsense I and Commonsense II thinking in the area of industrial relations. People frequently see reports of industrial disputes in which it is clear that there is a 'militant' leadership urging-on the workforce to fight the employer. The most obvious general explanation of the behaviour occurring here would be one which gave strong causal emphasis to the role of the strike leadership. The easy kind of everyday commonsense thinking would see it as fairly obvious that worker militance followed from the militance of their shop stewards or union officials. This kind of 'theory' of strike behaviour is frequently to be found among the public, among journalists and among public policy-makers as well as among some managers. However, a little more critical thought and an application of some cold logic would suggest the possibility that the employees were perhaps sorely aggrieved *first* and that the militance of their leaders was a reaction to this. It could well be that the officials involved felt bound to reflect the feelings of their members and to direct constructively the already existing militance of the membership.

Commonsense II thinking in this case would go on to examine this logical possibility. Anti or pro-trade union sentiments would be taken into account as influencing one's thinking. Attention would be paid to existing knowledge and research findings on industrial disputes and on, say, shop steward behaviour. And consideration would be given to whether or not one believes that employed people readily enter disputes which may lose them money, at least in the short term, just because certain officials tell them they should. The thinkers might well ask themselves whether they personally would go on strike unless they felt a very strong sense of grievance in the first place.

We cannot say what the outcome of this application of critical commonsense might be in any particular case. Critical commonsense always attempts to combine general principles with attention to the particularities of the case being considered. But what we can expect is a more balanced and intelligent understanding of this case by the person applying the Commonsense II style of thinking. And this means that if they are involved in any practical way in the matter then they are more likely to act wisely than if they depended on the simpler form of analysis of Commonsense I.

The two types of commonsense thinking which we have considered and which are summarised in Fig. 1.2 are clearly related to the difference between everyday thinking and social scientific thinking. But too much must not be made of this. Although I would argue that a social science training should enhance the analytical powers of any individual, we should nevertheless

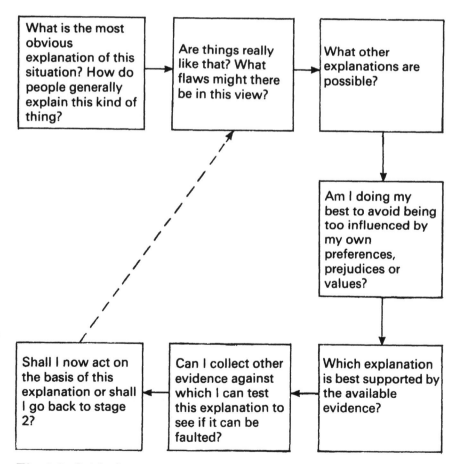

Fig. 1.2 Critical commonsense: seven stages of problem analysis

recognise that a critical commonsense style of thinking is by no means the sole prerogative of the behavioural scientist – even in the sphere of social behaviour. And, by the same token, social scientists often fall far short of the ideals of Commonsense II thinking. I believe this to be especially so in those areas where behavioural scientists have attempted to influence managerial behaviour in their publications and consultancies. What is therefore required is an attitude of constructive scepticism on the part of the student of organisational social or behavioural science.

Constructive scepticism

Although the social scientist might be expected to be professionally committed to some kind of objectivity, we nevertheless have to recognise that they too are influenced by personal preferences and values. Just like the lay person, they will be influenced by feelings about how they would like the world to be. This inevitably colours how they see the world around them. In addition to this, they are always likely to be influenced by a concern to impress. In this they are no different from any other 'professional' type of occupation. They will tend to be anxious to establish their expertise and to show that, in some important ways, they can see things that the lay person cannot. A degree of mystification is commonly to be expected: what could vulgarly be described as the 'bullshit factor'. This does not mean that we have to be cynical about behavioural science material. It does, however, suggest that we should always be sceptical; not in a negative or carping way but in a way which is guided by experience and whatever other information we have. Hence the principle of *informed constructive scepticism* – an accompanying principle to that of critical commonsense discussed above.

It may seem strange that I, as a teacher, writer and researcher in the social sciences, should be encouraging a sceptical approach to social science material. In part I do this because I believe such a stance itself to be an important element of what I see as a 'scientific style'. But there is more to it than that. I am much influenced by my own industrial experience. As a person trained in the social sciences, I found that much of the managerial thinking which I encountered seemed naive and even gullible. Yet I recognised that these practical men and women knew about things and understood aspects of working life about which the social scientists one met and read seemed correspondingly naive and, yes, gullible in their thinking. Practical experience undoubtedly has much to offer as does academic study and research. But the fact that these pursuits are all too often engaged in by different people in isolation from each other means that the strengths and weaknesses of each side rarely come to balance each other out. This state of affairs, which we will come back to later on, means that we need to stay alert and sceptical at all times.

The type of problem being considered here can be illustrated by reference to how people think about the relationship between productivity and work satisfaction. It is not uncommon to hear people working in the personnel management field say that it is commonsense to believe that good productivity comes from people 'giving of their best' which, in turn, will be dependent on their being happy and satisfied in what they do. Now, it is clear that this will often be the case. But how good a generalisation or 'theory' of work motivation can be derived from the point? As soon as we apply a little scepticism and some critical commonsense to the issue we begin to question the implicit theory being applied. Are there not, we would ask, cases where people have worked hard and effectively because they have had guns or whips flourished before them? Just because any civilised person would see this as 'a bad thing' does not mean that we can rule it out as something which can work. And we could go on to ask whether there are not cases in which people have slogged away productively at unsatisfying jobs to obtain the pay that results? And, to continue in this vein, we might ask whether an increase in job satisfaction might not make people more relaxed and hence lead to a fall in the amount they produce?

What is becoming obvious is that all sorts of things are possible in this area. In looking at just what the connections are between productivity and job satisfaction we soon find ourselves saying 'Ah well, it all depends ...'. What the systematic thinker needs to do is to theorise about the nature of and the connection between those factors on which it 'depends'. We begin to think then about the culture in which the workers are operating, the expectations which they bring to work, the technology being used and so on. This is the very kind of thing that we will be doing in later chapters when we come to consider available theories in this area. And when we do this we will soon find that behavioural scientists have been almost as ready as laypeople to make unwarranted connections between phenomena, to use simplistic notions of human nature, and the rest. But this work is still worthy of consideration, not least because critical examination of it helps sharpen up our own analytical powers.

A notorious example of social scientists lacking the kind of self-critical scepticism which we might expect from people committed to the idea of scientific procedure, is that of the influential Hawthorne Experiments carried out in the United States in the 1930s. These experiments, which will be discussed in detail later (pp. 98–100), together with the way they were reported and interpreted, persuaded many people that friendly and relaxed supervision in the factory causes higher productivity. It was true that there was an association between these two phenomena in the experimental situation. But commentators who have looked closely and sceptically at this work have suggested that the causal link was quite the opposite way round from what so many people had been led to infer. Productivity increases were not *caused* by the more relaxed managerial style. Instead, the management had begun to be more easy-going as a *consequence* of the productivity's having been increased. These increases had resulted from quite different pressures which had been applied by the managers.

Why was this not seen earlier? Again, we have to take into account the tendency we all have to see things in a way which supports what we would like to be the case. Behind the way these studies were analysed and reported to the world was a belief on the part of the social scientists that growing tendencies in industrial management at that time were ethically and practically unsound (see pp. 56–7). There was thus a pressure to use scientific work to 'do battle'. The Human Relationists had to undermine the so-called Scientific Managers!

This tendency to fall into that trap long recognised by philosophers whereby we confuse *is* and *ought* statements is just as prevalent in more recent behavioural science writings. Saul Gellerman (1974), in a popular book explaining the relevance and value of behavioural science in management, suggests that managers can choose between 'the rigorous, experimental or evidence-based studies of behaviour in work settings' which constitute behavioural science and the 'accumulated folklore, mythology and superstition that all too often passes for traditional managerial wisdom'. He suggests that behavioural scientists are helping to 'make productivity more of a triumphant personal experience and less of a humiliation or a bore'. This, he explains, is not being done out of charity but out of a hard practicality 'since triumphant men are ultimately more productive than defeated men'.

We are bound to ask, when we meet this kind of claim, whether a new mythology is not being created which may be as fragile as the old ones. Sceptical and critical thought leads us to wonder whether there is not a confusion between what the author thinks ought to be the case and what is possible in reality. We have to ask whether it is conceivable that scientific investigation, with all its limitations and its appropriately characteristic tentativeness, can possibly support such a massive and supremely optimistic generalisation.

The values underlying this humanistic kind of behavioural-science writing are laudable: the preference for forms of work in which people are fulfilled is good and kind. I share this preference and believe that it is a morally good thing to attempt to achieve a world in which this is possible. However, I believe that the kind of social scientific work which will help us achieve anything worthwhile in this direction must avoid naivety and any tinge of utopianism. If we want to organise work in such a way that people can enjoy doing it, we must be made aware of the costs and the limitations which are involved. Careful examination of social science evidence and attention to social scientific theories in this area suggest that, although there are many cases where a higher level of satisfaction may lead to better or cheaper output, there are other cases where this may not be the case. It is no good trying to bring about changes by only pointing to the evidence which suits our preferences. In doing this, the social scientist is ethically wrong and is also asking for eventual loss of credibility once he or she is rumbled. Further, people are being discouraged from considering alternative possibilities such as that suggested by Robert Dubin (1956): that we should concentrate on making our non-work lives more fulfilling and worthwhile. We might well want to consider accepting work roles which are highly efficient but unfulfilling and which we can get out of the way to enable us to get on with 'real living' away from the workplace.

It is not up to social scientists to tell us how we can best organise work, either from the point of view of human satisfactions or that of organisational productivity. But they should assist in opening up the possibilities. They should help inform the choices that are made by those with the responsibilities for decision-making. To this end they can provide us with useful evidence. But, far more importantly, they can provide us with frameworks for analysis – with systematic generalisations about how different phenomena in social behaviour connect with and affect each other. To put it another way, the main function of the social sciences is to provide us with useful *theories*. However, as soon as one begins to talk of theory, one comes up against that very popular view that theory is in some way the very antithesis of practice. Nothing could be more wrong.

Theorists and practitioners

Most human actions – including many of those which have become almost habitual – are informed by ideas of how one thing connects with another or how one event or action leads to another. These, in effect, are theories and, in this sense, poor practice is likely to follow from poor theory. Yet many people like to question the relevance of theory to practical matters even though to abjure theory in this way is to refuse to recognise that actions, if they are to be effective, often benefit enormously from having been thought out. The psychologist Kurt Lewin neatly made this point in his famous dictum that there is nothing so practical as a good theory.

The point of careful and systematic theorising is that it can inform practice by making clearer what actions might have what effects, so helping people achieve more readily desired effects and avoid undesired ones. But this is not likely to be widely recognised if too many of the theories which are available look more like uninformed speculation, mystifications or doctrines about the way the world should be rather than the way it is. Yet this is the way theory often appears to be.

Although much of the theory available may not be 'good'

theory in the sense being applied here, there are nevertheless other quite considerable blocks to our gaining recognition of the need to inform practice with theory. It is possible that there is, within our culture, a debilitating tendency to insist on an opposition between theory and practice. There are deeply held prejudices operating here and their continued existence would not bode well for our chances of dealing wisely with the major changes in work practices and organisation which are going to be needed in our changing societies and economies in the closing decades of the twentieth century. We cannot afford to base our actions entirely on poor or scarcely articulated theories about work and organisation. No more can we rely on the traditional managerial and political philosophy of simply muddling through and getting by.

The tendency to divorce theory and practice is particularly reinforced by the effects of certain deep-rooted features of British society and culture. Traditional status divisions and their influence on the occupational division of labour have played a major part here. The awarding of higher prestige to learned occupations or 'professions' than to industrial undertakings is in part a hangover from an era in which the elite of society was a leisured class. As patterns of status and prestige have changed, they have retained an element in which the more 'genteel' work of thinking, advising or professing is more highly honoured and desired than that involving making things or organising the provision of services. This leads to a division of labour in which those concerned with developing and disseminating ideas, knowledge and theories tend to do so in splendid isolation from those whose lives and efforts are often the subjects of these ideas and theories.

The quality and even intelligibility of the thinking which results from this division of effort and the associated status gulf is bound to be put in doubt. And the problems which arise can only be exacerbated by the resentments and bad feelings which are engendered by the status element in all this. It leads to the observable tendency of 'practical' men and women in industry to reject the theoretical. It leads to words like 'theoretical' or 'academic' becoming automatic insults. And it encourages practical people to celebrate their own supposed being in touch with reality by scorning as 'theorists' those who they see as afraid to 'dirty their hands' or 'get their feet wet'. This celebration of hard-headed atheoretical practicality partly reflects the abstraction, opaqueness and even silliness of much theory that is on offer. But it is also a defence mechanism which functions as a two-fingered salute to those who stay away from the coal-face yet who often claim to understand it better than those who work there.

Hard head and soft hearts

The difficulties which arise in the relationship between knowledge and action in the area of work organisation generally are compounded when we come to the employee relations or 'personnel' side of management. Personnel management has historically been associated with welfare and philanthropy. Its 'feminine' and tender-hearted ethos is partly derived from its historical associations with upper-class, educated female social improvers. But it is also reflected in the way it currently attracts a relatively high proportion of women recruits and is seen by many graduates as a more socially respectable area of industry and as one which provides an alternative career to that of social work (Pitfield and Palmer, 1981). This ethos of tender-heartedness and even social superiority presents appreciable problems to those concerned with building up personnel functions. It arouses suspicions in the minds of the hard-headed profit-oriented object-oriented masculine occupants of the key 'line' management and financial roles. And related to it are tendencies in some areas to replace philanthropy with profit-emphasis, women personnel officers with men personnel managers and human beings with 'human resources'.

Since there is often an association between personnel management and social-science thinking, difficulties are created for both by the general problems which exist with regard to the relationship between theory and practice. There is a basic need for a change of attitudes in both work and academic organisations. But it also requires a lot of effort on the part of the social scientists working in this area to develop usable frameworks, ideas and research findings. And one of the first things that has to be done here is to establish some more 'realistic' ways of looking at organisations than have often been adopted by theorists and practitioners alike.

People and systems

In the attempts which have been made to develop an understanding of how human organising activity works there have been two general types of approach. Each of these on its own is inadequate. The first concentrates on individuals and tries to understand or explain work behaviour in terms of human nature, needs, personality, leadership characteristics and so on. In simple terms, it is believed that to manage work activities effectively you need to know 'how people tick'. The contrasting approach emphasises instead the importance of 'setting up the right system'. Organising

Behavioural emphasis	*System emphasis*
Personality, needs and behaviour of individuals stressed	Organisational arrangements stressed
Focus on motivation, leadership and group dynamics	Focus on organisation design, technique selection, procedural arrangements
Practitioners concerned with 'how people tick'	Practitioners concerned with setting up the right system
Theorists lean towards psychology	Theorists lean towards sociology
Is weak because it places too little emphasis on situational factors and on structural constraints	Is weak because it is too little concerned with human individuality and independence and the unintended consequences of arrangements

Preferred alternative

Approaches which recognise that systems are made up of creative, questioning and choice-making individuals and that behaviour occurs within structures which help shape it.

Fig. 1.3 Two approaches to thinking about organising and managing

is to be understood in terms of the setting of goals, the passing of decisions up and down the reporting hierarchy, the monitoring and feeding back of results and so on. Structures rather than people are emphasised here.

In practice, people tend to veer between these two perspectives. My own research suggests that personnel specialists, for instance, tend towards the individualistic approach in their thinking. In spite of the fact that many of these people are educated in the social sciences – where there is usually a strong emphasis on structural factors – I reported a fondness for depending rather heavily on a sort of individualistic folk psychology rather than on assumptions which recognise the subtle interplay of structural and behavioural variables which social scientists discuss (Watson, 1977). Understanding 'how people tick' was indeed emphasised more than 'setting up the right organisation'. This can be explained in terms of the pressure which is typically put upon these people to be constantly 'fire-fighting' and thus be left with too little time to reflect on problems at a structural level. Nevertheless, one does still find personnel specialists who see the key to their effectiveness lying in the devising of the right personnel techniques, manpower planning systems, job evaluation schemes, pay structures and the rest.

A fundamental question to be faced is that of whether we can put together these two sides of the matter, as suggested in Fig. 1.3. In Chapters 3 and 4 the principle of separating behavioural and structural emphases will be used as a recognition of the fact that there have tended to be two traditions of study based on this dichotomy. But it will become clear, as the existing work is reviewed, that these two aspects are increasingly coming to be seen as the two sides of the same coin. You cannot deal with the one without dealing with the other. The new direction recognised by Chapter 5, whereby thought is increasingly being given to overall employment strategies reflects a growing recognition of this truth.

It has long been realised in the social sciences that organisational arrangements almost have a logic of their own. Once you have a number of people working together, what goes on is more than the outcome of the individuals' personalities, needs and motives added together. The organisation is more than a sum of its human parts, we might say. Consequently, organisation theorists, with the exception of those very firmly rooted in the tradition of psychology, have tended to lean rather heavily towards a 'system perspective'. This turns out to be a rather one-sided approach, not only in its playing down of the creative and assertive roles of individuals but in its tendency to encourage what might be called *an over-rationalised conception of organisation.*

It helps to make us comfortable in the potentially chaotic world of social relationships if we can assume that everybody is acting sensibly or reasonably: that they decide what they want, take the relevant circumstances into account, and act accordingly. As long as people act in this way, life is ordered because there is a degree of predictability about it. A preference for seeing things in this way has underpinned much of what I have been arguing for in this chapter so far about the value of sensibly linking theories and practice. But this can be overstressed. And where it has tended to be overstressed is where this emphasis on individual rationality has been carried over in organisational thinking into the explanation of and design of organisations – which have come to be seen as 'rational' themselves.

Pervading much organisational theory, administrative science, managerial economics and business studies texts is an image or myth of the organisation as a goal-seeking entity or *system* whose components can be carefully arranged to process various inputs into the kind of outputs required by the original goal. The organisational system is the means of achieving the organisational goal. The system, or rather the procedures which compose it, is rational because decisions about appropriate actions are based on the systematic or calculated relating of organisational consequences to organisational objectives. We cannot say that this is wrong, but we can argue that it is only half the truth. In this view there is more the ideal blueprint of the master organiser than a model which is anything like an adequate guide to what goes on in reality. The image is often preferred because it makes comfortable both the academic theorists and the senior executives who would find it too discomforting to have to come fully to terms with the degree of randomness, ambiguity and, above all, human cussedness with which those nearer to the settings in which real work is done are all too familiar.

Coming to terms with conflict and ambiguity

Organisational theorists have slowly been moving towards a re-cognition that the rationality component in their models has to be seen as more limited than they might have preferred. Thus, one of their number, Charles Perrow (1977), has called for analyses which acknowledge what, it is argued, most managers know but social scientists are reluctant to admit. This is that complex social systems are

> greatly influenced by sheer chance, accident and luck; that most decisions are very ambiguous, preference orderings are incoherent and unstable, efforts at communication and understanding are often ineffective, subsystems are often loosely connected, and most attempts at social control are clumsy and unpredictable.

The danger here, however, is that an over-reaction sets in and we get alternative images of the kind which have tended to fill the gap left by formal organisation theorists. These are the images to be found on the semi-humorous non-fiction bookstalls.

Robert Townsend's book *Up the Organisation* (1970) poured general scorn on those who believed in conventional organisation structures and business practices whilst Peter and Hull (1969) cynically pointed to the 'Peter Principle' whereby each employee in the hierarchy is said to rise to their level of incompetence. Northcote Parkinson (1957) and others, on the other hand, suggested that naked and calculated sectional self-interest on the part of executives is the prime mover in organisational behaviour. The cynicism of all this and the popularity which these books achieved among executives themselves can be interpreted as a turning to-wards one mythical picture of the organisation to compensate for and reduce the frustration with the other mythical picture: the official and preferred academic one of the rational, neutral, hier-archical goal-seeking system. Like most myths, these two both contain truths. But would it not be valuable to develop a model of frame of reference to use in thinking about work organisation which takes account of the systematic elements of organising *and* the conflicts, tensions, ambiguities and contradictions which arise?

The rational system myth

The organisation is made up of
a system of jobs, procedures
and operations which function
to meet the purposes for which
the organisation was set up

The jungle myth

The organisation is made up of
a collection of self-interested
and competing groups and
individuals who only cooperate
when to do so suits their
private or sectional purposes

*Preferred
approaches*
Ones which incorporate the
insights of both of these myths
and recognise that
organisations are cooperative
interactive systems which
nevertheless contain
fundamental conflicts and
tensions resulting from the fact
that employees use
organisations as much as
organisations use their
employees

Fig. 1.4 Two myths about how organisations function

A more detailed consideration of organisational theories will be
a central concern of a later chapter, but an outline of a general
conception of organising activity which indicates the direction to
be taken in this book can be put forward at this stage. This will
enable us to proceed towards a consideration of the nature of
management generally.

Organisations do have systematic aspects to them and they are
managed in order to achieve certain goals and policies which are
articulated by those who are at the top or are 'in charge'. But
these goals, as well as the procedures and arrangements which are
associated with them are as much the *outcomes* of the conflicts,
negotiations and indeed confusions existing among the various
individuals and groups which make up the organisation as they
are pregiven elements into which people fit. The organisation,
then, is an association of people with often widely differing and
indeed conflicting interests, preferences and purpose who are
willing, within rather rightly defined limits, to carry out tasks
which help meet the requirements of those in charge.

Organisations are cooperative and rational systems but this co-operation and rationality is strictly limited. People cooperate with each other at work to complete certain tasks which need to be done for their involvement in the organisation to continue. That cooperation is limited by the fact that the cooperators all have their own private interests and goals to pursue or defend. The production manager, for example, will cooperate with the quality control manager to keep their factory working. But the two managers may well, in the kind of hierarchical career structure which is typical, be rivals for a promotional post. This puts them into competition and possibly conflict with each other. It makes their relationship at first sight a rather odd one. But in reality, we have here a fairly normal situation: one which combines cooperative and conflicting elements. In a similar way, the machine operator cooperates with the supervisor to keep the job going but conflicts come to the surface the minute the supervisor makes demands that are seen as unfair or calls for an increase in effort without offering a consequent increase in reward.

The *rationality* of the organisational system is also limited. Systems are rational to the extent to which decisions and procedures are based on careful consideration of the appropriate means to achieving system ends, as was suggested above. This occurs, but it is limited by the extent to which the individuals or groups involved bias the information which is taken into account to encourage outcomes which meet their own preferences. And it is further limited by the highly ambiguous nature of the information which is used. As March and Olsen (1976) point out, there is typically ambiguity about what objectives are meant to be set, there is ambiguity about the nature of the technologies which are being used (because their nature is unclear) and the environments which prevail (they are difficult to interpret); important knowledge about the past is obscure because so much history is reconstructed or twisted and, finally, there is ambiguity about the involvement of the individuals employed in the organisation itself. This is because people's attention varies and their pattern of participation is uncertain and ever-changing. Karl Weick (1979) points out that in the real world of organising, people tend to deal with the 'here and now' in a way involving the least possible effort. This means that we do not get the degree of what he calls the 'review of all possible circumstances' which is implied in what I labelled the over-rationalised conception of organisation.

What all of this comes down to is that, although organisations do have machine-like aspects, they are nevertheless not machines because they are made up of human beings and their actions. Organisations are to an extent run as though they were machines converting inputs into outputs. But their reliability as machines is grossly compromised by the fact that the central means of goal achievement is human effort. To state it brutally: in modern work organisations people are used as means towards ends. And, because human beings generally and those in advanced western cultures especially, are assertive, questioning and self-considering animals, this renders work organisations essentially problematic – a theme which is fully developed in Chapter 5.

Discomforting as it may be to those who would prefer it otherwise, organisations are not only rational systems of procedures and techniques in which people are employed, they are also political arenas shot through with both conflicts and ambiguities. We all know this of course. But our organisational literature and much of our organisational policy-making proceeds as if this were not the case. Both understanding and practical policy can be improved by taking these challenging facts of life more centrally and systematically into account. Conflicts and ambiguities have to be lived with in organisations if we are to cope effectively or, as we might say, *manage*. And, in this spirit, we can now move on to consider the nature of managerial work.

Chapter 2

Management and managing: images and reality

In a sense, everybody in a work organisation 'manages'. Even the most junior employee has decisions to make, tools or materials to organise and tasks to coordinate. Nevertheless, it would appear that some people 'manage' more than others. This is suggested by the large number of people formally employed as managers, officials, administrators and supervisors. To sort out just what management is about and just what those called managers do is by no means a straightforward matter.

It has often been observed by those who have done research on managerial work that many of the prevailing ideas about what managerial work is are based upon myths. Myths are stories about the way the world is. Anthropologists have shown that myths serve the purpose of helping people make sense of the world in a comforting or reassuring way. They are not 'true' or 'false' in a simple scientific sense. They deal with what might be called truths but they do so in a partial way. And, because this partiality is often a reflection of the concern of the mythic to reassure, myths are not necessarily the most useful guides to action. Nevertheless, to understand management in a fuller and therefore more useful way, it can be valuable to look at the various myths and popular images which are around and to draw out whatever worthwhile insights they might contain.

To achieve this purpose, we need to treat management thought in the same spirit of *constructive scepticism* which was advocated in Chapter 1 as appropriate for considering social science thinking. And we also need to apply some of the *critical commonsense* which was advocated, especially with regard to the need to consider available research evidence on managerial activity. The outcome of this, I hope, will be a clearer conceptual view of what management is – what the basic principles of its role within or-ganisations are – and a clearer view of what managers do in prac-tice. A major problem which has hampered our understanding of management is that we have tended to operate with too big a gap between how we look at management in principle and how we find it when we examine its practices. Our conceptualisations, or theories of management, need to be better informed by knowledge of actual managerial practices. And our views of managerial prac-tice need to be informed by a more realistic appreciation of the essential nature of managerial work.

Managerial insecurity and defensiveness

At the heart of the problems we face in understanding manage-ment, whether in theory or practice, is that so much of what is written and said about it is concerned to *justify* or give legitimacy to managerial work. This is perhaps to be expected, given that managers are usually – by definition – people who have authority over others. And to have authority is usually to have to justify to those over whom you are set your right to command or instruct.

We could say that, because management involves both technical and social or power elements, management thought can be ex-pected to have to serve two functions which relate to these two aspects. John Child (1969) describes these as the 'technical func-tion', which is involved with the practical means of carrying out tasks, and the 'legitimatory function', which is 'primarily linked to the securing of social recognition and approval for managerial authority and the way it is used'. Because the carrying out of the technical aspects of management (devising budgets, applying operational research techniques, setting up payment systems) is constantly done in the context of managers having to persuade others to go along with them (to accept and follow the budget, provide information for analysis, recognise pay relativities as fair), we can expect everything that managers and their spokespersons say or write about their activities to be coloured by the constant concern to defend their authority. The right to manage, in the sense of the right to command, has constantly to be reestablished.

The fact that most of the managerial work with which we are concerned here is performed in societies which have democratic and relatively non-deferential cultures tends to mean that a certain amount of managerial anxiety can arise about this need constantly to maintain legitimacy. But there are additional sources of anxiety which colour the way managers see themselves and the way they encourage others to view them.

Winifred Marks (1978) has commented that, despite what she sees as their essential role in creating real wealth for the nation, managers have never been the best loved members of the community: 'industrial and commercial managers are associated with trade and no Jane Austen heroine would marry into that circle.' This historical legacy has continued in force, it is suggested: 'members of the learned professions, regular officers in the armed forces, gentry (preferably landed) of private means, senior civil servants and, latterly, social workers all enjoy a higher social cachet.' The worries that could be caused by this have only come to the surface in the 1970s, suggests Marks, as inflation and incomes policies eroded the financial advantage associated with managerial work and as challenges from legislation, trade unions and subordinates themselves challenged their 'right to manage'.

These insecurities about social status suffered by managers derive in part from the historical and cultural legacies of the ruling class values of an earlier age, as was suggested in Chapter 1 with regard to the divide between theory and practice (see p. 15). Alistair Mant (1979) sets these issues in the context of what he calls 'British binary thought', whereby activities are divided into the clean and respectable or U category and the dirty and disreputable non-U one. Being a gentleman, a pure scientist or a professional is valued in the culture above being a 'hard man', an applied scientist or an industrially employed person. To avoid the contamination of their association with the dirty world of industry, managers and their spokesmen have followed various legitimatory tactics ranging from the pursuit of professionalism (see pp. 187-91) to the claim to be exponents of a *science* of management. Both of these strategies, it can be argued, are double-edged for the managers. Whereas they might give some credibility which would enhance their performance, they might equally undermine credibility and effectiveness by drawing too heavy a dividing line between the managers and those with whom they have to work.

Although the influence of cultural factors creates problems for managers, another major ambiguity in the manager's social position can be seen to arise from the fact that practically all of them are both bosses and subordinates. Managers are asked to control and yet are themselves controlled. They employ others yet they too are employees. In the great majority of cases they are the hirelings put in charge of the slaves. They are not the masters. The ultimate benefits of their efforts generally lie with others than the managers themselves and this means that the managers are required to *make use* of people whilst constantly needing to be looking back anxiously over their shoulders as they become increasingly aware that they themselves are *being used*.

These ambiguities are ones deriving from the large-scale societal and economic context of management. But managerial insecurity also relates to the kind of internal everyday ambiguities that pervade organisational activity. On the basis of close observation of managerial activity in one large American corporation, Campanis (1970) suggested that the manager is often confused and frustrated by situations which do not have firm precedents. In a way similar to that followed in Chapter 1, this researcher attacked the tendency of the literature to 'promote the myths of rational organisation' which depict the manager as a 'kind of moral computer choosing from among rational decisions to reach known goals'. Managers, he says, are in the business of finding 'situational solutions', something with which they are not helped a great deal by either their academic training or their experience. This kind of argument can be exaggerated but I feel sure that most people's personal observation of managers at work would support those research findings which suggest that managerial work is very often a matter of managing in the sense of 'coping'. It often looks and feels more like 'flying by the seat of the pants' than anything else. We will shortly look at what systematic evidence there is on this. First, however, we need to consider some of the popular basic images of managerial work.

Management: art, science, politics or magic?

To make sense of the complex and highly ambiguous situations in which managers find themselves, there are on offer a variety of basic images of managerial work. Some of these tend to reassure the managers themselves and help them justify their position.

Views of management as an art or as a science are examples of these. But other images first appeared as something of a reaction to these first two alternative but equally comforting images. Views of managerial work as political or as involving 'magic' are examples of this.

The views of management as art, science, magic and politics are summarised in Fig. 2.1 by bringing out what each of them implies about what a 'successful' manager is.

Management ideologists have fluctuated in their preference for an image of management between an image of the manager as a scientist and an image of the manager as applier of an art. The view of management as a science is based on the view that there is a body of knowledge either in existence or awaiting discovery which can be learned and acted upon to achieve effectiveness. This view is likely to be preferred by those with an interest in management education or with an interest in supplying either techniques or equipment to managers. And, given that there does exist a range of demonstrably useful management techniques and as there are useful devices such as telephones and computers, we must recognise an element of truth in this picture. Yet the view of management as an art, if taken to its logical conclusion, questions this. The image of management as an art implies that managerial ability is a matter of intuition, native wit and personality. Management involves those undefinable, and hence unteachable, qualities associated with the idea of leadership. Leadership skills can be developed but cannot be acquired. To have an art is to possess inborn talents.

The art versus science debate in management circles is by no means an irrelevant one given its implications for how managers are educated, trained and developed. And both sides in the debate can be supported by the evidence of observation and experience. In the same way that we can recognise learnable techniques which contribute to effectiveness we can find cases where highly trained individuals turn out to be disastrous managers. We can also find managers to whom effective performance appears to come almost naturally. Could it not be that management is best seen as both an art and a science? Given that the implications of rationality and predictability implied in the science view are too comforting to abandon and, given that evidence and experience suggest the importance of various indefinable personal qualities in management,

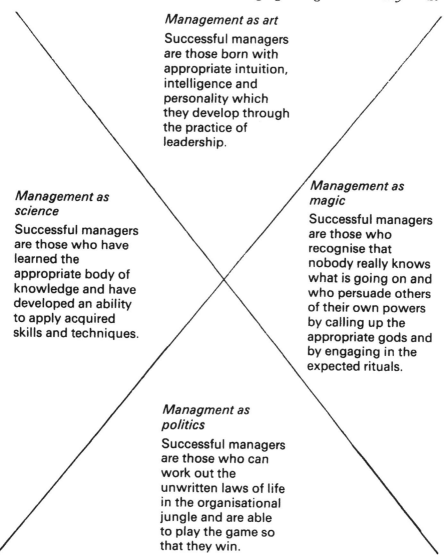

Management as art
Successful managers
are those born with
appropriate intuition,
intelligence and
personality which
they develop through
the practice of
leadership.

*Management as
science*

Successful managers
are those who have
learned the
appropriate body of
knowledge and have
developed an ability
to apply acquired
skills and techniques.

*Management as
magic*

Successful managers
are those who
recognise that
nobody really knows
what is going on and
who persuade others
of their own powers
by calling up the
appropriate gods and
by engaging in the
expected rituals.

*Managment as
politics*

Successful managers
are those who can
work out the
unwritten laws of life
in the organisational
jungle and are able
to play the game so
that they win.

Fig. 2.1 Management as art, science, magc and politics

we should not be surprised to find contemporary management
writers trying to have it both ways. Thus, for example, we find
Koontz, O'Donnell and Weihrich (1980) saying in their widely
used textbook that management is 'the most important of all arts'.
But they add to this the statement that 'the most productive art
is always based on an understanding of the science underlying it'.

At the same time as those working within the management and management education world worked towards a compromise between these views of management as art and as science, various other commentators began to develop a more irreverent interpretation of what goes on. One of these was the view that managers try to play the magician in a lot of what they do. Alistair Mant (1979), in his critique of British management, suggested that useful and directly productive work is often downgraded by managers whilst there is much 'building around the idea of "management" a plethora of myths, shibboleths and incantations which our most successful competitors seem able to do without'. Mant's view is that this resorting to magical devices is somehow pathological. The view that there is a resorting to magic and that it does not work too well is also implied by Charles Handy (1978) in his discussion of the 'gods of management'. Yet Handy goes some way beyond this view with his implication that perhaps it is not a matter of doing away with the magical if one seeks success in management but is more a matter of finding the right magic. He suggests that the management of organisations is 'more a set of values than a science, more a cult or a fashion than a theory'. But he implies that if we choose our gods more carefully, if we devise the appropriate cult, then we may do better (see below, p. 68).

Perhaps the most sustained analysis of management which uses the magic type of allegory is that of Graham Cleverley (1971). He puts forward the argument that much of what occurs is magico-religious rather than scientific or technical. He then very perceptively goes on to picture the management conference as a prayer meeting, the accountants as priests (the keepers of the books), the consultants as sorcerers, market research exercises as fertility rites and so on. Shareholders represent a supernatural force whilst 'The Company' may be ascribed supernatural qualities. The market plays a growing role as a 'new deity'. As with all magic there is a desire of the managers who use it to control the elements. In this case the elements are not the sea or the weather but human beings. It is in this light that we are to see the occasional resorting to the ritualistic following of behavioural scientists. This action of managers can only be ritualistic since there is no evidence as to whether following behavioural science 'principles' is good or bad for the organisation economically. When managers speak reverently of the Hawthorne Experiments they are, in fact, doing the same as an ancient people who looked to Greek myths to find comfort in the face of the chaotic nature of the world around them.

Cleverley's amusing book has a very serious point to it. He describes how he watched a speech by the head of a consultancy firm and how he noticed that every time the man mentioned *people* he clenched his teeth. To Cleverley, this was highly significant: 'it seems easily understandable that anyone attempting to apply rational principles and thinking to the practice of management should be forced to clench his teeth whenever he is reminded that ultimately he has to deal with people.' He argues that this is because people are irrational and therefore are not susceptible to rational control systems. The view taken here, however, is that it is not human irrationality that reduces the effectiveness of the control systems and hence encourages the turning to 'magic'. Rather, it is the fact that people follow their own rationales as well those of the organisers. And these rationales do not coincide a great deal of the time. What can be argued is that managerial work is made so difficult and uncomfortable by the independent-mindedness and sheer unpredictability of the human beings involved that there is a strong and widespread inclination to resort to magic, myths, fads, panaceas and a general mystification of the very idea of 'management'.

As we shall see in the next two chapters (pp. 66–71, 129–31) when we examine some of the important recent developments in organisation and management theory, this approach, which might at first sight seem facetious, can be built upon to help understand some very fundamental aspects of successful organising effort. Research work has shown that to achieve the kind of integrated but flexible employee efforts that make organisations effective, managers need to recognise a *symbolic* element to their work. To create the kind of ethos or 'culture' that enables people to commit themselves to the organisation in the required way, a lot of effort has to be put in to creating meanings for organisational members. Symbols, rituals, myths and other such cultural devices are vital tools of those who wish to weld together the efforts of human beings into a coherent pattern. Organisations are, in a sense, small-scale and artificially constructed societies. For them to function well, therefore, they will need a set of general meanings, a language, a history and a sense of belonging in the same way that a society does. But since an organisation is an especially focussed or purposive miniature society, these have been all the more carefully and deliberately constructed to have the desired effect.

The argument that managers are involved in manipulating symbols in a quasi-magical way to achieve some kind of constructive integration of activities easily leads us on to that view of management as involving essentially political behaviour. No intelligent politician sees politics as only a matter of rationality. As much as some of us may regret it, political success is greatly to do with 'image', with charisma, with faith and, yes, with magic. But in spite of this clear connection between magic and politics, the view of management as politics came into the contemporary managerial consciousness with a more particular thrust of its own. As was explained earlier, the image of the power-seeking, combative, competitive and career-obsessed manager was developed as an almost cynical attempt to sink the dominant 'rational systems myth' of the organisation with a 'jungle myth' (see p. 21). Yet, as we shall also see from our later review of how the study of organisation has developed, there is no doubt that much managerial activity is correctly to be understood as political (p. 71ff). As was stressed in the last chapter, power and conflict are pervasive in organisations. Managers are involved in power relationships with those whose efforts they are there to manage and they also find themselves in competition for scarce resources with their fellow managers.

The most sensible way to deal with this range of different views of what management is may well be to say that, in the end, management is indeed both an art and a science and that, at the same time, it is involved in both magic-making and politicking. And, if we think on, we could soon find other images to add to this. The mention of dealing with scarcity of resources could usefully lead us to claim that managers are applied economists, for example. On the other hand, the recognition of managers' involvement in the complexities of human behaviour could encourage us to paint a picture of the successful manager as an accomplished applied psychologist! However, I would argue that we will not achieve the most useful overall understanding of what management is simply by adding up all the various partial images of management. To make the best use of the particular insights which each of these images offers we need to do some basic conceptual work. We need to create a model which will enable us to bring together all of these insights. But in order to do this we have, first, to take fully into account the ways in which the traditional model of managerial work has in recent years been severely questioned by careful studies of how managers actually behave and by studies which show that all work generally labelled as managerial cannot easily be lumped together as being the same thing.

What do managers do?

The traditional, or we might even say 'official' approach to conceptualising managerial work has been to portray managers as the people who operate that rational and goal-seeking system which is the organisation. In the previous chapter, the rational-system view of the organisation was severely questioned. There are clearly very strong grounds for questioning the assumption that managers operate by systematically gathering information relevant to their responsibilities in the system and then carefully analysing that material with a view to making a decision about how to act in order to further the 'goals' of the system. And among the grounds for questioning these assumptions is the evidence which has been gathered by a number of researchers on real-life managerial behaviour.

The picture of managers as people who are reflective, analytical and systematic planners and decision-makers whose basic raw materials are objective data first began to be dented by the publication of research findings when Sune Carlson (1951) produced his study of the day-to-day work of a sample of company managing directors. Carlson showed that these people were rarely alone and uninterrupted for periods long enough to engage in systematic reading or thought. This is supported by what is perhaps the most comprehensive collection of evidence that we have about managerial behaviour: that brought together by Henry Mintzberg (1973) from his own and other people's studies. He concludes that managers' activities are 'characterised by brevity, variety, and fragmentation'. He sees this as applying to virtually all managers' jobs but especially to those 'closest to the action'.

Most activities are brief, taking seconds for the supervisor and minutes for the chief executives. The activities are highly varied and exhibit little pattern, with the trivial being interspersed with the consequential. Both fragmentation and frequent interruptions are commonplace.

It would appear from Mintzberg's information that the managers happily go along with this, for whatever reason. He suggests that they gravitate towards 'the current, the well-defined, the non-routine', prefer 'gossip, hearsay, speculation to routine reports and tend to deal with specific rather than general issues'. This applies to all levels, it is important to note. And Mintzberg is led to conclude that the manager's job is 'not one that breeds reflective planners; rather, it produces adaptive information manipulators who favour a stimulus-response milieu'. He therefore argues that 'there is no science in managerial work'. Work is not done according to procedures prescribed by scientific analysis. Most information comes by word of mouth and, although decisions involving modern technologies are made, these are done following intuitive or non-explicit procedures.

Managerial work can be seen, then, as very much a 'seat of the pants' activity. Much of it is opportunistic, habitual, almost 'instinctual'. Yet we should not go so far as to deny this picture any underlying pattern whatsoever. Research by J. P. Kotter (1978, 1982) is particularly helpful in revealing a significant pattern. Underlying the work of both the mayors of American cities and the general managers studied is a key concern with developing and maintaining a network of relationships with people at any level or in any sphere from whom they needed cooperation to get their job done. This does help explain the at-first-sight excessive preoccupation with talking to people as opposed to reading and analysing observed by many researchers. In the end, organisations are networks of cooperating individuals and groups whose cooperation always has to be won. For any manager to get done the job to which they have been appointed, they inevitably have to look after those relationships with people upon whom they are dependent for cooperation.

Variety in managerial work

One question which has engaged the attention of researchers on managerial behaviour has been that of whether there is or there is not one overall activity which can be called management. Related to this is the question of the extent to which, even if where there are similarities in the ways in which managerial jobs are conceived, different people will do the job differently. Henry Mintzberg, in his survey of the evidence, concluded that managers' jobs are remarkably alike. Managerial work involves fulfilling a combination of ten roles which can be grouped under three headings, he suggests. These are the *interpersonal* roles of figurehead, leader and liaisor; the *informational* roles of monitor, disseminator and spokesman, and the *decisional* roles of entrepreneur, disturbance-handler, resource-allocator and negotiator. But it is then accepted that there is variety within the overall managerial role in that different managerial jobs do require different degrees of emphasis on each of these component roles. Some managers, for example, are on their feet a lot of the time handling disturbances and negotiating whilst others spend much more of their time at their desks processing and monitoring information.

Rosemary Stewart's (1976) research has made a particularly significant contribution to understanding precisely how managers' jobs vary in practice. She goes beyond the traditional approach to recognising distinctions within managerial jobs which is to distinguish jobs by level (senior, middle, junior and the rest) and by function (production, finance, personnel and so on). She recognises two new basic differentiating factors. First, she shows that jobs can be differentiated according to whether the *contacts* which occur are largely internal, external or mixed internal/external to the organisation. Second she shows that jobs can be differentiated according to the *shape* of those contacts. We thus get the 'hub manager' whose interactions are upwards, downwards and sideways in the hierarchy; the 'peer dependent manager' whose interactions are sideways; the 'man manager' whose interactions are downwards and the 'solo manager' who is a specialist with limited contacts. The same study also showed that jobs vary in the extent to which they follow a pattern of fragmentation and interruption in the working day and a further difference detected was between those jobs in which the job holder was *exposed* in the sense that mistakes and poor performance could be individually identified and those jobs in which performance could not accurately be judged. Later Stewart (1982), showed that an important difference between jobs which does not necessarily relate to level or function lies in the amount and the nature of the *choices* which the job offers. The degree of discretion varies from one managerial job to another.

This research on variations between jobs has a clear practical relevance in that it can intelligently inform organisation design and can assist in fitting people to jobs or jobs to people. To know something about a range of managerial jobs in terms of the criteria recognised by Stewart would also be valuable to any individual making judgments about their own managerial career choices and aspirations. But, in addition to this, it is also clear that we have to be careful when it comes to getting to grips with identifying the essential nature of managerial work that we can account for managerial diversity as well as for consistency of function.

Variety within managerial work comes not only from the nature of the jobs themselves. It is also to be found in the sets of attitudes, predispositions and types of approach which develop among managers located in different kinds of job. These 'orientations' may result from the type of self-selection which goes on, from the type of training which is experienced as well as from the pressures of the job itself. Ellis and Child (1973) investigated managerial orientations among a large sample of managers in a variety of industries whose senior job level might well lead one to expect relatively little variation in orientation. Clear distinctions emerged. Finance and quality control managers appeared to exhibit significantly less mental flexibility in their approach than did personnel, research or marketing managers, for example. There were corresponding distinctions between functions in attitudes towards formal authority and procedure and in the extent to which managers were 'radically inclined' (marketing, personnel, research and production) or 'conservative' (finance and quality control).

In addition to the distinctions which can be drawn between different types of role and the orientations of those who occupy them within managements, there is also the possibility of there developing very general *management types* either in different cultures or societies or at different times in a society's or an economy's history. Michael Maccoby (1978), for instance, has noted the emergence in recent years of a new type of manager, *The Gamesman* – one who seeks out challenging and competitive activities and enjoys trying new techniques and approaches which may help the corporation. The Gamesman is seen as becoming more appropriate to the modern corporation than the other types who nevertheless exist alongside him or her. These are the *Jungle Fighter* whose main goal is power and who is happy to see winners destroy losers; the *Company Man* who depends on the protectiveness of the powerful corporation for his identity; and the *Craftsman* who is typified by the scientist who prefers to get on with their own specialism rather than to take over or change the system. Maccoby claims that in the United States in the 1960s the Gamesman went 'all out to win' but the changes that came about in the 1970s – especially the Watergate experience and the growing importance of cost reduction and conserving of resources – led to the *Modified Gamesman*. This managerial type is more 'sober and realistic' and recognises that 'winning is not everything'. But in Britain, Maccoby observed in 1978, management was still dominated by a variant of the jungle fighter who likes to be armed for the battle with tradition and titles. And, here, we are back to questions of symbol and culture.

Attention to certain aspects of the culture of managers themselves may, in fact, help us get to grips with the question of the essential nature of managerial work. If we look at the language of managers we may be able to find some clues as to what there is in common in the work of all managers, regardless of the specificities of the particular post which they occupy.

Managerial language: battling and surviving

One way to understand the underlying nature and assumptions of any area of human activity is to examine closely the language which is used to describe that activity and the language which is drawn upon to label specific aspects of it. Out of this may come some indication of what the people involved feel to be the guiding features of their behaviour. In particular, the metaphors used by people to make more concrete the abstract nature of what they are involved in can be enlightening. Nowhere is this more the case than in the sphere of work organisation and management.

In his survey of the 'key words' in English-speaking culture, Raymond Williams (1976) shows how the idea of 'management', seen historically, combines the Italian sense *maneggiare*, to handle or train (especially horses), with the French *ménager*, to keep house. Williams notes that soon after the word appears in the English language, in the first of these senses, we find its being 'extended to operations of war'. Examination of the *Oxford English Dictionary* reveals that 'to manage arms' was adopted as a synonym for fighting or conducting a war in the sixteenth century. It subsequently became applied in a general way to the taking of control, taking charge or directing. However, it is fascinating to note that this very early military connotation of the idea of managing is still very current.

Managerial work is frequently conceptualised in military terms, often one suspects, without those so doing being particularly conscious of the extent to which they are using an implicit metaphor of their organisation as an army. The language of managerial life is a language of *strategies* (from the Greek for generalship), of advertising *campaigns*, of *company headquarters*, of *divisions*, of *canteens*, of managerial *staffs* (staffs being those appointed to assist a general), of *line* managers and of personnel *officers*. The term *esprit de corps* is an obvious military borrowing and the fondness among managers for referring to *exercises* (marketing exercise, manpower planning exercise, redundancy exercise) is highly reminiscent of military talk. Even the word *personnel* has military connections deriving from its nineteenth-century appearance to distinguish between the human (personnel) and the material (materiel) in a service.

Why should military terminology be so central in managerial discourse? What is the deeper level significance of this surface-level talk? It is used, I suggest, as a kind of semi-covert reference to the essential corporate purposiveness of organisations. An army is the clearest case of an organisation which survives or dies, wins or loses, succeeds or fails on the basis of its controlling and coordinating its various parts and directing them as a whole to achieve certain specific purposes. In real or everyday managerial life or in the lessons taught by contemporary social science research, it is clear that organisations in practice amount to being rather tense and temporary coalitions involved in a series of ambiguous and often conflicting purposes. Yet at the heart of how managers ultimately think in an organisation is a recognition that organisational management does, in the end, come down to *pulling along* all the various interests and influences in some specific direction which will ensure some kind of success and, at the very least, survival. The organisation is not a goal-seeking system or entity. But it is an essential requirement of management to act as if it were, or rather, as if it could be. Hence the frequent calling for the devising of explicit corporate strategies as an essential part of good managerial practice.

The nature of management

Perhaps the most quoted definition of managment of all time is that of Henri Fayol (1949) which says that to manage is 'to forecast and plan, to organise, to command, to coordinate and control'. A more recent popular definition is that of Rosemary wart (1963) which says that management is 'deciding what should should be done and getting other people to do it'. Both of these definitions provide useful starting points for anyone trying to clarify the nature of management. However, they do not really get to the essence of the managerial phenomenon. They both usefully recognise that management involves a task element together with a political dimension but they stop short of recognising the immense complexity of what this implies and they both stop short of coming to terms with the implications of the variety of different kinds of work which is done by those generally recognised as working within management. Managers can be people who go out and sell products, people who analyse financial information, people who supervise production, people who negotiate with trade unions, people who buy raw materials and people who present organisational interests to the public. Some of these do very little, if any, 'commanding'; others 'organise' very little other than their own desks, and yet others are too involved in implementing the plans of other individuals to do much 'forecasting and planning' of their own.

Some management writers have tried to deal with this problem by suggesting that the only 'real' managers are those who actually direct subordinates. One organisational behaviour text, for example, suggests that the most useful definition of a manager is 'someone who is directly responsible for getting work done by other people' (Smith et al., 1982). There are other individuals with high status and salary in the organisation who are 'specialists' but not managers, it is suggested. They only become managers in this view when they become responsible for the work of others. This is ludicrous. It would mean, for example, that if we found a company who appointed an expert in industrial relations or an expert in investment to advise the other managers on strategy (but did not allocate them even a secretary), then we would have to deny them a managerial label, despite the fact that they would demonstrably be involved in directing the organisation. Surely we are getting nearer to the idea of management which is used in practice if we recognise that *it is what the work of any individual contributes to the steering of the organisation as a whole that makes their job a managerial one or not.*

A common mistake made by those trying to clarify what managers do or should do is to suggest that the work of the individual manager can be understood in isolation from the work of other managers in the same organisation. This leads to highly inadequate and ultimately misleading conceptions of managers as, typically, either 'decision-makers' or 'people who get other people to do things'. Managers are much more usefully seen as people who are part of a management. And a management is most usefully seen as a component of an organisation. In effect, managing is most usefully seen as the initiating aspect of the organisation itself. Put more simply: managing is organising. And a manager is a manager if they contribute to the general task of organising work, regardless of whether, in their everyday job, they directly organise others or not.

The hidden priorities of managerial language and its fondness for military terminology recognised above can help us develop this point. Managers are pushed towards talking in the language of armies and wars by their sensing of the fact that what they are essentially engaged in is the *pulling together* of the various bits and pieces of the organisation and a *pulling along* of the organisation in some general direction. And that direction is the one which enables the organisation to survive the slings and arrows of the potential misfortunes which confront it in its dealing with

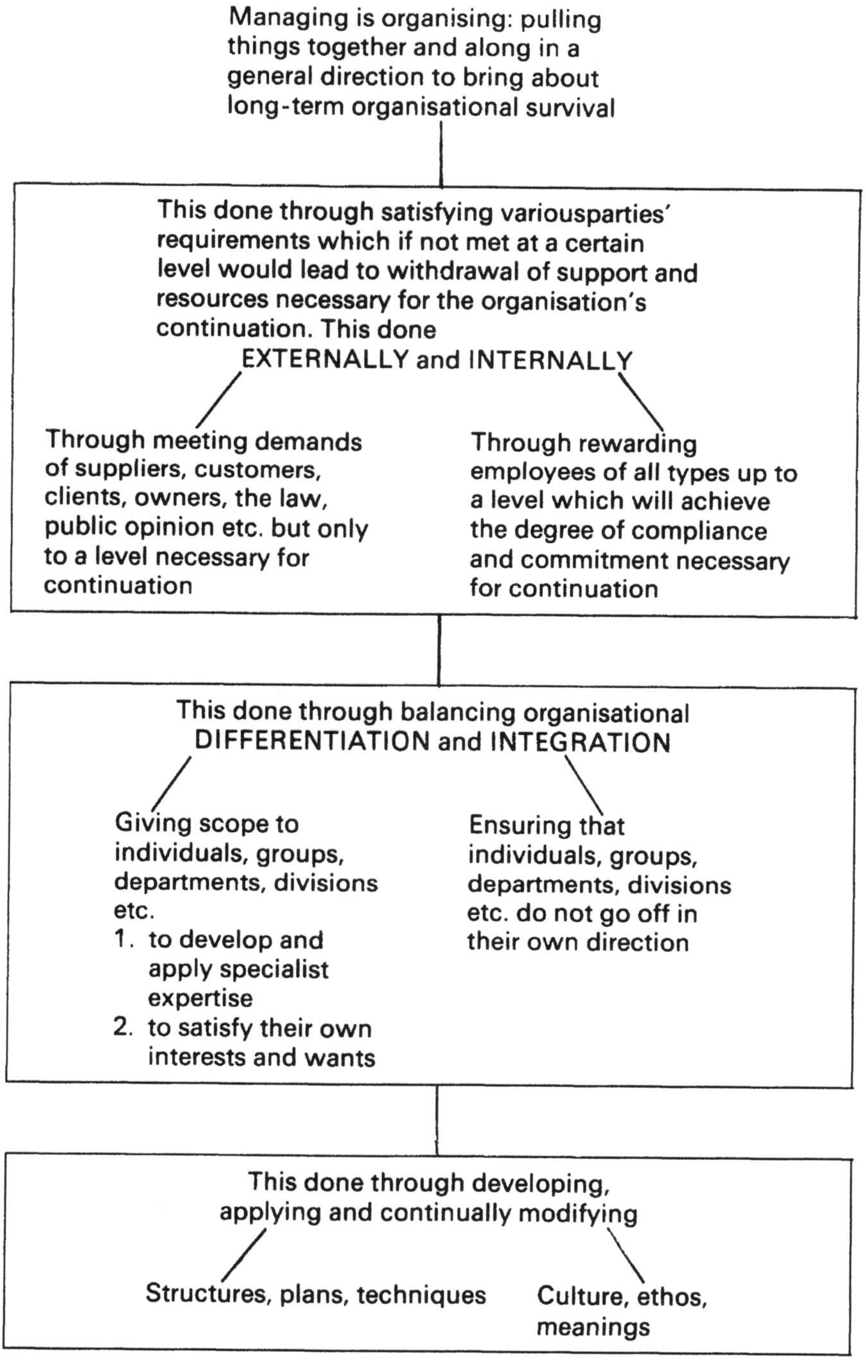

Managing is organising: pulling
things together and along in a
general direction to bring about
long-term organisational survival

This done through satisfying variousparties'
requirements which if not met at a certain
level would lead to withdrawal of support and
resources necessary for the organisation's
continuation. This done
EXTERNALLY and INTERNALLY

Through meeting demands
of suppliers, customers,
clients, owners, the law,
public opinion etc. but only
to a level necessary for
continuation

Through rewarding
employees of all types up to
a level which will achieve
the degree of compliance
and commitment necessary
for continuation

This done through balancing organisational
DIFFERENTIATION and INTEGRATION

Giving scope to
individuals, groups,
departments, divisions
etc.
1. to develop and
apply specialist
expertise
2. to satisfy their own
interests and wants

Ensuring that
individuals, groups,
departments, divisions
etc. do not go off in
their own direction

This done through developing,
applying and continually modifying

Structures, plans, techniques

Culture, ethos,
meanings

Fig. 2.2 The nature and tasks of management

markets, states, suppliers, employees, clients and so on. That
direction is what can be identified as the organisation's strategy.

Figure 2.2 sets out in a schematic form a conception of what
management is and what the tasks undertaken by managers
amount to. The thinking behind this scheme is complex and extensive. In fact, the scheme represents the way in which I have
personally come to understand managerial work in the light of
my reading of the whole range of theoretical and research material
which analyses organisational and managerial behaviour. It is the
intention of the next two chapters to survey and review that
material and the full implications of the present thinking will
become much clearer after these chapters have been read. The
scheme starts with the notion of managing as 'organising' and
then considers the means which are used to do this. Three levels
of managerial activity are identified. And at each level managers
are involved in economic and political processes, at each level
they work with limited predictability and at each level they find
themselves in situations of considerable ambiguity and conflict of
interest.

The *first level* recognises the essentially political-economic
nature of managerial work. Organisational continuation is dependent upon the organisation's conforming in a minimal way
with the requirements of all those parties who make demands upon
it. Externally, the managers have to ensure that tax bills are met,
goods or services supplied, the law and local bye-laws complied
with, suppliers paid, public opinion and the press kept sweet,
external organised labour interests discouraged from mounting
challenges and so on. Every one of these has a cost and each cost
must be balanced with the others within what can be afforded.
To meet any one of these requirements at a higher level than is
necessary for survival risks that survival itself. And the same
applies with the multiplicity of interests internal to the organisation which have to be balanced the one against the other: this
department against that, this group of employees against that
group, this individual against that one and so on. And, all the
time, the internal has to be balanced with the external.

At the *second level* we recognise that the extent that there are
different groups or parties within the organisation is itself an
outcome of managerial activity. It is an outcome of way in which
tasks have been divided, allocated or delegated across the corpor-

ation. Levels and sub-units are established to enable an efficient deployment of specialist expertise and, at the same time, to make it more likely that people will be able to satisfy their own interests and wants through their being located in groups of people with common interests or purposes. However, whenever such a grouping is set up there is created the potentially divisive possibility of that grouping (or even individual) going off in their own direction: putting their sectional interest above that of those running the organisation. This means that there must be a constant balancing of differentiation with integration. For every act of dividing there must be an act of uniting. Too much dividing can lead to divisiveness and disintegration and too much unity can lead to overconformity, to complacency and to individuals' becoming lost in the mass.

At the *third level* we see this need to achieve a balance of integration and differentiation being met by a range of structural means (organisational design, application of techniques, etc.) and what we might call qualitative, symbolic or cultural means. As suggested earlier, the creation of meanings is an important aspect of managerial work and its full import will become clear when we consider some of the most striking trends in recent managerial and organisational research. Structures are clearly important but their role has carefully to be balanced with the cultural.

What all this adds up to is a view of managerial work, whether it be at a senior, middle or junior level, which treats it as a social, economic and political process which goes on within work organisations. It is a process which, as the words above strongly imply, centrally involves an ability to balance. This is an ability to balance interest against interest, differentiation against integration, the use of structure against the use of the cultural. And to do all this, we might say, the manager will have to be a scientist, an artist, a magician and a politician. But before any of these skills can be deployed, the manager will need to have an *overview* of the organisation in which they are employed; a conception of where the organisation is going – an idea of organisational strategy. They will also need to understand the concepts of structure, culture, process, work meanings and so on. And all of these will now be dealt with in our survey of established and emerging ideas of organisation, motivation and employee management. It is to this that the next two chapters are devoted.

Chapter 3

Organisations: structure, process and effectiveness

In the process of looking at the nature of management, managerial work and how these activities are to be studied, we have necessarily established an image of the work organisation. This is an image which differs quite considerably from that typically found in standard managerial and organisation theory texts. It is also very much at odds with the official kind of image generally preferred by those who run organisations. In place of the managerially popular and comforting picture of the work organisation as a rationally planned system, carefully conceived and directed towards the meeting of clearly established goals, we have sketched a more complex and potentially more discomforting outline. This depicts the organisation less as a pregiven structure into which people fit and more as an ongoing and ever-changing association of people with potentially widely differing and conflicting interests, preferences and purposes who are willing, within rather closely defined limits, to carry out tasks which help to meet the requirements of those in charge.

In the pursuit of an image or model of the organisation which fits better with the realities of organisational life than do the neat schemes of official orthodoxy, full recognition has been given in both previous chapters to conflicts, politics, ambiguities and contradictions. These are seen as essential features of organising rather than as occasional morbidities. The purpose of the present chapter is to develop in a more systematic way a framework or general approach for the analysis of work organisations and to highlight the key issues which arise for those having to design and manage such organisations – especially with regard to the human element. This, however, is not to be done in a spirit which rejects as simply 'wrong' the various models and theories which have been developed in the past and which have different emphases and purposes.

The considerable variety of existing schools and schemes of organisational thinking provides us with a rich source of insights and suggestions even if many of these approaches are, in themselves, partial and inadequate. The intention here, therefore, is to review the existing body of thought not only to enable some kind of synthesis to be attempted but also to help present to readers a map of the organisation theory world which can help them find their way through a fascinating but too often confusing literature.

Our concern in this chapter is with what might be called the structural and wider processual aspects of organisational life: the patterns, processes, designs, systems, arrangements and procedures which add up to that 'whole' which people recognise as 'the organisation'. As we stressed in the first chapter, this structural aspect should not be viewed as really or ultimately separable from the other aspect of organisational existence: the 'behavioural'. Our separating the two is merely a matter of analytical convenience which recognises that in the past there have been these two traditions of thinking about organisational work. One of the significant directions which thinking is now beginning to take is away from this kind of division and towards the 'preferred alternative' identified in Fig. 1.3 in Chapter 1. The pattern for this integration will become apparent in the conception of managerial effectiveness with which this chapter will conclude. And it will be within this pattern that we will look at thinking on motivation, leadership and other behavioural dimensions of organisations in the following chapter.

Designing and managing work organisations at all levels involves the making of choices and the coming to terms with constraints. The constant search for a set of design rules, for a theory of organisations or for a usable analytical scheme is a reflection of a widely felt need to understand the nature of the relationship between the various choices and constraints which present themselves to organisational managers and to those simply trying to understand organisations alike. As we argued earlier, a good theory will inevitably have the potential to inform practice, irrespective of the original reason behind the theory's development. In the organisational sphere theories have to address a range of dilemmas of organisation design and management.

The dilemmas of organisational design are plentiful, perplexing and continually present. In any organisation there is the problem of deciding how the various tasks to be done are to be split into various jobs and how these in turn are to be grouped into sections, departments or divisions. There are problems of establishing the number of levels of authority, the proportions of supervised to supervising, the balance of centralisation to decentralisation and authority to delegation, the degree of formalisation and standardisation of procedures and instructions, and so on. But none of these problems is ever conclusively solved. There is never a completely right answer to any of these questions and any answer which is good enough for the present is not likely to last for too long. For every specialist department which is set up there is an added problem of integrating that part of the organisation into the whole. For every short-term problem that is expediently dealt with there is the danger of compromising longer-term aims. With every drive to emphasise production or output is the risk of under-emphasising the requirements of employees. And with every achievement of control and unpredictability there is a possible threat to any necessary willingness to take risks or seek innovation.

Different aspects of these dilemmas are addressed by various of the existing organisational theories. And to help us cope with the range and variety of material here I have grouped into three a selection of the more important contributions to understanding organisations. Each of these groupings is conceived as a *wave* of organisation theory. The three waves have arrived on the scene in the order in which they are introduced here. That is, the first wave represents the oldest type of thinking, the second wave brings along a more recent set of developments whilst the third wave carries the most up-to-date set of ideas. However, it would be utterly false to see each of these waves as replacing the one that went before it: as negating or somehow 'disproving' the older idea. Although there is frequently this kind of intent on the part of the researcher or theorist, we find that the ideas from the past remain current long after their successors had hoped to buy them and we often find them existing alongside their would-be successors.

To get away from what might be termed the 'serial error' of so much writing and teaching in this area in which one 'school' is seen as appearing in place of another only to be replaced by yet another, it is helpful to use this image of waves. Waves do arrive on the shore one after the other but the impact of each one does not replace the impact of what came before. Every wave both collides with its predecessor and combines with it. And the pattern that is left is rarely a neat one and it is never predictable.

The first group of approaches have in common a conception of the organisation as a *machine*. The second wave is made up of approaches which encourage us to see the organisation as a living *organism* and the third wave includes a number of contributions to a view of the organisation as a cluster of social, economic and political *processes*. The pattern underlying this is one in which there is a movement through two metaphors and then into a more abstract view which frees us from the restrictions of operating with these potentially simplistic analogies. As was recognised in the previous chapter, analogies are useful but they are limiting if taken too far. To be able to analyse organisations in terms of human social processes instead of as machines or biological systems does perhaps represent progress. This we will judge when we come to these ideas.

Organisations as machines	Organisations as organisms	Organisations as processes
Classical administrative principles	Human relations	Negotiated order approach (social action)
Scientific management	Equilibrium theory	Decision process theory
Theories of bureaucracy	Socio-technical systems	Culture-excellence school
	Contingency theory	Micropolitics
		Power strategy perspectives
		Political economy
		Resource dependence (and population ecology)

Fig. 3.1 Three waves of organisation theory

The organisation as a machine

Much of the early thinking on work organisations was wedded to the image of the organisation as a machine. This was not simply because mechanical imagery happened to provide a convenient metaphor but because many organisational designers in effect *aspired* to build great human engines for production and administration. The bureaucratisation of work was part of the historical rationalisation process whereby more and more aspects of life in Western societies were being subjected to a more instrumental or calculative style of thinking. This was a style which was associated with the growth of science and with technological developments. With regard to work organisation, it was felt that by carefully calculating the most appropriate way of achieving tasks and then basing on this formalised roles, procedures and arrangements within which people would be rewarded only in terms of their contribution to officially set task achievement, the efforts of large numbers of people could be coordinated and controlled and large and complex jobs done.

The potential costs to individuals of this newer approach in terms of lost autonomy and subjection to work instructions and office procedures would be outweighed by the advantages. In the production sphere there was the promise of much increased output and enhanced quality. And in the sphere of state administration there was the promise of the kind of fairness which was expected in the democratising societies of the time. This would come from the following of procedural neutrality and impartiality. The no longer tolerable evils of favouritism, nepotism and capriciousness would be removed from administration. Efficiency and fairness could both be increased.

Undoubtedly, employees were increasingly seen as means towards ends other than their own in the developing world of formal organisation and paid employment. But it was thought that this was rendered unproblematic by the rewards to be derived by employees. These would come in the form of increased wages and salaries and in the form of the wider benefits to be shared out as a result of the inevitable economic growth and the spread of democratic values and practices.

These assumptions underlie the varieties of 'classical' organisation and management theory we are now to examine. We shall consider two prescriptive schools of thought: Classical Administrative Principles and Scientific Management. These were clearly informed by an aspiration to give human work organisation the efficiency and precision of the machine. We shall then turn to a more descriptive and analytical strand of thinking which was concerned with developing Theories of Bureaucracy and which, although working with the image of the organisation as a machine, began to highlight its inadequacies.

Classical administrative principles

This was a somewhat atheoretical body of work. The writings of people like Henri Fayol (1916), Mooney and Reiley (1931), Gulik and Urwick (1937) were based on their own experiences and reflections. On the basis of these they attempted to establish universally applicable principles upon which organisational and management structures could be based. Among the mixture of exhortations, moral precepts and design principles to be found in the writing of the main inspirer of this literature, Henri Fayol, are some of the following suggestions. There should always be a 'unity of command' (no employee should have to take orders from more than one superior), a 'unity of direction' (there should be one head and one plan for a group of activities having the same objective) and regular efforts to maintain the harmony and union encouraged by an 'esprit de corps'. Although the contributors to this body of work vary in their sophistication and in the extent to which they see their principles as relevant to all conditions, there is nevertheless an underlying assumption of there always being a 'one best way'. This might be a matter of always differentiating 'line' and 'staff' departments (those directly concerned with producing the main output of the organisation and those who service this process) or perhaps fixing a *correct* 'span of control' (the number of subordinates any superior can effectively direct).

Scientific management

This shares the implicit philosophy of there always being a 'one best way' to organise and manage. According to the key inspirational figure of this school, F. W. Taylor (1911a, 1911b; and see below, p. 93), the application of scientific logic to the organisation of the workshop would achieve a level of efficiency which would remove any necessity for conflict between managers and workers. He saw employees who do manual work as basically asocial, economically motivated and self-seeking creatures who would generally prefer the management to do their task-related thinking for them. Given this, the management simply had to work out the most efficient way of organising work and then tie the monetary rewards of the work to the level of output achieved by each individual. This would produce results which would benefit employer and employee alike.

To make the organisation of the workshop maximally efficient the managers would need scientifically to analyse all the tasks to be done. They would then design jobs to achieve the maximum technical division of labour through advanced task fragmentation. They would ensure that the planning of work and its execution should be divorced and that skill requirements and job-learning times be reduced to a minimum. Materials-handling by operators would be minimised and indirect or preparatory tasks would be separated from direct or productive ones. To coordinate these now fragmented elements and these deskilled workers, such devices as time-study and monitoring systems would be established whilst worker effort would be both stabilised and intensified by the use of incentive payment systems.

Frederick Taylor, as the key figure in this movement which has given the world work study, bonus schemes, time and motion study and the like, is best seen as an advocate and systematiser rather than the inventor of what came to be called Taylorism. But it is probably no accident that this figurehead of the workplace rationalisation movement was an engineer by background and training. And whilst Taylor, in the early years of the twentieth century, was pulling together ideas about how to turn the human organisation of the workshop into a smooth-running and efficient machine, Fayol was following the spirit of his engineering training in trying to achieve something similar for the higher managerial and administrative levels of organisations.

As we move on to look at subsequent ideas on organising we shall see that many of the theoretical assumptions of these classical approaches have fallen under the onslaught of critical analysis and research investigation. Nevertheless, the major practices advocated by these schools are still central to the way much modern work is organised. Although the rationales put forward by the classical writers have proved defective in some important respects, their schemes for the building of machine-like bureaucracies with managers and officials strongly in control of activities have continued to be applied. These are not schools of thought to be dragged out merely to give historical background to contemporary practices. They are a lot more than fossils from the ancient past to be held up in front of each generation of management students. Botched and compromised as these schemes necessarily are, they have proved to have a great deal to offer to contemporary managers and organisers. At the heart of the major debates about how work is going to be organised in the future will be considerations of what place there will be for both big tightly integrated bureaucracies and for the fragmented and deskilled type of work advocated by these historical figures and still closely pursued by many contemporary managements. But, for the present, we can understand more about both the strength and the weaknesses of the mechanical bureaucratic form by turning to a more analytical group of writers who are part of this wave of thinking.

Theories of bureaucracy

These have been developed by a number of writers and researchers who have taken as their inspiration the ideas of the highly influential but much misrepresented Max Weber (1968). Weber was a German academic whose interests covered economics, sociology, political science and history. Although a figure of the same historical period as Fayol and Taylor, his role is entirely different. He was concerned to analyse and understand what was going on throughout the modernising world. Central to what he saw was the general process of 'rationalisation' referred to earlier (p. 48). Bureaucratisation was a key part of this process. Bureaucracy, like the growth of money economies and formalised markets, the spread of scientific and technological thinking, and the codifying of rules and laws, was a facet of a general trend in social life. This was one in which people increasingly make decisions and act on the basis of calculatingly devising the most appropriate means to meet specified goals throughout social life. To help analyse and understand the process of bureaucratisation, Weber devised a model of what a bureaucracy would look like if it existed in a pure form. This is the famous Weberian *ideal type* of bureaucracy. It is often taken to be the starting point for the discipline of organisation theory and much of what followed develops, refines or takes issue with what it is taken to imply.

In ideal-type form a bureaucracy has the following features. It has a clear *hierarchy* of offices whose functions are clearly specified. Officials are subject to a *unified control* and disciplinary system and are appointed on a contractual basis after being selected because of their specific *expertise*. The officials' posts constitute their sole employment or career and they are rewarded by a money salary paid according to their position in the hierarchy. They may be promoted up the hierarchy at the discretion of their superiors. This is the model which provides the launching pad for the great bulk of modern organisation theory. It is simply an outlining of the basic principles of bureaucratic organisation. It is a sketch of an impossibly pure and unachievable structure against which reality could be compared. Yet the status of the model has been widely misunderstood.

There have been two main reasons for the ideal type's being so misunderstood. First the term 'ideal type' has been taken to imply desirability instead of the intended notion of a pure mental construct or 'idea'. And, second, Weber has been taken to be an advocate of bureaucracy as a result of his pointing to the 'technical superiority' of bureaucracy. In pointing to this he was noting the *potential* efficiency of bureaucracy and not the actual or the inevitable efficiency which would be achieved by bureaucratising. In fact, Max Weber was anything but an advocate of bureaucracy. He was ambivalent in that he liked some of the potential which it held whilst he feared and despaired at aspects of the bureaucratising world around him. This was a world in which people could be turned into the small cogs of big machines. It was a world in which human beings would be prisoners in an 'iron cage'.

If we set Weber's thinking on bureaucracy in the context of his larger body of work we see that he provides us with a key to understanding why machine-like bureaucratic work organisations can achieve a great deal more than traditional ways of organising human efforts yet do not in fact anything like fulfil the promise of efficiency implicit in the notion of the machine. The key notion here is that of the *paradox of consequences.*

Bureaucracies or formal organisations are part of the social life of the society and culture in which they are set. And, in Weber's view, human social life is characterised by diversity of interests, values and perspectives, by conflict and by power struggles. Humans are seen as rational human beings pursuing ends, but there is no direct relationship between their efforts and the resulting social arrangements. The structures or patterns we see, whether in society generally or in the specific form of bureaucracy, never function in the way any social designer or engineer might have intended. The idea of the paradox of consequences refers to the fact that human actions often have unintended consequences. These may not only differ from what was intended but may even be in direct opposition to it.

This principle may be illustrated by the tendency noted by Weber's associate and fellow theorist of bureaucracy, Robert Michels (1949). This is the tendency, elevated by the pessimistic Michels to 'iron law' status, whereby a democratic organisation such as a political party or a trade union choosing to appoint a body of officials to serve its democratic purposes would find those officials using their posts and the associated resources to protect or further their own private interests. Here we see a means chosen to fulfil a particular purpose – that of democracy in this case – ending up subverting that very purpose. Weber himself saw this kind of danger present whenever social arrangements are deliberately set up to achieve certain things. The rationality of such attempts is clearly to be recognised. But that rationality is always liable to be compromised to a greater or lesser extent by the nature of the social and political world in which it occurs.

Whereas in the world in general, Robert Burns was able to note that the 'best laid schemes of mice and men gang aft agley', we can say that in the world of work organisations the best laid plans of managers and organisers always 'gang agley' – to some extent at least. Just how far wrong things go, we might argue, is a matter of how sensitive to this paradox-of-consequences tendency are those managing any given organisation.

A number of other theorists of bureaucracy have shown various ways in which unintended consequences undermine the potential efficiency of any social machine. It is ironic, however, that a number of these mistakenly saw themselves as correcting the drift of Weber's analysis rather than, as is really the case, following it. Robert Merton (1940), for example, argued that the emphasis on employee rule-following at the heart of bureaucratic rationality would encourage a counter-productive inflexibility on the part of those employees. This 'dysfunction' of bureaucracy, as he labels it, is the hatching of the dreaded 'bureaucratic personality'. Employing people in the bureaucratic setting encourages them to become the instigators of those kinds of petty officiousness and red tape which have turned the very word 'bureaucratic' into an epithet of distinctly negative character.

Philip Selznick (1966) also pointed to tendencies in organisations to trip themselves up, so to speak. He observed that the division of an organisation into departments intended to enable overall purposes to be more efficiently served can easily see those departments developing purposes of their own which come into conflict with the aims that inspired their establishment. Alvin Gouldner (1964), correspondingly, shows that, although the impersonal kind of rule which characterises formal organisations contributes to control and predictability in task-performance and keeps power relations more or less invisible, it also tends to be interpreted as a minimum performance standard. There is always the tendency for performance to be reduced to the 'official' minimum. If this occurs, it is likely to be met with the managerial reaction of tightened rules or closer supervision. This then makes power relations more visible and thus increases the likelihood of conflict between managers and managed.

These various dysfunctions, unintended consequences and vicious circles show us that the view of the organisation as a machine has major inadequacies. The problem, put simply, is that organisations are not, like machines, composed of inanimate bits and pieces – metallic cogs, levers and axles – but are made up of living, thinking, choice-making beings. The latter group of theorists, who studied rather than advocated bureaucratic organisation, have been discussed under this heading of 'organisations as machines' because they were initially engaging with that image in their work. However, several of these theorists, in recognising the living or organic nature of organisations, came to a preferred image of the organisation as a natural system, a kind of living organism which adapts to its circumstances. It is to this image that we now turn.

The organisation as a living organism

The bureaucratic character of modern work organisations at first seemed to make appropriate an idea of the organisation as a machine – as an instrument rationally and logically designed to meet certain purposes. However, as people's experience of such organisations grew and as academic studies of how they operate appeared, it became clear that, in a sense, they do take on a life of their own. Organisations seem to operate at times more in terms of their own inherent logic than as tools serving the purposes of their designers. If one looks at a sample of organisations and how they have changed over time it soon becomes apparent that it is quite normal for the original purpose for which an organisation is set up to become obscure or for it to change entirely. A profitable arms manufacturer becomes a semi-profitable bicycle producer or an orphanage becomes a school. The organisation is still a purposive or task-oriented structure in some sense but it does appear to have a facility for developing, adapting or modifying its form in the light of what is going on in its context. It is almost like a living creature adapting to its habitat. The appeal of the organic analogy as an image for conceptualising organisations soon becomes clear.

The various systems models which underpin many of the most influential schools of organisation theory have been inspired by a variety of sources including ones in engineering, biology and cybernetics. Ultimately, however, they all hark back to one of the most ancient metaphors for social organisation: the biological one of the natural living organism. Ever since human beings first began to devise models within which to think about how people might organise cooperative social life the suggestion has been made that, like a living creature, any society or organisation must be differentiated into head, stomach, arms, legs and so on and, most importantly, that all these parts are interdependent and need to be kept in a harmonious relationship with each other if the overall body is to survive fit and healthy within a potentially hostile environment.

Many valuable insights are offered by the organisation theorists who base their analysis on the organic image. They vary in the degree of sophistication with which they use the system idea, particularly with regard to how far they see the organisation as an 'open system' interacting with and adapting to the environment rather than simply a 'closed system' of interlocking parts. This second wave of organisation theories, all reacting to the mechanistic and one-best-way ethos of the first wave, has the main strength of highlighting two aspects of organisational functioning. These are, first, the ways in which what occurs in one part or 'sub-system' of the organisation has implications for what goes on in another and, second, the ways in which the various sub-systems, taken together as a whole system, interact with environment. However, the weakness of this general approach is that, as with any analytical scheme based on one clear metaphor, there is always the danger that the limits of metaphor-based thinking become forgotten. As we shall see when we come to the developments of our 'third wave', it is important to recognise that to treat an organisation as if it really were a system or an independently existing entity is to play down too much the fact that organisations ultimately only exist in the minds and actions of *people*, with all their variety, fickleness, ambition and individuality.

The four approaches characterised by this organic emphasis that we shall consider here are the human relations writers, the equilibrium theorists, the socio-technical school and the contingency theorists.

The human relations school

This school of writers on organisations is best known for the famous Hawthorne experiments which form the research basis for much of what they say. As we suggested earlier (p. 12), and will come back to later (pp. 98–101), the findings of these experiments can be interpreted in various ways. The various writers in this tradition, ranging from the careful reporters of the basic research, Roethlisberger and Dickson (1939), to the arch publicist, Elton Mayo (1933, 1949), and the British interpreter, J.A.C. Brown (1954), have all barbed their analytical arrows so as to damage as much as possible the body of Taylorist assumptions with which they want to take issue.

Scientific Management thinking implied that effective workplace organisation was a matter of giving appropriate levels of monetary reward to each individual in return for that individual's carrying out tasks precisely laid down by the more intelligent and expert 'scientific' managers. To the Human Relations writers this is to deny the social nature and social needs of human beings. To treat employees as a rabble of self-seeking and economistic individuals is to fail to see that the consensual cooperative interdependence vital to any effective social system cannot be achieved unless the basic human need to 'belong' is met. People are fuelled not by bread alone. The ever-improving productivity of the Hawthorne works' Relay Assembly Test Room (see below, p. 98) – occurring whether the changes made were of the kind scientific managers would expect to lead to deterioration as well as to improvement – could thus only be explained by the fact that the close interest shown in the workers by the investigators encouraged an effective pattern of communication and strong feelings of social cohesion. This made it possible for the needs of the group members for rewarding social interaction to be brought together with meeting the output needs of the management. The system worked because it met both the task requirements necessary for its economic survival and the emotional requirements of its human constituents – these being equally necessary for survival.

A great deal is not made of the 'open system' aspects of organisational functioning by the Human Relations school. Less is made of the adaptiveness of the organism within its environment than of the necessity of achieving a harmonious interdependence of what amounts to the two sub-systems of the organisation. These are the rational *managerial* sub-system on the one hand and the largely emotional, sentiment-based or affective *employee* sub-system on the other. We could say that the emphasis is on a harmony of the head and the heart of the organism rather than on an adaptive struggle for survival.

Equilibrium theory

This can be identified as a separate tradition within organisation theory, although at times it has aspired to becoming *the* organisation theory, bringing together as it does ideas from economics as well as from psychology and sociology. Its origins lie in the massively influential book by Chester Barnard, *The Functions of the Executive*, which was published in 1938. Much encouraged by his contacts with the Human Relations theorists and their intellectual supporters, this successful businessman set about producing a systematic theory of the organisation and of the role of the management within it. He conceives of the organisation as a cooperative grouping of individuals who are committed to a common purpose. This commitment is not unproblematic, however. It has to be worked for by the executive's involvement in training, inculcation of appropriate attitudes and by the provision of incentives.

The variety of human needs of the employees have to be met if the system is to be kept in the state of *equilibrium* which is vital for survival. What we can clearly see in Barnard's work is a conception of the managerial role which is implicit in the whole organic or systems tradition and which differs from that of the classical or machine tradition. Here the managers are not the people who run or operate the organisational machine in some sense from outside it. Instead, they are part of the organisational organism themselves. Their function within the system is to help it adapt to its environment. They are not outside the machine directing it towards pre-set goals as are the scientific managers of the classical scheme.

The decision-making aspect of organisational management came increasingly to the fore in those who followed Barnard. In the influential work of Herbert Simon (1948), March and Simon (1958) and Cyert and March (1963) we see a struggle to bring together the rationalistic aspects of organisational structures with the limited or 'bounded rationality' of the individuals who have, in various ways, to be 'induced' to 'contribute' so as to maintain the equilibrium of the system. Although this work is clearly dependent on the organic image, we shall see when we come to our 'third wave', that the later thinking of J. G. March on the limits of rationality and the interest of Cyert and March in the political dimension of organisational life opens the way to a different conception of organising.

Socio-technical systems theory

This theory differs from all the preceding work considered in largely having been developed in Britain rather than in the United States. Central to this approach, associated with people like Eric Trist, Fred Emery and A. K. Rice, is the notion that, to achieve its 'primary task', the technical and the social components of the overall system must be designed to take each other into account. This may sound obvious but, as these authors set out to demonstrate, the more normal procedure is to design a structure of technically defined tasks and only once this is done to fix onto it a set of human arrangements. Typically, a factory is designed and the layout of the plant decided prior to a choice of organisational structure (Miller and Rice, 1967). The socio-technical approach suggests instead that the two should be designed alongside each other in order to jointly optimise the two. It is assumed that the precise technical form required to achieve tasks is variable, as is the social structure to accompany it. Each can therefore be *chosen* to get the best fit with the other.

The principles of socio-technical design are clearly illustrated in the famous study done by Eric Trist and colleagues (1963) which tackled the problem of why the technical innovations introduced into certain post-war British coal mines gave neither the level of work satisfaction traditionally expected by the miners nor the levels of productivity sought by the management. They argued that the technical pattern of such things as the new occupational roles and shift arrangements associated with the newly introduced machinery took away the relative autonomy of work groups and removed the previously existing opportunity for each miner to use a variety of skills in his daily work. Because the social arrangements were designed primarily to suit the machinery rather than to accord with both technical constraints *and* the workforce's social and psychological requirements, the system worked poorly. The researchers devised a different approach to the use of new machinery which allowed retention of some of the traditional features of the social and cultural arrangements preferred by miners. A better *fit* having been achieved between the social and technical arrangements, there was said to be a marked improvement in productivity, worker-management co-operation and absenteeism levels.

The socio-technical systems perspective can be seen as one which incorporates into the framework of the organisation as a living organism certain of the ideas of both the Scientific Management and the Human Relations Schools. Both technical and social constraints are recognised but, instead of one side's being emphasised at the expense of the other, they are seen as inter-penetrating. We will see these ideas in practice again later when we consider the autonomous workgroup (p. 104), a characteristic development of this school of thought. This idea, like the rest of their thinking, involves a very clear rejection of the one-best-way ethos of the classical approaches. The key ideas here are ones of *fit* and *appropriateness*. These are also the themes of the various contingency theory contributions to what has become practically an orthodoxy in many places where organisation theory is taught.

Contingency theory

This is a grouping of contributions to organisation studies which share similar central concerns rather than a single body of theory. It applies insights similar to those developed by the socio-technical theorists at the workshop level to the whole organisation. Where the classical theorists sought to establish the universally applicable *best* vertical and horizontal span of hierarchies and the *best* degree of specialisation, formalisation, centralisation, delegation and the rest, this approach suggests that managements should seek the most *appropriate* organisational shape to achieve their purposes, given prevailing circumstances of *contingencies*.

Although the contingency theory terminology was not introduced until the later 1960s, the studies which established this tradition of seeking ways in which various contingent factors have to be taken into account when selecting structural schemes were done in the late 1950s. This new flexible approach was established by Joan Woodward and by Burns and Stalker.

Joan Woodward's study (1958, 1965) of a hundred manufacturing firms in Essex began along lines consistent with classical administrative thinking. The aim was to establish, on the basis of solid research, just which patterns of organisational structure lead to successful business performance. However, the data collected did not at first allow any kind of generalisations to be made. Using conventional definitions of business success, it appeared that there were no clear factors in common between either the successful or the unsuccessful enterprises. It was only when the variable of manufacturing technology was introduced that a pattern emerged. When firms were grouped in terms of the complexity of their technology (after being located on a scale running from unit and small batch production through large batch and mass production to process production) it appeared that different structural arrangements were appropriate for different technologies. Effective petrochemical companies (process-flow) would, for example, tend to have relatively tall and narrow hierarchical shapes whilst effective producers of custom-built cabinet-work (unit production) would tend to have a short and wide profile.

Where the Woodward study stresses *technology* as the key contingency, Burns and Stalker (1961) interpreted their research findings as pointing to the importance of the organisation's *environment*. From their study of organisations in the electronics and the textiles industries they concluded that a different organisational pattern is likely to be appropriate in an industry like textiles, where the business environment is relatively stable, compared to the pattern appropriate in an industry like electronics where the environment produces a constant pressure for innovation. To cope with pressures for innovation, an *organic* type of structure will be appropriate. The structure here will be loose and flexible with a relatively low degree of formalisation and task prescription. Where conditions are more stable, however, *mechanistic* structures may be more appropriate. These are ones closer to the ideal type of bureaucracy and the prescriptions of the classical administrative writers. What we see being established here as a trend in organisation theory is an unwillingness simply to reject older ideas about organising. Instead, there is a search for frameworks which can give guidance on how organisers do select or should select the appropriate arrangements for their particular circumstances.

The framework which emerges from this thinking is generally an open systems one in which the organisational structure somehow adapts itself or is adapted to enable it to function successfully in its environment. Researchers who followed those described above have both pointed to alternative key contingencies to those of technology and environment or have refined the way those contingencies are to be understood. The Aston University group led by Derek Pugh (Pugh and Hickson, 1976, Pugh and Hinings, 1976, Pugh and Payne, 1977), for example, put their greatest emphasis on the organisation's size. They accepted Woodward's stress on technology in the case of smaller organisations and in those areas of larger organisations close to the production process itself. However, they argued that, once you move away from the shop-floor level of an organisation of any size, then it will be that very issue of size, together with the extent of the organisation's independence from other organisations (such as parent organisations) that will influence the structural pattern necessary for effective organisational performance. Other researchers such as Blau (1970) in the United States and Child and Mansfield (1972) in Britain have shown a corresponding tendency towards increased level of bureaucratisation with increase in organisational size.

Lawrence and Lorsch (1967) refined the existing thinking on how environmental contingencies apply. They concentrated on the fact that different departments of any given organisation will vary in the degree to which they have to cope with environmental uncertainty and diversity. Thus, a production department and a research department within the same organisation might have quite different structures and operating styles. In another industry, however, this difference might not apply. But the nature of the *differentiation* pattern of any given organisation necessarily has implications for the devices chosen to achieve *integration* of these units. Therefore an organisation whose sub-units do not vary in the way they have to cope with their environment will be appropriately integrated by the normal chain of command and standard operating procedures whereas an organisation with greater differentiation will need, say, special committees, coordinating departments or liaison specialists.

In terms of both analytical and practical value this second wave of organisation theory improves on the first. To see the organisation as a living ever-changing organism whose form has to vary according to its circumstances is an improvement on seeing it as a machine whose success is only really dependent on the quality of the blueprint from which it is engineered. But both of these approaches use metaphors which too readily encourage us to see the organisation as an actually existing social entity. We are encouraged to *reify* the organisation; to commit the 'fallacy of misplaced concreteness'. And, by being so encouraged to say 'the organisation does this' or 'the organisation did that' we are being encouraged to forget that, real as organisations sometimes seem to be when we get paid by one, sacked by one or taxed by one, they are really only highly fragile sets of cooperative arrangements tentatively agreed by individuals and groups who have a variety of social, political and economic interests.

With the third wave of organisation theory we see various moves towards accepting this reality. The organic metaphor of the second wave valuably drew attention to the *process* of organising. But the third wave confronts the fact that the processes involved are not biological processes going on in the brains, bones and guts of big organisms but are social, political and economic processes going on in complex human arenas.

The organisation as a social, political and economic process

The variety of different approaches considered as part of this third wave of organisation theory vary in the way that some very clearly derive from the type of model introduced in the second wave whilst others come from quite contrary traditions within the social sciences. But, whether these contributions derive from the holistic systems tradition considered above or have been prompted by the more individualistic or interactional tradition of social scientific thought which we have not yet met, they all take us in the direction of a new general perspective. This is one which stresses three aspects of organisational life. First, it stresses the importance of the creative, critical and situation-defining characteristics of the individuals who make up the organisation. Second, it recognises the varieties of interest and goal among individuals and groups in the organisation, with a consequent emphasis on conflict and political behaviour. And, third, it tries to come to terms with the fact that organisations are not simply entities which react to the general environment which surrounds them.

Organisations make their 'environment' as much as it makes them.

Under the present heading we shall consider the Negotiated Order (or Social Action) approach, Decision Process Theory, the Culture-Excellence School, the Micropolitics Perspective, the Power-Strategy Emphasis, the Political Economy Approach and the Resource Dependence Perspective.

The negotiated order (social action) approach

The negotiated order approach has its roots partly in the methodological thinking of the German sociologist Max Weber and partly in the interactionist tradition of American social psychology. The fullest statement of the position is that of David Silverman (1970). And the main insight operating here is the one that social structures – be they societies, organisations or groups – are not pregiven structures or systems into which people are slotted. Instead, they are the outcome of the interactive patterns of human activity. Social structures are often experienced as if they are things which precede human activity but what are really being experienced are institutional *processes*.

What society or the organisation *is*, in this view, is continually being negotiated and renegotiated by the inter-subjective relating of its members to each other. For example, one does not obey an organisational rule because, as we might typically say, the organisation requires it. Rather, we obey that rule because we go along with a set of expectations that we should, with a greater or a lesser degree of willingness, obey it. And those expectations are ones partly imposed upon organisational members by those holding power and partly negotiated between the variety of parties involved in that situation. Those with power, and especially the management, attempt to create definitions of the situation among the employees which make the prevailing pattern of power acceptable. In Weber's terms, power is made legitimate and thus converted to 'authority'. This means that managerial work is involved in the creation of meanings for organisational members. But these are not meanings which can ever be unilaterally imposed. All realities are to some degree negotiated. And we shall return to issues of meaning later (pp. 129–31).

Decision process theory

This has much in common with the view of organisational patterns or structures as the outcomes of the activities of individuals and groups rather than as the set of slots into which people are fitted and controlled. It focuses on the ways in which decisions are made in organisations and derives from the equilibrium theory described earlier (p. 58) and, especially, from Herbert Simon's notion of 'bounded rationality'. Central stress is placed on the fact that organisational members, in making sense of their situations in order to make choices or decisions, typically have very limited or ambiguous information. And what information they do have is going to be processed neither with the cold calculative efficiency of a human computer nor with the disinterested and unemotional coolness of a perfect bureaucrat.

This basic insight is developed to show that organisations are far less rational, consistent, purposive and integrated than either the mechanical or the organic perspectives would suggest. Ambiguity, randomness, chance and accident are realities too often played down, as was suggested in Chapter 1 when it was argued that coming to terms with ambiguity when studying or managing organisations is an important necessity (pp. 20-3).

Decision-making is clearly central to organisational life but people, in taking part in decision-making, are typically involved in a lot more than operating a system. As March and Olsen (1976) point out, choice processes provide occasions for a number of things to be done. These range from fulfilling duties and meeting commitments, through justifying oneself; distributing glory or blame; exercising, challenging or reaffirming friendships; power and status-seeking; expressing group or self-interest to having a good time and simply enjoying the experience of taking part in the making of a decision. In this view, the organisation begins to look like a stage for dramas rather than a system or organism. The organisation is like an everlasting administrative soap opera. But the launching of new metaphors does not stop here.

Cohen, March and Olsen (1972) introduce the image of the dustbin in their analysis of organisational decision-making. They base their 'garbage can model of organisational choice' on research done in American universities, which they conceptualise as 'organised anarchies'. However, their analysis can, I believe, be realistically applied to most if not to all types of organisation.

It is suggested that the decision opportunity operates like a garbage can. Just what transpires in a particular situation depends on what happens to have been thrown into the bin in terms of what problems are around at the time, what solutions are available which might be attached to those problems, which people happen to be about and how much time they have available. The organised anarchy has fairly unclear goals and technologies and a fluid pattern of participation. Although organisations may vary in the extent to which they are anarchic in this sense, we can reasonably say that all decision opportunities are dustbins which collect a muddled assortment of problems, solutions and participants. As these authors put it, we get choices looking for problems, issues and feelings looking for decision situations, solutions looking for issues and decision-makers looking for work!

March and Romelaer (1976) talk of decisions as streams rather than as events and, after implying that people 'drift' into decisions, they switch their metaphor to that of the organisation as a game. They suggest that the organisation can be seen as a round-sloped multi-goal soccer field with many players joining and leaving at different times. Some people can throw balls in and some can remove them. The players try to kick whichever ball comes near them in the direction of the goal they like and away from the goal they wish to avoid. The slope of the field produces a bias in how the balls roll and what goals are reached but, nevertheless, the course of the particular decision and the actual outcomes are not easily anticipated. The inclusion of bias in the game as described here is important because it draws attention to the fact that organisations are not made up of equal partners or even equal antagonists.

The culture-excellence school

This takes from decision-process theory the idea of the organisation as loosely structured and full of ambiguity. However, it attempts to bring some pattern into the picture by showing that, in the more effective or 'excellent' organisations, there are some basic values and orientations which ensure that organisational efforts are not dissipated as a result of these factors. What brings the activities of the organisational members to focus upon those purposes which lead to effective performance is the existence of a strong and clearly articulated culture.

The idea that any social organisation – be it a society, a community or a corporation – has a culture as well as a structure is as old as the disciplines of sociology and social anthropology. Perhaps its first impact on organisational thinking is to be seen in Philip Selznick's (1948, 1949) contrast between the mechanical idea of an 'organisation' and the more culturally developed 'institution'. Organisations are set up to act as tools to meet certain purposes, he argues, but a process of institutionalisation occurs whereby the organisation becomes a more responsive and adaptive social organism with an identity and set of values which integrate it in such a way that its existence has a significance for its members far greater than one of simply achieving the tasks for which it was set up. Selznick recognises that the management has to be involved in moulding what he calls the 'character' of the organisation. And in this he is in accord with the approach to the managerial role as conceived by Chester Barnard (see p. 58), an important inspiring figure for the culture-excellence school. Barnard's importance is seen as arising from his stress on the management of the organisation as a whole and from his recognition that to achieve this the manager must act as the shaper and communicator of a set of shared values for the organisation.

Values are at the heart of most of the concepts of culture which are used. They underpin the essential idea of culture, which is one of a set of shared beliefs about how one properly behaves in the context in which the culture prevails. This notion of 'proper' behaviour is present in one of the first explicit uses of the idea of culture in the managerial literature. Elliot Jaques (1951) writes of the culture of the factory as 'its customary and traditional way of thinking and doing things, which is shared to a greater or lesser degree by all its members'. He suggests that culture becomes second nature to those who have been in the organisation for some time whilst ignorance of culture 'marks out the newcomers' and whilst 'maladjusted members are recognised as those who reject or are otherwise unable to use the culture of the firm'.

The idea that there are different types of culture to be found in different organisations was popularised by Charles Handy (1976) who developed his views in his 1978 book in which he argued that bad management is mixed-up management. It operates with a confusion of managerial philosophies rather than with a carefully thought-out culture which embraces an appropriate mixture of the basic management cult ideas. He argues for mixed management rather than mixed-up management: for 'cultural propriety'. The four basic cults are those following the four 'gods of management'. Zeus is the god of the dynamic entrepreneur who rules through snap decisions, Apollo is the god of bureaucracy and order whilst Athena represents the craft approach with its emphasis on technical expertise and Dionysus inspires those of an artistic or professional temperament who dislike owing allegiance to any boss. Successful management is a matter of choosing the appropriate mixture of these influences.

Andrew Pettigrew (1979) argued strongly for the integration of the notion of culture into the language of organisational studies, suggesting that in the pursuit of 'everyday tasks and objectives, it is all too easy to forget the less rational and instrumental, the more expressive social tissue around us that gives those tasks meaning'. He sees culture as the system of 'publicly and collectively accepted meanings operating for a given group at a given time' and he sees it as an important role of the leader not only to create the 'rational and tangible aspects of organisations, such as structure and technology', but also 'symbols, ideologies, language, beliefs, rituals and myths'. There are clear echoes in this of the discussion in Chapter 2 of the idea of management as magic.

The pulling together of a lot of this kind of thinking and its relating to organisational effectiveness or 'excellence' has been done by a group of researchers in the United States who can be seen as forming the group which I am labelling as the culture-excellence school. This research was done under the auspices of the McKinsey consulting organisation and was concerned to locate the characteristics which were common to those American businesses which were generally regarded in the business community as outstandingly successful. The major statement of their findings and their interpretations are to be found in Peters and Waterman's (1982) highly influential *In Search of Excellence*.

This work attacks what the authors call the 'rational model' of organisation, in terms not dissimilar from those used in the first chapter of this book. They argue that what makes for excellence in the management of organisations is not the rigorous use of techniques of organisational design, of financial planning and analysis, of computerised control systems and the rest. These may be used but what makes the difference is attention to something much more qualitative. Success comes from the use of a certain kind of simplicity. There is reliance on simple structures, simple strategies, simple goals and simple communications. And the key to managing in a basically simple way in what are often large and potentially complex organisations is the use of a clear and 'tight' culture.

Peters and Waterman see the main function of the organisation's culture as one of giving meaning to the organisational members, often through such media as what they call the 'rich tapestries of anecdote, myth and fairy tale'. These devices all serve to communicate and reinforce the 'shared values' which constitute the culture. The authors suggest that it was the 'dominance and coherence' of culture that was essential to the excellent companies. They say that the stronger was the culture and the more it was directed towards the marketplace, the 'less need there was for policy manuals, organisation charts, or detailed procedures and rules'.

An example of the sort of cultural device which can be used in this way and which is often quoted by the members of this school is the slogan 'IBM means service'. This provides a central value orientation in that company which meets the success criterion identified by Peters and Waterman: that the organisation's 'value set' integrate 'the notions of economic health, serving customers, and making meanings down the line'. What this device can also be used to illustrate is the central principle advocated by these writers whereby the excellent organisation operates with a combination of 'loose' and 'tight' controls.

With the concept of simultaneously loose and tight controls, these writers move away from the older style of managerial debate in which argument is based on the question of whether it is better to operate with tight managerial controls or to operate on the basis of a relatively easy-going control structure which gives employees autonomy and discretion. The IBM slogan is an illustration of how this either-or view is contradicted in practice in one organisation: the slogan 'underscores the company's overpowering devotion to the individual customer' whilst the formulation 'also provides remarkable space'. As Peters and Waterman say:

> In the same institutions in which culture is so dominant, the highest levels of true autonomy occur. The culture regulates rigorously the few variables that do count, and it provides meaning. But within those qualitative values (and in almost all other dimensions), people are encouraged to stick out, to innovate.

Deal and Kennedy (1982) are associates of the above authors and their research follows very similar lines. Using words which clearly echo Selznick's thinking mentioned earlier, they say that they wanted to see 'what had made America's great companies not merely organisations, but successful human institutions'. And they claim that their research showed that the 'consistently high performers' among the 80 companies studied could be character- ised as 'strong culture companies'. These authors, in effect, treat culture as simply amounting to 'the way we do things around here' and see a strong culture as a 'powerful lever for guiding behaviour'. It does this through spelling out how people are ex- pected to behave most of the time (through 'informal rules') and through 'making people feel better about what they do, so that they are more likely to work harder'. People are not managed 'directly by computer reports, but by the subtle cues of a culture'. This culture, in which 'nothing is too trivial' involves key values, heroes, rites, rituals and myths. There is a variety of cultural types but what counts is the strength and the consistency of the culture which prevails.

The attending to the cultures of organisations and the mana- gerial role in developing and maintaining them has proved to represent an important new direction in organisational analysis and, indeed, in managerial practice. The great importance of the concept of culture, I suggest, is that it can be seen as the glue which holds an organisation together and as the key concept which can link the largely structural or patterning concerns of this chapter with the largely behavioural or leadership concerns of the next. It is a concept to which we will return more than once, not least when we come to consider the ways in which managers can be seen as dealing with symbols and meanings in performing a leadership role within the organisation (p. 129). And, if this is to be seen as corresponding to discussion in the previous chapter of management as magic, then we now turn to the approach which provides the theoretical underpinning to the managerial politics theme which was present in both of our previous chapters.

The micropolitics perspective

This is rooted in a conception of the organisation as a political arena in which individuals both cooperate and compete in a series of groups and coalitions. This can be related to the stress put in the previous two approaches on the ambiguity which pervades organisational life. As Jeffrey Pfeffer (1978) puts it, organisational politics involves 'those activities taken within organisations to acquire, develop, and use power and other resources to obtain one's preferred outcomes in a situation in which there is uncertainty or dissensus about choices'. Most contributors to this approach concentrate on the behaviour of managers and other decision-makers but the basic insight that people tend to act both individually and in groups or coalitions within organisations in order to further or defend their interests applies across the board.

The clearest analysis of micropolitics in organisations is to be found in the works of Tom Burns (1961, 1977). He suggests that organisational participants can be seen to be acting politically when they are making use of both physical and human resources in competitive situations in order to achieve greater control over others. They thus make their situation safer or more comfortable or generally more satisfying. But the fact that such behaviour is normal in organisations is not simply a reflection of some general attribute like 'human nature'. It is a built-in feature of organisations which always have two sides to them. On the one hand they are cooperative systems which are 'assembled out of the usable attributes of people'. And on the other hand they are also social systems within which people compete for advancement. In doing this they make use of others. The whole perspective is summarised in Burns's (1961) words:

> members of a corporation are at one and the same time
> cooperators in a common enterprise and rivals for the material

and intangible rewards of successful competition with each other. The hierarchic order of rank and power that prevails in them is at the same time a single control system and a career ladder.

Politicking is a normal part of organisational life and not a pathology within it. It is normal because all organisations use people who, in turn, use the organisation. And, because of the hierarchic nature of organisation structures, people use and compete with each other in the process of managing resources. But it is not only the hierarchic aspect of structures that leads to what Ian Mangham (1979) calls a view of the organisation as a 'more or less complex arena for internal bargaining among the bureaucratic elements and personalities who collectively comprise its working apparatus'. The horizontal dimension also contributes.

The horizontal division of the organisation into departments or sub-units is emphasised by Andrew Pettigrew (1973) who points out that individuals laying claim to resources necessarily operate within the departmental structure. Since such sub-units have differentiated interests, individuals tend to operate by relating themselves to sub-unit competition for scarce resources. As Pettigrew shows from his research, their politicking skills and, especially, their ability to manage information is important in how successful any given individual tends to be in the competition for resources. However, it is nevertheless the case that certain departments often have a better chance of becoming more powerful than others. To understand this we have to turn to thinking which has attempted to connect power issues in organisations to questions of how organisations relate to their environments and to how strategies are developed within organisations.

The power-strategy emphasis

I am using this heading to cover contributions from a variety of sources which all concern themselves with the connection between questions of power and the general direction which the organisation takes in relating to its environment. An early contribution to the thinking here was made by Charles Perrow (1970) in the way he interpreted his finding that in eleven of the twelve

industrial firms which he studied the managers felt the sales department to be the most powerful. Perrow put this down to 'their
strategic position with respect to the environment'. Both Michel
Crozier (1964) and J. D. Thompson (1967) had pointed out that
this power or leadership among organisational sub-units goes to
those who deal with the sources of the greatest uncertainty for
the organisation.

The insight that there is a relationship between the power of a
section of an organisation and the way it deals with problems for
the organisation was systematically developed by David Hickson
and his colleagues (1971) in what they called a *strategic contingency theory of power*. This suggests that the power of a sub-unit
depends on three things. First, it depends on the extent to which
the sub-unit is not dependent or 'contingent' on other sub-units;
second, on its not being substitutable by any other sub-unit and,
third, on its centrality to the organisation. Centrality derives from
the part played in coping with strategically important uncertainties. This would mean, for example, that if an organisation faced
its severest problems in the area of finance, we would expect the
finance specialists to become the most powerful group within the
management. If, however, these problems eased only to find the
organisation's continuation dependent on having to find new
markets, we might find the marketing function coming to the
fore. But these two outcomes would only occur if the role of,
respectively, the finance and the marketing people could
not be carried out by any other section and as long as, in each
case, the section was not under the control of another group or
department.

The strategic contingency approach emphasises the political
dimension of organising but its clear origins in the systems thinking of our second wave of organisation theory means that it is not
as strong as it might be on the processual side. Little is said about
how the uncertainties in the environment are actually mediated
by the members of those units. As with the wider contingency
approach, there is an implication that the organism – or system
– reacts to its circumstances in some almost automatic way. As
contingencies or uncertainties arise, the structure adapts to cope
with them so that the organisation can continue to follow its
strategy. To make use of the insight being offered here without
losing sight of the fact that organisations are the outcomes of

human processes and, to some extent, choices, we must turn to those approaches which stress *strategic choice*.

Both contingency theory of the type considered as part of our second wave of organisation theories and traditional thinking in economics see organisational structures as following in a fairly automatic – or at least unexamined – way from factors in the environment. Economic thinking tends to see the major force influencing events as the 'invisible hand' of the market. However, there have been a number of economists who have been willing to recognise the significance of the role of managers as mediators between market circumstances and organisational structures.

Oliver Williamson (1975) stresses the ways in which managerial decision-making takes into account 'transaction costs'. These are such costs to the organisation as those of constantly seeking market information and the making and policing of contractual arrangements. Strategies therefore tend to be followed which bring into the organisational 'hierarchy' those activities which create such costs. This leads to such structural developments as the vertical integration of operations. Sources of uncertainty and problems of bounded rationality in analysing information, as well as the difficulties of opportunism, encourage organisational managers to bring activities 'in house', so to speak. Closer control is thus made possible. Yet, to cope with what are called 'market failures' in this way creates further problems of managing efficiently.

Organisations exist and grow because markets fail but, points out Williamson, managers, in large part for reasons of self-interest, come to favour in-house sources of supply. They also like to see their own organisation grow (this being to do with perceived connections between employer size and executive remuneration level) and they tend to want to defend current programmes of action or ways of doing things, regardless of whether there exist alternative and more efficient ways of proceeding. As a result of this there will arise an efficiency pressure for those at the top to structure the organisation to reduce these effects. The adoption of the multi-divisional corporate form within large businesses is to be understood in this way. The tendencies towards the above organisational inefficiencies are seen to be reduced if people are located in smaller units or profit-centres where they have to be more sensitive to external pressures whilst still being under surveillance from the centre and subject to central control on matters of capital allocation.

Although this kind of 'behavioural economics' analysis concentrates on how activities are 'efficiency-led', it does recognise that outcomes such as the adoption of certain basic organisational structures result from strategic choices made by those directing organisations. This notion is important in the work of another economist and business historian, Alfred Chandler, who, significantly, entitled one of his major works *The Visible Hand* (1977). Organisational structures are seen to follow from choices made by the organisational strategists and Chandler (1962) defines strategy as 'the determination of the basic long-term goals and objectives of an enterprise and the adoption of courses of action and the allocation of resources necessary for carrying out those goals'. Because businesses have to face exigencies of shifting demands, changing sources of supply, fluctuating economic conditions, new technological developments and the actions of competitors, new patterns of action and resource allocation continually need to be sought. The particular organisational form which Chandler observes as being chosen by those heading large businesses (especially in America) has again been the multi-divisional structure or what Chandler calls the 'M-form'.

The importance of *strategic choices* was brought into the mainstream of organisation theory in a seminal article by John Child (1972). This takes ideas from behavioural economics as a means of going beyond the deterministic implications of contingency thinking. The emphasis here is on the latitude of choice which the key decision-makers are said to have. Those who make the strategic decisions are conceptualised in the terms suggested by Cyert and March (1963). They are members of the *dominant coalition*: that group within the politics of managerial behaviour who have won for themselves the capacity to make key decisions. The contingencies of size, technology, environmental conditions and so on do indeed influence decisions made. But these are not simply 'givens' requiring reactions. The dominant coalition can decide to influence or change the contingencies or the constraints surrounding it as well as the structures which are adopted in the light of these. Organisational leaders manipulate their environments using methods varying from advertising to takeovers and from political lobbying to wholesale manipulation of governments.

If we accept that organisations follow strategies in a general sense of following a particular direction in their relationship with their environment, and we accept that this is an outcome of political choices made in the light of various (partly-manipulable) constraints, we still have to note two things. First, we must note the danger of slipping back towards an over-rationalised conception of the organisation which sees it as a structure straightforwardly designed to meet 'goals'. Goals, objectives and strategies must be seen as emergent rather than as pre-existing. We need a conception of strategy formation which recognises both the rational aspects and the 'behavioural'.

J. B. Quinn (1980) attempts to do this in his attempted synthesis of what he calls the 'formal planning approach' of traditional business-strategy thinking and the 'power-behavioural' approach which emphasises the realities of multiple goals, politics, bargaining and muddling through. He interprets his own research findings as showing that strategic decisions come neither from 'power-political interplay' nor from processes of 'aggregation in a single massive decision matrix where all factors can be treated quantitatively ... to arrive at a holistic optimum'. Strategy is something which emerges at the top. But it is not created by strategic specialists located at the top. The studies show that what are judged to be 'effective' strategies arise out of a whole series of experiments and probes into the future made in various parts of the organisation and at various levels. Strategy-making is – or should be – a matter of *'logical incrementalism'*. It is incremental because it is built up from lessons which are learned and it is logical because managers are aware of these processes and consciously develop their ability to direct them. At least this is what happens in the organisations which Quinn sees as successful strategically.

The second factor which we must bear in mind is the role played by organisational cultures or managerial philosophies in both strategy formation and structural choice. The research of Miles and Snow (1978) is helpful here and shows how in a sample of both business and non-business organisations, there can be seen a variety of 'strategic types'. The four basic types which were identified can be seen as operating with their own distinct ethos. In *domain defenders* those at the top perceive little or no change or uncertainty in the environment and they are not inclined to do more than adjust structures and processes in a minor way. *Reluctant reactors* have top managers who see change and uncertainty but leave adjustments until conditions in the environment force them to make changes. An alternative reaction to perceived uncertainty and change is that of the *anxious analysers*, who wait until competitors develop a suitable response which they, too, adopt. *Enthusiastic prospectors*, on the other hand, have leaders who continually perceive and almost create change and uncertainty. They regularly experiment with potential responses to new environmental trends.

The political economy approach

This approach to organisational analysis is based upon a desire to understand organisations in terms of social, political and economic processes like much of what we have considered so far. However, its level of analysis tends to be rather different. The approach is one favoured by sociologists concerned primarily with the structures of societies. Organisations are considered in terms of their relationship with the overall political economy of which they are a part and, in particular, with how they both contribute to and derive from the general societal pattern of advantage and disadvantage in power, prestige, wealth and income. A number of British organisation analysts, when writing primarily as sociologists, have adopted this perspective (Clegg and Dunkerley, 1980; Watson, 1980a; Littler and Salaman, 1984). The central idea here is one of recognising the correspondence between the way in which society is patterned and the way organisations are shaped. In each case there is a hierarchy, with discretion, power, prestige, and material advantage both going together and being distributed to the advantage of those in the 'higher' positions. And it is typically observed that the people in the higher positions in organisations are not only those who occupy, or are connected with those who occupy, the higher 'class' positions in society. They tend also to be predominantly male and white, thus giving us a further correspondence between societal and organisational structures.

The emphasis in this approach on class and other inequalities and on the role of capitalist priorities in the structuring and managing of organisations has meant that there has been a significant drawing on ideas from the Marxist tradition of social and political thought. But this by no means can be taken to imply that ideas developed here are solely relevant to those interested in bringing about radical social and political changes. They are equally relevant to those wishing to know how organisations work for any other kind of reason. We will have to consider the political economy context of organisations, for example, when we examine the institution of employment in Chapter 5.

The resource dependence approach

This can be understood as based on strong political economy assumptions. It recognises that managing organisations is both political and economic and always occurs in the context of what is happening in the wider environment. However, this approach focuses on the organisation itself rather than on the structural context. It is nevertheless perfectly compatible with more macro-sociological concerns of the political economy approach described above.

In its origins, this approach was close to the 'population ecology' perspective (Hannan and Freeman, 1977; Aldrich, 1979). Strictly speaking, we should be describing this approach as part of our second wave of organisational thinking since it borrows very heavily from biology. It stresses that organisations have to be seen as components of their own environment, this being conceptualised as an ecological system populated by other organisations. Attention is then paid to the relationship between organisations and, especially, to the processes whereby organisations adapt and evolve in order to survive. Successful evolution is a matter of the survival of the fittest in the environment in a way paralleling that of the evolutionary model of Darwinian biology. Organisations go through both planned and unplanned 'variations' in their form, and the environment 'selects' the form which best suits it, primarily through competitive processes. Organisations then 'retain' the form which best suits the 'niche' or 'domain' which they have found in the ecological system of which they are a part. Retention includes all those standard practices – ranging from the use of operating manuals to socialisation activities – which organisations use to maintain stability.

The resource dependence theorists have developed these 'natural selection' assumptions away from the biological starting point and into a more political-economic framework (Pfeffer and Salancik, 1978; Miles, 1980). What is retained, however, is the key idea of organisational strategies and activities being ultimately to do with issues of survival in an environment which contains other organisations. Any given organisation does not simply compete with others. It is dependent upon a whole series of them for the supply of resources upon which its continued life depends. What makes this a political model is the recognition that these suppliers of resources are *constituencies*: coalitions of actors with interests or concerns of their own. The environment is seen therefore as a mixture of a political arena and a marketplace rather than as an ecological environment of the type studied by the naturalist. And the organic analogy is further rejected in the all-important recognition that the organisation's survival is also dependent for 'resources' on internal constituencies. The processual ideas of the micropolitical perspective (p. 71) are thus incorporated and the ideas of the strategic contingency theory of power are exploited to relate the activities of organisational sub-units to the actions of external resource suppliers, as we shall see in a moment.

The resource dependence approach sees the organisation as dependent for its continued existence on a whole range of constituencies, internal and external. These may be key individuals, materials suppliers, customers and clients, departments or divisions, owners or shareholders, workers and trade unions, government agencies, consumer bodies, a managerial elite, pressure groups, and so on. And at any given time, certain constituencies will be more *strategic* than others in the sense of posing a threat of resource withdrawal, be these resources material or symbolic. Shareholders threatening to withdraw capital could be the focus of attention one day and a workforce threatening to withdraw labour could be of central concern on another day. And if, on another occasion, the press were tending to create damaging publicity then attention to that question would become strategic just as would, in yet another circumstance, a question of the state or the courts acting in a way which could lead to withdrawal of that vital symbolic resource, legality.

Both internal structures and internal power distribution – and how these change – will reflect resource dependence trends. We can see internal power and resource distribution potentially shifting with the above set of circumstances from finance, to personnel, to public relations to legal specialists. Organisational effectiveness – an ability to survive long term – requires an ability to monitor the behaviour and demands of constituencies, both inside and outside the organisation, and to economically and in a balanced way meet the demands of those constituencies with whom an exchange relationship exists. For any particular organisation, it is possible to chart the set of constituencies which have to be considered. A scheme on the lines suggested in Fig. 3.2 can be used for this. It will be noticed that competitors are treated slightly differently from other constituencies here. I have done this because they do not strictly provide resources on which the organisation is dependent. Yet they are clearly very important

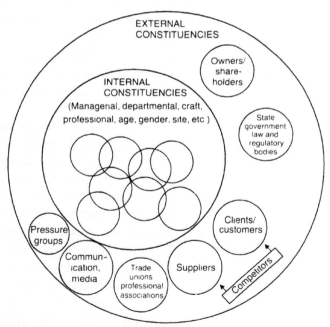

Fig. 3.2 Organisational constituencies:
    groups upon which the organisation is dependent for
    resources

influences on those organisations which have competitors. They are therefore most usefully represented as having an influence which is mediated by the client or customer constituencies. The threat posed by a rival organisation is one of persuading clients to transfer resources away from the focal organisation.

Organisational and managerial effectiveness

The resource dependence approach significantly informed the conception of management introduced in the previous chapter (p. 41). Its value as a basis for understanding organisations and their managerial component derives in particular from two features of the framework. The first of these relates to the fact that it incorporates ideas from many other processual approaches which are available (the micropolitics and power-strategy approaches especially) and yet also has the scope to be made compatible with other useful perspectives. For example, in both its focus on holding together internal constituencies to cope with a difficult environment and in its focus on the need to be sensitive to the requirements of external constituencies such as customers, it can be connected up to the culture-excellence school's thinking. Culture can be seen as giving coherence to the idea of 'the organisation': giving coherence to what might otherwise look like too fluid a coalition of coalitions. All this makes the approach a promising basis for synthesis within organisational analysis.

The second feature making the resource dependence perspective so potentially valuable is its contribution towards that perpetually nagging question of how we are to conceptualise 'effectiveness' or, if you prefer, the question of what framework we can use to judge or evaluate organisational performance. There have been endless debates about just what it is that indicates effective organisational management: is it productivity, long-term profitability, employee satisfaction, return on capital, rate or degree of growth or what? And there has also been the vexed question of whether organisational effectiveness is the same thing or something entirely different in business organisations, welfare organisations, schools, hospitals, prisons and so on.

All types of organisations have managements and we face the challenge of answering a basic question: just because the indicators of successful performance usually applied to the management of a business (profit, growth, etc.) are clearly quite different from the indicators applied to the management of a school (exams passed, encouraging creativity, etc.), did it really have to mean that there was nothing in common between managerial work in each of these areas? The resource dependence framework helps considerably here: it suggests that the indicator of effectiveness which you choose is a matter of the circumstances of the particular organisation at a particular time. A business whose strategic constituency at a certain time is its shareholders could well have its management judged by their ability to produce profit. But this would only be insofar as it was not at the expense of an ability to deal successfully with whatever set of demands were likely to become strategic subsequently. But, more importantly, we would judge effectiveness in terms of balancing the range of often conflicting coalition-demands in combination with the ability to recognise and handle priorities – priorities in the sense of which constituencies are currently most 'strategic'.

This is especially useful in judging effectiveness in public-sector organisations where the range of relevant external constituencies tends to be especially complex. Think of a prison, for example, with pressures from various sources demanding that, at the same time, it punishes, reforms, treats and deters. Effective management here is not a matter of doing all of these but of minimally satisfying those upon whom the organisation depends for resources, both material and symbolic.

In a book dedicated to helping managers become more effective, R. E. Freeman (1984) argues for a conceptual shift in management thinking. This is vital, he argues, if managers are going to cope with the 'major strategic shifts' currently going on in the environments of organisations. He says that 'if you want to manage effectively, then you must take your stakeholders into account in a systematic fashion'. To help with this he puts forward his 'stakeholder approach', which is very much a resource-dependence type of model despite the fact that it does not treat internal groups as stakeholders. Managers must relate all their activities to the wider strategic picture, it is suggested. And that picture is a stakeholder map not unlike the scheme shown in Fig. 3.2.

If we bring together what was said about the nature of management in the previous chapter with what we have seen here of the various approaches available for understanding organisations, we can perhaps identify some of the basic ways in which 'the effective manager' thinks. The starting point here is the conceptualisation of management as *pulling things together and along in a general direction to bring about long-term organisational survival.* And this is seen to be done via three levels (as shown in Fig. 2.2, p. 41): minimally satisfying internal and external resource-providing constituencies, balancing differentiation and integration, and balancing the use of structural and cultural devices. In the light of this we can say that *effective managers are those who attend to both organisational arrangements and the staff for which they are responsible in such a way that efforts are directed to the greatest possible extent towards the overall effectiveness of the organisation.* This suggests that there are three areas of attention: those of structure, people and strategy.

We can go on to say that managerial effectiveness is a matter of attending to three types of question, each always in the light of the other:

The strategic questions

What strategies are being followed or might be followed by the organisation to ensure its long-term survival given the various constituencies which are looking to it to be satisfied? What specific objectives can be derived from this for my area of responsibility?

The structure questions

What pattern of work roles, task allocation, job specifications, teams, departments, authority and communication channels, appraisal and reward systems will meet the above objectives in the light of the prevailing circumstances or 'contingencies'? Do we accept these contingent factors as requiring a reaction or should we try to change them?

The people questions

What are the appropriate styles and practices of leadership, motivation, delegation and communication to be followed given the concerns and expectations of the staff and in the light of the structural circumstances? How is one to relate to and negotiate arrangements with regard to superiors, peers and subordinates given (a) the career and departmental politics of the organisation and (b) the inadequate, ambiguous and partial nature of the information which is generally available? What might be the unintended consequences of any particular measure taken, given both the psychological and the sociological characteristics of the organisation? How appropriate, clear and consistent is the culture or the ethos of the organisation or the part of it for which I am responsible?

This analysis provides guidance to those involved in work organisations as long as they are aware of the range of insights, theories and findings reviewed in this or the next chapter and which are behind these specific questions. Fig. 3.3 represents this thinking in the form of a model showing the influences and constraints on managerial choices. It is important to stress, however, that this is only a model or simplification. The areas identified – strategy, structure, people, culture – are nothing like as separate as the scheme implies in practice. And each aspect could be represented differently. For example, the 'people' element could

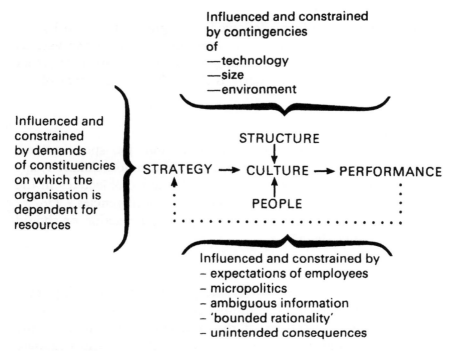

Fig. 3.3 Influences and constraints on managerial choice

readily be treated as a direct influence on strategy since the employees are inevitably a significant 'constituency'. And they could equally well be represented as one of the 'contingencies' which influence structure.

It is within this general framework that we can now pay attention to the more detailed aspects of the human aspects of managerial work. The focus of the next chapter is on the ways in which we can understand how managers relate to the staff for which they are responsible and how they attempt to influence employee performance.

Chapter 4

Motivation, leadership and employee management

The view of management which we have been developing is one which firmly identifies managerial effort with the functioning of the overall organisation in which the manager is located. Effective managers locate the carrying out of their particular responsibilities within the existing and emerging strategies of the organisation – these strategies amounting to the general way in which the range of constituencies on whom the organisation depends for resources vital to survival are to be satisfied. In the previous chapter we concentrated on these strategic matters and upon the structures or patterns which are either formally designed or emerge from the interaction of organisational participants. It was suggested, however, that effective managers not only attend to strategic questions and questions of structure but continually attend to a range of what were called people questions. It is to these that we now turn.

The area of managerial or organisational thought upon which we are concentrating here is similar to that which is still referred to by some, who are still attached to archaic usages, as 'man management'. The basic practical concern here is that of how managers go about or might go about ensuring that employees (male and female!) behave or 'perform' in a way which enables those managers to meet the objectives attached to their particular roles within the organisation. It is that part of managerial work which involves 'getting people to do things'.

A lot of academic attention has been paid to these issues, particularly by people working in the academic field of 'Organisational Behaviour'. Unfortunately, however, the picture tends to be somewhat confused by the fact that different theorists and researchers tend to approach what amount to basically similar issues from rather different angles and in a way which suggests that there are more basic issues here than there perhaps really are. Thus, some researchers see the issue as one of 'leadership' whilst others see it as a question of 'motivation'. And very similar matters are considered by yet another group who focus on questions of job design or job redesign (job enlargement, job enrichment and the like). We thus get several different literatures which are perhaps better seen as different facets of one. The intention here is to attempt to bring ideas from these various contributions together.

Linking many of these applied or prescriptive pieces of social science thinking about employee behaviour is a debate represented in Fig. 4.1 about which general approach managers should take in order to get employees to behave in the required way: should people be closely controlled and treated more-or-less explicitly as means towards ends on a basis of simple cash reward or should they be given more personal scope in how they do the job and be treated as the junior colleagues of the manager rather than as their tools?

To appreciate fully the complexities of employee behaviour we have to go beyond the ideas which have been developed on

To achieve the employee
performance which they
require should managers/
supervisors/job designers
lean towards . . .

OR

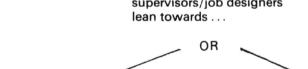

Low employee discretion,
Work only as a means to other
ends,

Distant management-worker/
organisation-individual
relations,

Hierarchical authority,
Boss-centred style?

High employee discretion,
Work in part as an end in itself,

Close management-worker/
organisation-individual
relations,
Participation/self-direction,
Employee-centred style?

Fig. 4.1 Motivation, leadership and job design theory: the underlying issue

motivation, leadership and job redesign. To get the full benefit of
social scientific thinking in this area it is vital, I suggest, to pay
additional attention to ideas which have been developed by industrial sociologists and organisational theorists who have been
less immediately concerned with instructing managers. The
application of our principle of constructive scepticism to much of
what has been produced by the applied behavioural scientists
shows that it is rather severely limited in a number of ways. One
aspect of the problem here was fairly forcefully dealt with in
Chapter 1 when it was suggested that much of what has been
advocated by some of the famous purveyors of behavioural science for managers has been more informed by their feelings about
how they would like the world to be rather than about how it
is or how real people actually behave in it (see pp. 12–14). This
point will be amplified when we come to examine some of
the apparently influential theories of motivation and job design
shortly.

A second major problem with much of the material on employee motivation is that it is limited by the particular psychological perspectives which are used. There is a tendency to look
at the individual human organism too much in isolation and,
especially, too much in terms of the 'needs' which that organism
is alleged to have. But, whilst it is by no means inappropriate to
consider the needs which people bring with them into their work
situation, it may be overly restrictive to concentrate on these at
the expense of paying attention to the considerable number of
ways in which people vary in how they interpret basic human
needs and at the expense of looking at how these interpretations
alter and shift in accord with the various social and situational
pressures which are experienced. What this means is that,
although we need to look at thinking and research on how needs
come into work behaviour, we need to set this kind of consideration within the various *processes* which go on both within people's
minds and within the social or group contexts in which individuals operate.

As with the kind of more strategic and structural thinking
which was examined in the previous chapter, we can see a clear
trend towards more *processual* styles of analysis in the thinking
about how people are motivated and behave in organisations.
In a corresponding way to that in which we saw a move from

mechanistic thinking through organic or systems thinking towards processual emphases in organisational analysis, we can see a trend from mechanistic through need-based to processual emphases in the analysis of motivation and behaviour in organisations. Accordingly, we can organise our material within a similar framework to that used in Chapter 3. Three waves of thinking about employee motivation and behaviour are recognised and these are headed with the simple labels of People as Machines, People with Needs, and People in Processes. The various approaches to be considered within this framework are shown in Fig. 4.2.

The three-wave scheme is being used for the same reasons and with the same qualifications as applied in the previous chapter (pp. 46–7). The three groupings have little validity beyond the function which they are intended to serve: that of helping the reader find a way through a potentially frightening mass of different ideas and theories. However, the claim that in both the structural and the behavioural areas of organisational and management thinking there is a movement towards stressing processes is an important one. It does, in effect, encourage us to believe that we may eventually achieve the sort of synthesis between the

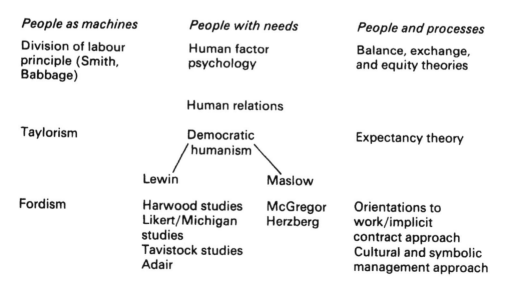

Fig. 4.2 Three waves of motivation, leadership and job design thinking

structural and the behavioural emphases which was called for in Chapter 1 (pp. 17-19, esp. Fig. 1.3).

In the last chapter's consideration of organisational analysis we saw that there has been increasing attention paid to such things as political behaviour within organisations, the importance of 'meanings' and cultures and the influence of factors external to the organisation. And in our present review of behavioural thinking we shall see that corresponding factors have increasingly come to be seen as relevant to understanding why and how people behave in the ways they do at work. This coming together of what have often been seen as different kinds of concern will, in fact, be developed in the next chapter when a trend towards joint consideration of structural and behavioural factors will be recognised in the increasing attention being given to the idea of overall *employment strategies* in organisations.

People as machines

As we saw in the previous chapter, much of the early formal thinking about work organisations was inspired by an aspiration to develop organisations which could be designed to function like large engines. It was believed that such organisations could make modern problems of both production and public administration manageable and fair. It was shown that people with a training and background in engineering were particularly influential in systematising ideas about building organisations. However, if we go further back than the writings of people like Fayol and Taylor to earlier periods of the industrialisation of societies, we find that there is, in the very fundamental principles of the new industrial capitalist order, a basic economistic and mechanistic way of looking at how people are to be involved as the employees of the new kind of work enterprise.

It is important to start our review of ideas about employee motivation and behaviour with the earliest thinking which was put forward. A great deal of what has been debated since, and perhaps even more significantly will be debated in the future, amounts to an engagement with principles set down early in the period of the industrial revolution. In this wave of ideas we shall first, therefore, look at principles discussed by Adam Smith and

Charles Babbage whereby work is subjected to a detailed division of labour. We can then come back to the development of these principles in the twentieth century forms of Taylorism and Fordism.

The division of labour principle

This underlies the forms of job design which are often seen to typify modern rationalised work organisations and were first systematically identified by Adam Smith in his *Wealth of Nations* of 1776. This classic work puts forward many of the main economic and social principles which underpinned the industrial capitalist type of political economy which was emerging at this time in Britain. Among these is the revolutionary idea of ruthlessly extending the way in which the work to be done in society is divided up and allocated to different parties. Every society has had some kind of general division of labour, a typical and basic example being the allocation of defence to men and childcare to women. On top of this we traditionally see the allocation of types of task to particular crafts or professions: weaver, baker, priest or mason. But with the industrial revolution we see a move beyond this *general* division of labour towards a *detailed* division of labour.

Smith explained that enormous gains in efficiency were to be made by splitting up what might be seen as a 'whole' task like the making of pins into a number of smaller-scale and less skilled tasks or jobs. In his famous example of such a reorganised pin factory he envisages up to eighteen such jobs. The effect of this would be that each worker could produce in one day 4,800 pins whereas, on his own, he could manage only one pin. Each job would be easy to learn and each operation readily repeatable. The advantages of this system to the employer would lie in the savings to accrue from the increased dexterity of each worker, the reduction of time for preparation and changeover from one operation to another, and the possibilities opened up for further mechanisation.

The recognition that the introduction of a detailed division of labour is a stimulus to further mechanisation reveals the implicit association of the human worker with the machine itself. The person and the machine are equivalents in this model of deskilled work. The view of the worker is a view of the person as an appendage to the machine. And the dehumanising – or at least the stultifying – implications of this were clear to Smith himself. He pointed out that the man 'whose life is spent in performing a few simple operations ... has no occasion to exert his understanding and generally becomes as ignorant as it is possible for a human creature to become'.

The importance of Charles Babbage to the analysis of the growing detailed division of labour is that he points out a basic advantage to the employer of the principle which he claimed, in 1832, had not yet been recognised. This was the advantage that the cost of the labour could be significantly reduced by deskilling. If you employed workers to perform whole tasks then you would have to pay each worker the rate which was appropriate to the most skilful element of their work or to the element which required the most strength. However, you can 'by dividing the work to be executed into different degrees of skill and force ... purchase the precise quantity of both that is necessary for each process'.

Babbage is probably best known as the deviser of the original computer and his work here is relevant to our claim that the philosophy underlying these ideas is one which sees people as machines. Part of the inspiration for Babbage's 'calculating engine' derived from his admiration of the way his fellow mathematicians in France had so speedily produced a series of mathematical tables. This had been done by identifying parts of the work that could be done by the less mathematically able staff and allocating it accordingly. The organisation of these tasks, thought Babbage, showed the way for the machines which would eventually replace people in this kind of work.

The motivational theory behind all this is implicit and is crude. The economic context in which this kind of work is offered is a free market one. The individual is not dependent on any kind of feudal lord or on the state. To survive he or she has to sell their capacity to work for the best price they can get. In the laissez-faire world implied by these principles of job design, one works to avoid hunger. And the extent to which one's hunger is assuaged depends on what quality of labour capacity one has to sell.

Taylorism

Taylorism or Scientific Management represents a further syste-
matisation of emerging ideas of rationalised work effort. The basic
principles laid down by Taylor and his fellow systematisers were
examined earlier (pp. 49–51) but there are several points which
need to be added in the present context. The earlier advocates of
work specialisation did not have a great deal to say about how the
work was to be 'managed' or about 'leadership' and 'rewards'. As
Craig Littler (1982) puts it, earlier theorists like Babbage had 'no
clear idea of the problems of, and the means of, re-integration of
the fragmented job roles'. To manage the fragmented work,
therefore, the managers would ensure that all the planning and
allocation work was done by themselves, that all work would be
monitored and allocated times and that a payment-by-results system would be introduced to motivate the workers to apply themselves to maximum effect in terms of output.

Leadership under Taylorism is a matter of applying science,
and motivation is a matter of offering a financial return commen-
surate with the steady application of effort to the tasks designed
by the managers. Workers are like machines, both in the manner
they are required to work and in the way they are 'fed' with cash
in proportion to their output – just as a motor is fed with petrol
in proportion to the mileage it covers.

Fordism

Fordism represents an extension of Taylorism in one respect and
a modification of it in another. The 'robotising' of the worker
implicit in Taylorism was extended by Henry Ford by the placing
of the worker on the assembly line. The cost of this, however,
was one of a counterproductively high level of labour turnover.
This was to be compensated for by a high guaranteed wage rate
– the famous Five Dollar Day. To obtain this the worker had to
have a minimum of six months continuous service and to comply
with certain standards of personal behaviour.

Taylorism and Fordism are not likely to be found applied in
practice in pure form. But it is of utmost importance to recognise
their nature as templates for a great deal of the job design which

has been done during the twentieth century. The most systematic evidence on this is the survey carried out by Davis, Canter and Hoffman in 1955 and followed up in 1976 by J. C. Taylor (Davis and Taylor, 1979) on a representative sample of American companies. This showed that job design practices in manufacturing were dominated by a concern to minimise the unit production time in order to minimise the cost of production. Job design criteria included skill specialisation, minimal skill requirements, minimal training times, maximum repetition and the general limiting of both the number of tasks in a job and the variation within those tasks and jobs. The people responsible for these decisions were predominantly production specialists, be they line managers, production engineers or systems analysts. In neither survey was there evidence of any significant contribution being made by personnel specialists. The studies showed that there was little change in approach over the two decades between the investigations: there was still the preference, as J. C. Taylor puts it, 'to minimise the immediate costs of production rather than to emphasise a longer-term approach ... which recognises the economic costs of worker frustration and acknowledges employee satisfaction and motivation.'

It will be a major objective of our next chapter to look at just what the factors are which encourage an employer to be more or less inclined to follow employment and management policies which take this mechanistic approach to their workforce. Although scientific management principles are still widely applied and, in some spheres may come to be pursued even more rigorously than in the past, there have increasingly been available alternative ways of looking at how and why people behave as they do in their jobs. It is to these alternatives that we now turn. But before we do so, we need to consider some of the basic factors which have led thinkers to develop alternative perspectives and offer alternative recommendations to managers.

The reasons why alternatives to the Taylorist style of thinking and practice have been developed are a mixture of the idealistically principled and the down-to-earth pragmatic. To put it another way: some think that these are wrong or 'bad' ways of proceeding whilst others see them as inappropriate or impractical. And, at times, the two things get rather muddled, with commentators being unclear as to whether the main grounds for change are moral or practical. Whilst both of these factors are undoubtedly important in all kinds of decision-making, it is nevertheless important to keep the two distinct, at least at the stage of analysing what actions will have what effect.

From early on in the growth of industrial capitalist societies, there were social and political commentators who disapproved of the basic principles of employment within a detailed division of labour on a basis of cold calculation and pure cash exchange. This humanistic dislike of reducing people to the commodity of a human 'resource' or 'factor of production' can be seen in the ideas of conservative and radical thinkers and writers alike. The attack on the dehumanising potential of employment within industrialism which came, in various forms, from nineteenth-century poets, novelists, philosophers and political writers has inevitably influenced much twentieth-century thinking about work. And we can expect this influence to have been particularly strong among the academics and intellectuals who have produced most of the alternative ideas to Taylorist thinking in the years which followed his systematising of rationalised work patterns and his advocacy of crude methods of motivation.

It is reasonable to assume, then, that a lot of the ideas of 'organisational behaviour', motivation theory and the rest have been inspired by a humanistic concern to improve the human lot – a concern in part informed by the intellectual heritage which will have informed the education of their producers. But the impact that this material has had on management thought – if less than the impact it has had on managerial practice – is also the result of pragmatic concerns. There was a recognition among certain practitioners that some more subtle understanding of work motivation and some more sophisticated styles of management might be necessary, at least in some spheres of employment. From the early days of the spread of scientific management practices there were reservations expressed about the longer-term sense of this approach to employment. Potential costs in terms of quality of work, of labour stability, of labour flexibility and of reasonable industrial relations could outweigh the short-term benefits of high quantity and low cost output. The nature of human beings' relationship to their work had to be looked at anew. And this was to involve an examination of the kinds of *need* that people take to their work.

People with needs

Our second wave of thinking represents the emergence onto the scene of the social or 'behavioural' scientists: sociologists and psychologists with a mixture of principled and pragmatic interests, all anxious to influence managerial practice. The basic assumption applying here is that people work in order to meet certain needs or wants. They therefore apply themselves in their work in whatever way will lead to their being provided with the means of satisfying those needs. Thus, the basic idea of 'work motivation' is a straightforward and commonsensical one.

Taylorism was clearly based on such a theory and it assumed that worker needs could all be subsumed within the economic reward to be gained by appropriate application of effort. Any human needs beyond the need for an income would presumably be met in the worker's private life outside the workplace. Work experience was only relevant to the meeting of these needs insofar as the money earned affected what sort of life the individual could lead outside work. And this was no concern of the employer. But, once the psychologists began to look at this, we see it being increasingly suggested that things are not as simple as this. Human needs are relevant to human behaviour at all times. The human does not become a machine at work whilst existing as a person only in the realms beyond the territory of the employer. People take their humanness to work with them. And the extent to which it is fulfilled is relevant to how they will perform. Managers therefore need to understand human psychology if they are to motivate their employees.

Human factor psychology

This represents the first important development in this direction. It grew out of the application of industrial psychology to problems of industrial production in Britain during the First World War and the key figure behind the movement was C. S. Myers. The emphasis of the early work, done under the auspices of the Health of Munitions Workers' Committee and its successors the Industrial Fatigue Research Board and the Health Research Board, was away from the Taylorian concern with increasing output through increased incentive and towards the easing of effort itself. Barriers to effective work were to be removed, these including in Myers' (1920) words, 'the effects of mental and nervous fatigue, monotony, want of interest, suspicion, hostility etc.'. He went on to say that 'the psychological factor must be the main consideration of industry and commerce in the future'.

This early application of psychology to work behaviour, which became institutionally embodied in the National Institute of Industrial Psychology, had a great deal in common with the rationalising spirit of Scientific Management and with it emphasis on measurement and on the worker as an individual. Yet it also involved a reaction to the human engineering ethos of Taylorist thinking. Myers refers to the Scientific Managers' neglect of the 'human factor'. He stressed the error of assuming that there can be a 'one best way' which applies to every worker. People vary in their motivations and the way people regard their work can vary with circumstances. There was a clear recognition that people's attitudes make a difference, and even that these attitudes can be influenced by social and political factors. Writing in the period after the Second World War, Myers (1920) pointed to the need for managerial policies to adjust their approach to leadership in recognition of the 'increasing democratic spirit in education, and of growth of personality and responsibility'.

The human relations school

This school of thought had its origins in work which was very similar to the industrial psychology investigations into such things as the effects of monotony and fatigue. But, as we showed earlier (p. 57), their approach soon became distinguished by an emphasis on the social needs of people at work. Workers did not simply bring economic needs to work with them, they also brought along their sentiment-based desire for 'belonging'. Co-operation and output would be compromised if this were not recognised and catered for by the management. Employees' morale and productivity is more affected by their need to be secure, involved and recognised than by either their physical conditions or the level of monetary reward. In fact, demands for more money could well be displaced pleas for managerial recognition of these deeper needs.

The claim was made that all this could be shown by careful scientific research. The Hawthorne Studies were seen as a breakthrough in their demonstration of the basically social nature of work motivation. The original investigations done at the Hawthorne plant of General Electric in Chicago by the company itself had attempted to relate changes in workshop illumination to productivity. No clear pattern could be found: productivity was liable to increase with a deterioration in lighting as readily as with an improvement, for instance. The social scientists from Harvard University, upon joining the investigation, attempted to discover just what other variables might be at work. The Relay Assembly Room experiment was designed to do this.

Six women, whose previous output levels had been secretly monitored, were put into a special room in which production could be systematically monitored as a series of changes were made to incentive schemes, rest periods, and the length of the working day. Various changes were made and withdrawn, some of these being potentially seen as improvements from the worker point of view and some of them as a worsening of conditions. But there was a steady rise throughout the twenty-six weeks of the experiment in the level of output, regardless of the nature of the changes made in any period. Whatever was measured, be it weather conditions, health factors or hours of sleep taken, it appeared not to be statistically significant as a possible causal factor. It was thus that the explanation in terms of the social characteristics of the test room was offered. The friendly atmosphere of the test room and the interest shown in the women by the experimenters were felt to be crucial.

The Bank Wiring Observation Room experiment focused on this social group factor and involved the study of the work of fourteen men who were employed to wire banks of telephone equipment. The group was observed to have fixed a level of output which was below what they might have achieved and which gave them a lower income than would have been possible under the incentive scheme. There were patterns of informal leadership within the group and the informal group output norm of two banks per day was enforced by the men themselves through a set of sanctions. Deviants who went above the accepted norm

were labelled 'ratebusters' and those who went below it, 'chisel-
lers'. Offenders were brought into line by a mixture of name-
calling, ostracism and the hitting or 'binging' of their arms. The
experimenters rejected the obvious commonsensical or rational
explanation of this kind of behaviour – that it might be a sensible
way of maintaining a level of output which would give a reasonable income under the group bonus scheme without risking either
the bonus rate or the level of employment being cut. They chose,
instead, to understand the behaviour in terms of some basic instinctive need of the workers to belong to a group. The behaviour
observed, they believed, functioned primarily to maintain the
group in such a way that this 'need' would be met.

Evidence from a programme of 21,000 non-directive interviews
which took place at the same time as the experiments were going
on was also used to show the importance of 'group sentiments'.
Although individuals varied to some extent in their reported
satisfactions and dissatisfactions, a pattern was noted whereby
what people said was related to what was said by other people
with whom they found themselves grouped in the workplace.

The advice given to managements on the basis of all this was
that they should attempt to integrate workers into the organisation. This would be done by ensuring that individuals were
socially integrated into primary groups of workers which would,
in turn, be managed so as to operate in a way consonant with
managerial interests. Colleague groups would be established and
fostered by management and recruits introduced into these. Individuals would be guided away from group loyalties which did
not fit with management aims and informal leaders would be
identified so that they could be used as communication channels.
Individuals could be helped to meet their own social needs by
psychological counsellors. These trained interviewers would help
individuals to handle any personal emotional problems so that
they could more easily fit into their group and hence into the
organisation.

The writings of the human relations school can be criticised on
numerous scores. They drastically play down the basic economic
conflict of interest which inevitably exists between employers and
employed. And they severely underestimate the degree of rationality on the part of workers whilst overestimating the rationality
of those who manage them. They fail to see that managers are

employees themselves and are likely to be born with the same 'instincts' as those who are employed in more junior capacities. There is an inconsistency in the desire to generalise about human instincts and needs at the same time as wanting to see one social group, the managers, as somehow above having these needs.

Despite these drawbacks and the further weaknesses which follow from the fact that such of the so-called evidence appears to be regularly and heavily interpreted to make it fit beliefs and hunches which derive from the writers' political preferences and social beliefs, this material is not to be consigned to the historical archive or to the practitioner's rubbish bin. The Hawthorne studies can perhaps be seen as an instructive set of half-true stories. Like all myths, they mix fiction, exaggeration, one-sidedness and an element of truth. The rhetoric within which the story is presented is one in which the intrepid scientists 'discover' the social aspects of people's involvement in work. But the hollowness of this rhetoric to the more sceptical social scientist of half-a-century later, should not prevent us from seeing that something important is being said. And neither should the bias and political naïvety of the writers persuade us that managers, in practice, are not well advised to think about the influence on work behaviour of the groups, official and otherwise, to which employees belong. Although, as we shall see, there are many more factors which operate, the social nature of people and the desire for some kind of meaningful involvement among many employees is not something to be dismissed.

It was in the two decades or so following the Second World War that human relations thinking had its real impact on management thought. This was not, however, to break the grip of scientific management thinking on job design but to overlay these now standard work structuring practices with some meliorating supervisory and 'welfare' practices. The exploitative and dehumanising edge could be taken off Taylorist practices in a way which made those practices tolerable in the new post-war world of full employment. The research evidence and scientific credibility of the human relations writers provided a rationale for an element of 'caring' in management which was more acceptable to the age than would now be the older rationales of paternalist and religious welfarism which had played a role something like this in the past. However, in the post-war world of American social psychology there was developing a newer and more humanistic approach to work motivation.

Although human relations probably made its greatest impact after the Second World War, its roots lay in a more pessimistic inter-war concern, not only with problems of worker productivity, but also with the basic problems of social integration in an industrial world. In fact, these were almost nineteenth-century concerns: Mayo in his work was addressing large-scale issues of the same kind addressed by the earlier founders of sociology such as Emile Durkheim. Consequently, we should not be surprised to see a new direction being taken in the much more optimistic America of the 1950s. And we should be even less surprised to see the emphasis of this new approach on democracy and humanism, given the influence within American social psychology of scholars who had fled from European totalitarianism and authoritarianism and who saw in American society the potential for human fulfilment and democratic involvement of a kind not previously possible.

Democratic humanism

As a general kind of approach to understanding work behaviour and motivation democratic humanism has, like human relations, to be seen less as a scientific 'breakthrough' in understanding and more as a way in which more sophisticated psychological assumptions together with value-based prescriptions were introduced into management thinking under the banner of scientific progress. The inspiring figures of this general style of thinking were Kurt Lewin and Abraham Maslow.

Kurt Lewin took with him to America, when he left Germany in 1933, a set of assumptions about human behaviour which strongly contrasted with the mechanistic approaches which dominated psychology at that time. The *gestalt* approach to understanding human behaviour sees human experience as essentially organised into a gestalt or 'whole'. Any particular experience or action has therefore to be understood as relating to a whole lot of other factors in the overall 'field' of the individual's experience. Especially important in this, according to Lewin's Field Theory, is the group context within which the individual feels, sees things and acts. How people are motivated, therefore, will be, in part, a function of group situation in which the individual operates. But, in addition to this, the individual will be influenced by factors about which he or she is not necessarily aware. These include events in the individual's past.

Although Lewin's terminology is more in terms of 'fields' and 'forces' than 'needs' and 'motives', it is possible to see implicit in the approach he established a notion of the needs which people bring to the work situation. These are not simply needs for belonging but a more complex yet specific type of need. Experiments and studies conducted under Lewin's supervision were interpreted to show two main things. First, they are alleged to show that decisions which emanate from and are backed by group agreement are more effective than ones imposed by a leader and, second, they are taken to show that democratic or participative leadership works better than authoritarian or 'laissez-faire' leadership. The basic assumption, then, appears to be that people have some kind of need to be actively involved in decision-making if they are to be fulfilled and effective in following up the decisions made. To put it more simply: people 'need' democracy and if the democratic need is met in any given activity then that activity will be better carried out.

The industrial application of Lewin's ideas is seen in the various Harwood Studies which were carried out in the late 1940s at the Harwood Manufacturing Corporation in Virginia. Various experiments which involved introducing a measure of participative management were conducted by associates of Lewin, Alex Bavelas and J.R.P. French but probably best known is the study of ways of 'overcoming resistance to change' (Coch and French, 1948). Frequent changes in manufacturing technique and market pressure meant that the company was frequently faced with the problem of moving the mainly women workers from jobs into which they had settled into different ones to which they had to adjust. This was commonly associated with hostility, resistance and a falling-off in production levels. Several different ways of introducing change were therefore tried out, the major difference between them being the degree to which worker participation was involved.

The first group simply had the intended changes explained to them whilst the second group had some representative members assigned to participating in the design of the changes to be made. The third group, which was matched with the other two in terms of their known level of efficiency and group cohesiveness, was allowed to participate as a whole in the choice of the ways in which the changes were to be implemented. And, whereas with the first group there followed conflict with supervision and engineers and a tendency to resist the changes, the second and third groups showed cooperation and a willingness to learn the new jobs at a better rate than was usual. The rate at which the output picked up was greatest, however, with the fully participative group and their subsequent level of output was as good as or better than that of the partially participative group.

The tradition established by Lewin (who died in 1947) and his colleagues was followed up by several other groups both in Britain and the USA. Rensis Likert and colleagues at the University of Michigan's Survey Research Center concentrated on supervisory style, having compared matched groups of high-producing and low-producing workers. Both workers and their supervisors were interviewed and it was established that there were generally two types of supervisor: *production-centred* and *employee-centred*. The production-centred supervisors, when interviewed, emphasised the part of the job which dealt with managing the production process itself rather than the people involved in it. The latter group appeared to see the maintenance of good human relationships as the priority, however. Their interest in their subordinates and their needs was clearly associated with good levels of output more than in the situations in which the output itself was the primary concern.

Likert (1961) developed this work to suggest that four basic styles of leadership can be seen in organisations. He called these systems one to four. System One management is 'exploitative autocratic' and involves imposed decisions, motivation by threat and low levels of communication and emphasis on teamwork, whilst System Two, the 'benevolent authoritative', motivates by reward and, although decisions are still imposed, it does use a degree of condescending or paternalistic interest in the employees as people. The System Three or 'participative' style shows more trust in employees and uses their ideas constructively, motivating through rewards and involvement. Yet decision-making is still controlled by the manager or supervisor. System Four, the 'democratic' approach, goes further than this by allowing subordinates to make decisions for themselves and letting them be motivated through the reward of achieving the goals they have set for themselves. Likert uses his research work to show that Systems Three and Four work better: the participative or democratic leaders achieved better results in terms of output as well as satisfaction showed by the group members.

The message emerging appears to be that democracy pays in management. Examination of this claim from the point of view of critical commonsense might encourage us to see that this is quite a reasonable pattern to expect from such research. Yet our application of a little constructive scepticism might lead us to ask whether this pattern is likely to apply in all work situations, in every society and in all socio-economic contexts and industrial relations climates. And, in addition to this, we might query whether a willingness to manage in a relatively open or participative way might not, in part, be a reflection of the relaxation which might arise managerially given the existence of a high-output group in the first place. That is, the participative style could logically be as much an outcome of good productivity as a cause of it.

In Britain and Scandinavia we can see a particular set of developments which have been influential in newer ideas about job design and which have their origins in thinking which parallels that of Lewin. These are the contributions made by members of the Tavistock Institute of Human Relations and the linked Industrial Democracy Programme in Norway. The socio-technical systems approach to organisational design looked at earlier (p. 60) emerged from this work but, central to the work, is a focus on job design in a work-group context and, especially, the idea of the autonomous work-group. The principle applying here is one in which work tasks are grouped together to form a logical 'whole task' which can then be performed by members of the group with minimal supervisory interference. The work designer devises a group which consists of 'the smallest number that can perform a whole task and can satisfy the social and psychological needs of its members' this being both 'from the point of view of task performance and of those performing it, the most satisfactory and efficient group' (Rice, 1958).

Quite explicit in the later theorising of the Tavistock group, when there is an apparent moving away from more psychoanalytic and Lewinian gestaltist concepts, is an emphasis on human needs. Emery and Thorsrud (1969) list a number of what they call 'general psychological requirements' of people at work. Among these are needs for a job to be 'reasonably demanding' in terms other than sheer endurance, to contain variety, to allow the individual to learn on the job and to go on learning, to allow the individual some area of decision-making they can call their own, to give individuals some social support and recognition in the workplace and to give them the feeling that the job leads to some sort of desirable future. All this is qualified with the warning that it is not possible to meet these needs 'in the same way in all work settings or for all kinds of people'. In these few simple words lie many questions to which we might have expected attempts at answers. To get them, however, we will have to wait until we move on to our third wave of thinking.

Another British contribution to this tradition which began with Lewin and which focuses on how managers interrelate their concern for task matters and their concern for subordinates is John Adair's (1968) notion of action-centred leadership. Adair argues that three types of needs have to be met if a group is going to be successful. First, there are the 'task needs' which relate to the job itself, second there are 'group needs' whereby maintenance work has to be done to keep the group cohesive and able to work cooperatively together and, third, there are the 'individual needs' which the group members bring to work and which require satisfaction within the work group context. Adair stresses that these three sets of needs have to be dealt with in a way in which they take account of each other. He represents the three sets of needs as circles which overlap with each other. Thus failure to deal with one set of needs, say group needs, can lead to both problems in the task requirement area and the extent to which individual needs are met. All three types of need have to be considered simultaneously, each acting to the benefit of the others as well as to itself.

Whereas the work following Lewin had stressed the role of groups and of democracy in its view of motivation, leadership and job design, that looking more towards Abraham Maslow has concentrated on the individual and the variety and range of needs which they have. The basic assumptions about people are not so much ones involving the idealising of democracy as a means to both personal fulfilment and productivity as ones idealising the notion of human 'fulfilment' itself. The inspiration is a 'humanistic' one: a belief that the key to understanding human and social life is a recognition of the potential that humans have. The starting point for the humanistic psychology movement of which Maslow was an important part is the belief that scientific investigation of human behaviour should be oriented towards releasing in people the potential they have. This is a strand of American thinking that has flourished in a variety of forms in the warmth and affluence of middle-class California ever since it first appeared. It is strange that a creed coming from this particularly rarefied and often self-indulgent quarter of the intellectual world should have been taken up so much in the traditionally hardheaded world of management thinking and organisational behaviour. But it has. And we must therefore look at it closely.

The hierarchy of needs model first appeared in Maslow's work in 1943. He was mainly interested in clinical work at this time and was pursuing the relationship between human needs and human personality. Behaviour was the outcome of the interaction of certain needs to be found within the individual and other biological, cultural and situational factors. The needs are genetic or instinctive in nature and can be understood better if categorised. He therefore groups needs into five main categories (although he does sometimes mention additional 'cognitive' and 'aesthetic' needs). First, there are *physiological* needs such as for food, drink, sex and sensory satisfactions. Second, there are *safety* needs which motivate people to avoid danger and, third, there are what he calls *love* needs. These include needs to belong and to affiliate with others in both a giving and a receiving sense. Fourth, there are *esteem* needs which cover prestige, status and appreciation coming from external sources as well as internal feelings of confidence, achievement, strength, adequacy and independence. And, fifth, there is the need for *self-actualisation* which is the desire to realise one's ultimate potential, 'to become more and more what one is, to become everything that one is capable of becoming' (1943).

The five sets of needs are related to each other through their forming a hierarchy of prepotency. Thus the lowest level needs, the physiological, are the most prepotent in that they need to be satisfied before the next level, the safety needs, come into play. This process continues until the peak of the need hierarchy is reached and one follows one's satisfaction in physical, safety, social and esteem needs with seeking the essentially human fulfilments of realising one's highest potential. Maslow does not claim that one completely fulfils every one of these types of need before one begins to look for satisfactions at the next level. And he does recognise exceptional cases, either of clinical deficiency or involving moral or political ideals where people cannot or do not follow the normal pattern. Certain people, such as religious martyrs, may be achieving such a high and lasting level of self-actualisation that they accept deprivations at the lowest levels, for example.

How valid is this model or theory of motivation? It undoubtedly has some basic credibility with those who read it – or read brief accounts of it in textbooks – as the hierarchy turned into a simple triangular diagram must have been drawn up on the blackboards of tens of thousands of management lectures and seminars over the years, not to mention possibly hundreds of thousands of essays and examination scripts submitted by students of business and management. I would suggest that it is popular because it makes look scientific and plausible an idea which is little more sophisticated than the run-of-mill Commonsense I type of assumption discussed in our first chapter (pp. 5–6). It has been taken up within management education discourse as a fancy way of saying that it is easy enough to motivate people with simple rewards when they are hungry and insecure but, once they are better off in these respects, then they look for something more. As a theory that can offer any more than this, Maslow's contribution is next to useless. And, if I am going to utter so blasphemously, I had better say why.

Although Maslow's theory is, in one sense, hardly worth wasting one's time on, a certain amount of demolition work is necessary if one is going to persuade teachers and students to give more serious attention to models and theories which better come to terms with the complexities of the real motivational world.

A small application of our constructive scepticism together with a little critical commonsense (Commonsense II) soon has the edifice crumbling. We only have to begin to think about situations in which the hierarchical pattern might not be followed to realise that the model breaks down as often as it works. For example, is it any more normal for one to satisfy physiological needs like hunger and thirst before one attends to matters which threaten one's security or safety? Does a hungry man have a bite to eat before he gets out of the sight of a prowling lion or does a thirsty woman take a drink before walking out of a bar in which she espies some dangerous looking characters? She might but, then again, she very much might not! We can go on and on with this, pointing to how people's social or affiliation needs, which might be reflected in a desire to be loyal to others or to help others, overrides concern for their own safety or hunger. We can point to people regularly forgoing various of the 'lower level' needs for the sake of prestige or status (just think of the uncomfortable clothes worn by people in order to look good!). And if we consider the sexual drive – which is identified as a prepotent need – we immediately come up against that powerful insight of Freud who suggests that civilisation itself (and hence the opportunity to fulfil every one of the allegedly higher needs) is dependent on people overcoming or 'repressing' sexual drives.

The theory can be strongly attacked from other angles too. One line of attack is to question the concepts used. Is a need of the hunger or warmth type really in any way conceptually equivalent to the self-actualisation need for instance? The former is specific, universally recognised and even more-or-less measurable in the laboratory. Yet the category of self-actualisation is more like a philosophical or even a religious ideal which can, as Maslow himself seems to recognise, mean different things to different people. The utopian strand in Maslow's thinking is never far from the surface in his work and is sometimes well above the surface, as in his notion of Eupsychia – an island whose culture is devised by the thousand self-actualising individuals who have been marooned there (1965). Self-actualisation, one begins to suspect, is more something on the agenda of the affluent North American professor of psychology than of the average employee, be they blue collar, white collar, working class or middle class.

Scientific attempts to test the hierarchy approach have not been any more supportive than conceptual critiques. Wahba and Bridwell's (1976) review of such work questioned whether it is feasible to find the five separate areas of need when one examines

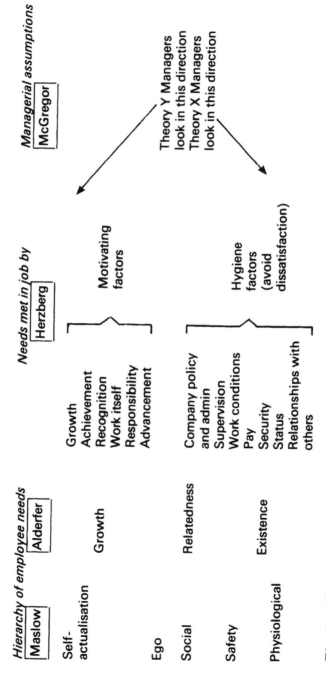

Fig. 4.3 Need-hierarchy based approaches to motivation

actual data on motives and Rauschenberger, Schmitt and Hunter (1980) in their longitudinal study using the 'improved' version of the hierarchy theory developed by Alderfer (1972) were similarly sceptical. When they analysed questionnaire data gathered from the same groups at different times they find that Maslow's view that a person's needs will be dominated by one of the five general categories at any given time did not stand. And Markov chain analysis of the data provided no evidence to suggest that when changes in needs did occur they changed hierarchically from lower to higher. These researchers comment that Maslow's work has provided a 'dominant theory of motivation in industrial and organisational psychology for some time'. Yet, they go on to say, 'almost all empirical evidence, like that in this study, had disconfirmed the theory'.

The significance of Maslow's work does not lie in its scientific validity. It clearly has little. Its role has really been as a propaganda device: propaganda in a good and humanistic cause, but propaganda nonetheless. It has been part of a cause to alter the way managers think about their employees; a cause, in effect, to make the world a better and more fulfilling place, albeit within the existing political, social and economic system. It is a cause which was also vigorously pressed by a writer who was much more directly concerned to address organisational managers than was Maslow. This is D. C. McGregor, the man who was perhaps more responsible than any other for putting across the Maslovian ideal for management practice.

In identifying two basic styles of management thought and practice which, with brilliant simplicity, he labelled Theory X and Theory Y, Douglas McGregor caught the imagination of those who were looking for a more enlightened way of managing people (1957, 1960). Theory X assumes that people generally dislike work and will avoid it if they can. They prefer to avoid responsibility and prefer to be given direction. They have limited ambitions and see security as a priority. The manager therefore controls and coerces people towards the meeting of organisational objectives. McGregor saw these principles as informing a great deal of managerial behaviour in industry and stressed that the theory operated as a 'self-fulfilling prophecy'. It actually brings about the kind of behaviour it assumes to be inevitable. This may be through either the employees' passive acceptance of the situation leading to a lack of initiative and creativity or through their becoming resentful and hence aggressive and uncooperative.

Theory Y involves fundamentally different assumptions. It assumes that people do want to take on responsibilities and that most of them have creative and imaginative abilities waiting to be tapped. To bring out all this, the individual needs to be integrated into the organisation in such a way that their own goals are fulfilled through their working towards the success of the enterprise. Managers working with these assumptions would release the full talents of their employees for the sake of the organisation through ensuring that the Maslovian higher-level needs are met at work. This would mean a participative style of leadership with the manager acting less as an authority figure and more as a consultant, teacher or professional helper.

The idealism of this is plain to see and, despite McGregor's claim that his arguments are solidly based on behavioural science research, it is difficult to see how research studies could possibly support such grandiose claims and vast generalisations. Yet, by setting up two stereotyped schemes of how managers tend to think about employee motivation and by pointing out the tendency for self-fulfilling prophecies to occur in the motivational area, McGregor was perhaps doing quite a useful service to managers who were beginning to give thought to how to improve employee performance. Although the formulations are simplistic, they do provide bench marks against which managers can put their own styles of thinking and behaviour. To invite managers to think about the behavioural assumptions they make in their work is in itself a useful thing, even if it has too often led managers to see the main issue as one of making a simple choice between Theory X and Theory Y styles of managing, regardless of the nature of either the specific work being done or the particular employees involved.

The motivation-hygiene or two-factor theory of work motivation developed by Frederick Herzberg (1959, 1966, 1976) was one of the sources which McGregor made use of in the more developed formulations of his approach. Like McGregor, Herzberg follows the humanistic path laid down by Maslow. However, the theory here is presented as emerging from the author's own research studies. The original study was of 203 Pittsburg engineers and accountants who were interviewed and asked to describe events in their working lives which made them feel good and also to describe events which made them feel bad about their jobs. The pattern which emerged from a content analysis of the replies was one which suggested that the factors which led to satisfaction at work are different from the ones which cause dissatisfaction.

It was suggested that, on the one hand, there are context or hygiene factors like salary, status, security, working conditions, supervision and company policy which can lead to dissatisfaction if absent but which do not lead to satisfaction as such if present. And, on the other hand, there are the content or motivating factors such as achievement, advancement, recognition, growth, responsibility and 'the work itself'. These have to be present, in addition to the contextual or 'hygiene' factors, before satisfactions can be produced and people motivated to perform well. These motivators clearly relate to Maslow's 'higher-level needs' whilst the hygiene factors only satisfy the 'lower-level' ones.

Like Maslow, Herzberg reveals a mystical element in his thinking when he relates these two aspects of people's lives to, on the one hand, the Adam view of man (mankind as sinful and fallen from grace) and, on the other, the Abraham view in which mankind is seen as created in the image of God and as possessing innate potential – as having a 'compelling urge to realise his own potentiality by continuous psychological growth'.

The prescriptions which followed from this were that managers should realise the very limited performance benefits of such things as improved salaries and working conditions, good supervision and the rest. Getting these right would avoid dissatisfactions among employees but would produce little positive motivation, however much they were improved. Instead, the 'motivators' have to be built into the very way jobs are designed. Motivation would thus be improved through 'job enrichment'. Jobs should be enlarged and managerial controls over how they are performed reduced. Workers themselves would set targets, plan the work and, as far as possible, choose the working methods to be used. In brief, this is a reversal of the job design principles advocated by the scientific managers or Taylorists.

Herzberg's concepts have become widely used and there have been successful applications of the type of job enrichment which he advocates (see below p. 121). However, this may be in spite of the underpinning theory being wrong. I suggest that later theories which we will consider better explain why job enrichment can succeed. The value of Herzberg's writing has been as a sensitiser: pointing out to managers that features intrinsic to the job itself have to be considered as possible motivators. What is questionable is whether they are, as Herzberg says, the things which motivate *instead of* pay, working conditions and the rest. It is probably better to see them as possible *additional* motivators. A better theory of motivation is needed which sees a range of factors, from pay to intrinsic satisfaction, all having potential as motivators, given appropriate circumstances.

It is doubtful whether we can accept the validity of the research upon which the two-factor theory depends (Locke, 1976). The results of the studies were perhaps inevitable given the research method used. First, the fact that different questions were asked to bring out the satisfiers on the one hand and the dissatisfiers on the other made the production of two sets of answers (giving motivators and hygiene factors) more likely than would otherwise have been the case. And, second, it is likely that the respondents followed the pattern well known to psychologists whereby people tend to attribute successes or positive effects to themselves or to their own actions whilst they attribute failures or negative effects to factors beyond themselves. This again would tend to push the responses to the two types of question into two apparently separate categories.

In this summary or review of what I suggest can be seen as a second wave of thinking about work behaviour, motivation, job design and leadership, we see what stands as the basis of the contribution of the behavioural or social scientists. Before we go on to summarise some of the very serious drawbacks of this work it is important to reiterate a general point hinted at several times in what I have already said. This is the point that this work is of very considerable significance despite its flaws. However much wish-fulfilment and idealistic over-sell there is on the part of the human relations and the democratic humanist writers, they have raised many basic questions about the ways in which managers have traditionally thought about employee behaviour.

The researches we have looked at may be less than 'scientifically pure' but they have shown the possibilities for change in managerial style and job organisation. The studies and the ways they have been interpreted are always well worth considering and reconsidering. To work through what has been produced in a spirit of constructive scepticism and of critical commonsense questioning is to make oneself do some very worthwhile thinking about one's own beliefs and preferences. Out of such a process can come some genuinely valuable understandings and an ability to generalise about work behaviour which can usefully inform practice. The third wave of academic thinking to which we will shortly move represents the formal attempt to do this. I would argue, however, that this third wave of thinking is best understood if the second wave, from which it has developed, is fully appreciated. This is not least the case because the second wave provides some of the important research studies which cry out for theoretical interpretation of a more sophisticated or 'realistic' kind than was achieved within the second wave itself. But, at this stage, we need to consider the kind of reservations about the above kind of work which has pushed thinking in the direction to be seen in the third wave.

The first reaction to second-wave thinking has been against its tendency towards psychological universalism. Although there are various references made to different human types on occasions, the general thrust of the thinking is towards analysing what people generally are like. The focus is on the human individual and the 'needs' or the 'potentials' which they are all said to have. This is not a bad thing to consider, but difficulties arise if this is too one-sided: if the human individual is considered too much outside the context of the social and cultural processes in which they are located. These factors are by no means ignored. They are firmly put on the agenda by the Hawthorne studies and by Lewin's and the Tavistock's work. Yet there has frequently been the tendency to reduce these kind of factors back to features of the 'standard' human individual. More attention is needed not only to the social context but to the ways in which different people might want different things from work, to the ways in which the same people might want different things at different times and to the ways in which the satisfaction of people's wants can occur outside work as well as within it. Does all fulfilment have to come in one's working life, for example?

One way in which more recent thinkers have tried to bring the 'logic of the situation' into these issues has been the attempt to put forward contingency frameworks of the kind seen in the previous chapter where they were applied to the level of organisational structure. Particularly well-known here is Fred Fiedler's Contingency Theory of Leadership (1967, 1977). This involves an invitation to leaders or managers to *diagnose* the structural and behavioural context in which they are working. Whether the style adopted should lean towards being task-centred or people-centred depends on the general quality of relationships between leaders and followers, the power which the leader derives from their formal position and the extent to which the tasks to be done are structured (how clear the goals are, how many appropriate outcomes are possible, how many ways of doing things there are and how clear are the criteria of success). Thus, for example, a task-oriented leader is likely to achieve better results than a people-oriented one when a job is highly structured, the leader has a high degree of organisational power and subordinates feel that relationships with their boss are good. The range of appropriate approaches for particular circumstances are set out on a chart by Fiedler and something similar for the extent to which managers should adopt 'participative' approaches is offered by Vroom and Yetton (1973).

Although the contingency-based behavioural models move us away from the universalism of the second-wave style of thinking, they are only ultimately as strong as the theory on which they depend. And this is not usually clear. Just what Fiedler's view is of the needs or wants people bring to work, for example, is not clear. We have to be careful not to overreact to the universalism of the second wave with a highly specific set of situational prescriptions which play down the generalities of work behaviour. The third wave takes on the challenge of balancing the general and the specific.

A further challenge to be taken up in the third wave is that of avoiding a basic trap so easily fallen into by those adopting the second-wave ideas. This is the trap pointed out in the first chapter (pp. 12–14) whereby logically unwarranted assumptions are made about the connection between organisational outcomes in terms of performance and the degree of satisfaction of needs experienced by employees. It simply does not automatically follow that, in every circumstance, either dissatisfaction leads to poor performance or high satisfaction leads to good performance. A miserable slave could do some jobs well and a blissfully satisfied worker could conceivably be doing a terrible job – they could, for example, be meeting all their psychological needs, higher and lower, and deriving all the rewards of democratic participation through producing items or services which are so wrong for the employing organisation that they eventually bankrupt it! Reviews of job satisfaction research support this (Brayfield and Crockett, 1955; Vroom, 1964), showing little connection between satisfaction and productivity. Stronger correlations are shown between satisfaction and lower labour turnover and absenteeism, however. These are not unconnected with productivity but are by no means the same thing.

Finally, the third wave has to produce a more sophisticated view of the human being and their mental or cognitive processes. People are not just need-led. They act politically and economically, they make meanings and they calculate what is worth putting into work for what they might get out of it. They have notions of fairness and justice and they have the capacity to adjust to their situation as well as a potential for resisting or challenging their circumstances. All this has to be taken into account in a way which balances the universal and general features of human beings and human behaviour with the specificities of the situations in which they find themselves. It also has to be done in a way which need not abandon idealism and humanistic aspirations but which avoids confusing what ought to be or what might be with what is the case or what is realistically possible.

People and processes

The third wave of theories of motivation, leadership and employee behaviour build on and develop what was established by the 'second-wave' social scientists who established the field of study often known as 'organisational behaviour'. But the third wave takes a new direction in a similar way to what we saw in the third wave of approaches considered in the previous chapter. As with the more recent thinking on organisations and their structures looked at in Chapter 3, we see here a turning to a view of the human individual as creative, assertive and concerned to make sense of the world. We see a recognition of economic and political factors in work behaviour and we note a stronger recognition of the role of the world outside the workplace as an influence on what goes on inside it. Above all, we see an emphasis on the processual. In the present area of interest this emphasis on processes will not be just with social, political and economic processes but also with people's mental or *cognitive* processes. Instead of the concentration on 'content' in the sense of what 'needs' people take to work, we have an emphasis on the processes whereby they think, calculate and pursue meanings and purposes.

Balance, exchange and equity theories

These theories represent one of the first attempts to produce process-type theories of work motivation. There are a number of contributions here which are all very similar in their being based upon a recognition that human beings have a tendency to seek cognitive balance. If we have notions in our mind which we cannot 'square' with each other or 'balance' we tend either to adjust our thinking or change our behaviour to restore equilibrium. There is a general tendency to reduce what Leon Festinger (1957) called 'cognitive dissonance'. If, for example, you have a job which requires you to work on Sundays at the same time as you have religious beliefs which regard Sunday working as sinful, then you have a difficulty. Consequently you may change your job, find another religion or, alternatively, you may decide that you can continue both affiliations through somehow 'rationalising' what you are doing. You might persuade yourself that the religious injunction to feed your children in the way that only this job allows outweighs the offence of breaking the sabbath. In this way, dissonance is removed. Cognitive balance is restored.

The aspect of balance theory which is perhaps most directly relevant to work motivation is equity or social comparison theory. This concentrates on the mental processes which involve the individual's perceptions of justice and fairness in respect of what they put into and what they get out of work. A classical contribution here is that of Stouffer and his colleagues (1949). They noted in their study of the American soldier that there was a greater dissatisfaction with promotional opportunities in the Army Corps than in the Military Police, in spite of the fact that, objectively, there were better opportunities in the former case than in the latter. The dissatisfactions and the demotivating influence of these were not the outcomes of what was objectively the case but resulted from the expectations of the people involved about promotional chances. There was a sense of unfairness, this in part coming about as a result of individuals comparing their own prospects with the way others had been treated.

J. S. Adams (1963, 1965) has systematically developed an equity theory of motivation suggesting that people balance what they put into their work with what they get out of it in the light of what they see other people putting in and taking out in similar situations. We can thus expect a person to achieve balance by reducing effort if the reward being reaped is judged unfair. Studies tend to support this suggestion but do not so readily support its obverse: that a perceived over-generous reward will lead to a move to increase output to reduce imbalance or guilt (see Mowday, 1979). Adams (1965) recognises this to some extent and suggests that the threshold of tolerance of incongruity in the direction of over-reward is probably higher since people can rationalise a certain degree of over-reward by noting their 'good fortune'.

Expectancy theory

This is another cognitive or process theory of motivation and its basic assumption is that human behaviour is strongly influenced by the rational *expectations* which people have about how their behaviour will lead to their fulfilling goals or achieving rewards in which they are interested. It is currently the most influential approach to motivation which derives from psychological thinking and the two major contributors to its development have been Victor Vroom (1964) and E. E. Lawler (1971). It goes much further than equity theory in that it points to the several interrelated conditions which have to apply before successful motivation by the management occurs.

Overall, there are five conditions needing to exist before successful motivation occurs. First, the employee must see that effort applied will in fact cause effective performance. It would not be appropriate for an individual output bonus to be paid to someone operating a machine which had a fixed rate or level of output, for example. Second, they must see that appropriate performance will lead to their receiving rewards. Promotion would not be a good motivator if the individual either sees people being promoted for reasons other than effective performance or if they see cases of such performance failing to lead to promotion. Third, it has to be the case that the rewards available are ones in which the employee is interested. The offer of rewards of meeting challenges and achieving status to people who simply want a quiet life and a good income would be a poor motivator. Fourth, the individual has to have the appropriate knowledge and skills to do the job and, fifth, they have to have an appropriate perception of the role they are filling. This last point means that the individual must be aware of all the factors which influence the extent to which personal objectives can be fulfilled. These may include informal aspects of the role, such as maintaining good relationships with key superiors, as well as the more formal ones of, say, meeting official targets.

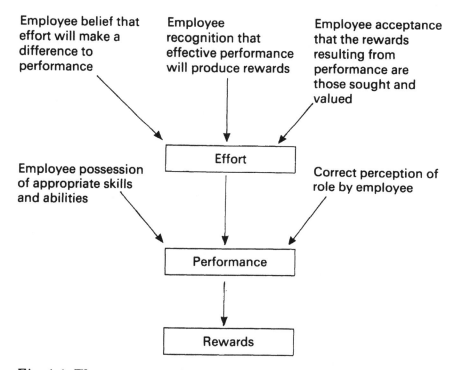

Fig. 4.4 The expectancy view of work motivation

Expectancy theory provides a framework for analysing work motivation which is eminently practical. It provides a checklist of factors to be considered in any managerial situation and it points to the links between the relevant factors and the direction which these factors tend to follow in their interrelationships. It is a good example of the similarity between effective social science thought and critical commonsense thinking (Commonsense II). Very significantly from this point of view, it rejects the Commonsense I type of assumption that job satisfaction leads to appropriate performance. Instead, it sees satisfaction as deriving from effective performance. Thus, a wise motivator does not set out to provide the things they think those being motivated would want from work, and then sit back and wait for the required performance to follow on the basis of some automatic kind of reciprocity. They are more commonsensical if they make the desired reward dependent on the required performance having occurred. However, we must remember that such good commonsense is often not applied in this way! Hence the need for the social scientists' theories and models to prompt commonsense and develop it systematically.

A further virtue of expectancy approaches lies in their recognition that employees are rational and thinking beings rather than Pavlovian dogs who can be conditioned to behave as desired at the sound of the dinner bell. Yet the theory does not assume a necessarily high level of rational-calculation on the part of employees. The theory copes perfectly well with the idea of 'bounded rationality' (see above pp. 58, 65). People make assumptions and operate with limited knowledge in their thinking and the theory, in its stress on people's perceptions and expectations, allows for this. Employees' perceptions about what is likely to happen at work might be wrong. They might have miscalculated the outcomes of particular acts. Yet those perceptions will nonetheless influence their behaviour. The manager sensitised to the role of expectations in cognitive processes would take this kind of factor into account and act accordingly.

The theory has a further strength in its openness with regard to the needs which people bring to work. Instead of assuming that most people have the same 'menu' or 'hierarchy' of needs, it treats as a variable to be investigated just what it is that particular employees are seeking in their work. This has been incorporated into job-design thinking by Hackman and Oldham (1976) in their attempt to make up for the deficiencies in the rationale for job redesign offered by Herzberg. Their 'job characteristics' model shows how, depending on the extent to which the workers themselves are interested in 'personal growth' in their jobs, certain psychological states can be achieved (such as the experience of meaningfulness of work) as a result of the job being given certain core dimensions such as autonomy, feedback, skill, variety and task identity. The outcomes of this can be such things as high motivation, high-quality performance, job satisfaction and low absenteeism and labour turnover. In addition to its virtue of treating the employees' wants as variables instead of as universal human attributes which apply in every situation – as in second-wave theories the model is valuable in that it specifies the particular dimensions of job design which can lead to particular effects in both performance and satisfaction. Figure 4.5 shows these relationships.

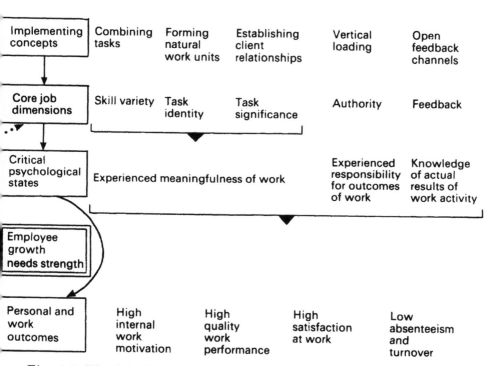

Fig. 4.5 The job characteristics view of motivation and job design (*Hackman and Oldham*)

Managers, then, are encouraged by the expectancy approaches to ask questions about the particular people with whom they are involved rather to agonise over the 'nature of mankind'! This is not, however, to suggest that such issues are not relevant. An awareness of the ideas of the content or need theorists looked at earlier would encourage an awareness of the range of needs which might be present. And, in addition to this, thinking like that of Maslow, McGregor and the rest about the hidden potential in people could usefully prompt the manager not to take too much at face value the salience or the fixed nature of the requirements which people claim or appear to have. To take for granted, for example, an employee's statement that they are only working for the money would be naïve. It might be appropriate to work on this assumption but, on the other hand, such a stated point of view might cover up other possibilities. The theory does not preclude the possibility that employees' perceived wants might change or, indeed, be changed. The 'orientation to work' approach, to which we now turn, develops this point.

The orientations to work/implicit contract approach

This approach to understanding employee behaviour has been developed by industrial sociologists rather than by psychologists. It incorporates a social psychology, however, which is consistent with the emphasis on 'expectations' which characterises the approach of the cognitive psychologists. For the practitioner, as well as for the disinterested analyst, it makes a useful complement to expectancy theory, stressing as it does the societal and group context in which work motivation occurs and bringing into the analysis issues of conflict of interest and industrial relations.

The theoretical roots of this approach lie in the Weberian and symbolic interactionist traditions in sociology which were referred to when the 'negotiated order' or 'social action' approach to organisational analysis was introduced in the last chapter (p. 64). The starting point for such analyses, as in cognitive psychology, is the (more-or-less) rational human individual.

The concept of 'orientation to work' was introduced into industrial sociology as one of the by-products of a study of changing patterns of class and political affiliation in Britain in the 1960s

(Goldthorpe, Lockwood et al., 1968) to help account for the varying patterns of work attachment found in different types of employee studied. The approach was suggested as an alternative to human relations thinking which stressed people's social needs, to democratic humanist thinking (which they called neo-human relations) stressing self-actualisation needs and to the systems approaches like that of Joan Woodward (pp. 60–1) which stressed the influence of technology on work behaviour. The latter type of approach would, for example, see the car assembly line itself as a major factor leading to particular patterns of behaviour among car workers. Most notorious here is the common assumption that working on an assembly line creates the frustrations which lie behind an alleged tendency of car workers to be strike-prone.

The distinctive line taken by Lockwood and his colleagues was to argue that, before it is assumed that a lack of higher-level or social needs on the assembly line leads to any particular pattern of behaviour, it is necessary to ask just what it is that those car workers are looking for when they take on this particular job. If, as they argued was the case with the car workers among the people they studied, individuals take a job in the full knowledge that intrinsic job satisfaction and social satisfaction are not available, then their behaviour in the job is not likely to be significantly influenced by the unavailability of such rewards.

Lockwood and Goldthorpe suggested, therefore, that we should differentiate between different kinds of work orientation. Some people might have an *instrumental* orientation whereby the key motivation is a monetary one, others might have a *bureaucratic* orientation whereby the key motivation is one of advancement up the organisational career hierarchy, and so on. To understand people's motivation at work therefore, attention needs to be paid to the expectations which are brought to the workplace in the first place. This corresponds with expectancy theory.

Where the work orientation approach goes beyond expectancy theory is in its concern to locate the particular orientations – the expectations and meanings of work which predispose behaviour in a particular general direction – of employees in their social context outside work. Lockwood and Goldthorpe did this with regard to the car workers they studied by showing that their 'instrumentality' derived from a tendency for the car workers to be people who wanted to improve the material position of themselves and their families even at the cost of their work's being intrinsically unfulfilling. They therefore 'traded off' the satisfaction they might get in other jobs (and had often experienced) for the relatively high pay levels available at the time in the car factory. This corresponds to the arguments put forward by Robert Dubin (1956) on the basis of his study of the 'central life interests' of various types ofworker. Three out of four of the manual workers he studied reported central life interests outside ofwork. This leads Dubin to argue that attempting to motivate workers who are more centrally involved in their non-work lives with fulfilling involvements at work is unwise.

Other studies point to a significant role for external influences on people's work motivations. Turner and Lawrence (1965) looked at the extent to which a sample of 470 workers found satisfactions in jobs which had various allegedly desirable job characteristics such as variety, responsibility and autonomy. Unexpectedly, no relationship was found between the existence of these job attributes and the levels of reported satisfaction. There was a small negative association with absenteeism, however. But when the sample was differentiated in terms of whether the workers were rural and largely Protestant or urban and largely Catholic a distinct pattern emerged. The rural workers were more satisfied and less absent from jobs with the hypothetically desirable features whilst the urban workers were more satisfied with and less absent from those jobs with less of these features.

Similar patterns are evident in the study by Hulin and Blood (1968) of manual workers in 21 different plants located in a range of types of American community. Workers in communities where there was high alienation from middle-class norms of achievement, hard work and responsibility appeared to prefer jobs with less responsibility and personal involvement. Individuals from communities where such norms were more acceptable expressed satisfaction with jobs which were more demanding in terms of involvement and responsibility.

With all these demonstrations of the importance of the expectations which people bring to their jobs there is a danger of our being drawn into a pessimistic determinism about the possibilities for innovation in work organisation and motivation. Although this evidence is a useful corrective to the psychological universalism of second-wave theories and to much everyday commonsense thinking, it could lead us to under-estimate the extent to which people's orientations might change or be changed once they are in work. An important study of an attempt to enrich the work experience of manual workers in a British nylon spinning plant shows the possibilities here (Cotgrove et al., 1971). Although the men's orientations were predominantly 'instrumental', their orientations did not preclude their being persuaded to accept some job redesign which increased the potential for intrinsic satisfactions and better motivation. But, significantly, the study showed that, when it came round to pay-bargaining times, instrumental concerns came to the fore again.

As W. W. Daniel (1973) points out, in criticising Lockwood and Goldthorpe's work, the nylon plant study shows that people at work have different priorities at different times and in different contexts. Employees acting to improve their pay packet are not likely to stress job satisfaction *at that time*. However, once individuals return to their machines or their desks, the intrinsic satisfaction to be gained *in that specific context* may become important again.

In my own work (Watson, 1980a), I have suggested that we should distinguish between the 'prior orientations' to work and the 'dynamic orientations' which prevail once the individual has joined an organisation. Orientations should be seen as dynamic in several respects. First, they may change with the particular circumstances in which they become relevant to behaviour - as in the case pointed to by Daniel. Second, they may change with a shift in non-work circumstances. For example, the orientation of a breadwinner who finds that their children have left home and that their level of take-home pay is now less crucial may well alter. Attention may turn to the quality of the experience in the job now that there is no longer the same urgent need to be instrumental. Similarly, it is conceivable that the orientations of a whole workforce could be modified if they perceived a growing level of unemployment in their locality. Job security could become a greater priority than pay or job interest.

The third way in which the orientation to work of an individual or a group could change would be as a result of changing circumstances within the organisation itself. There are numerous possibilities here, from a trade union representative's influencing people's expectations to the effects of a management's either creating suspicion among employees or inspiring them to feel a sense of commitment and enthusiasm for achievement. To help the analysis of changing orientations in the workplace I have suggested that we take the notion of the employee's 'effort bargain' with the employer (Baldamus, 1961), set it out in a schematic form which lists potential employee inputs alongside potential employee rewards and treats it as forming the core of the employee's orientation to their job. This gives us a version of the 'implicit contract' view of the employee's attachment to their job. It is suggested that a person's orientation to work, as it stands at a particular moment, and functioning as a predisposition to

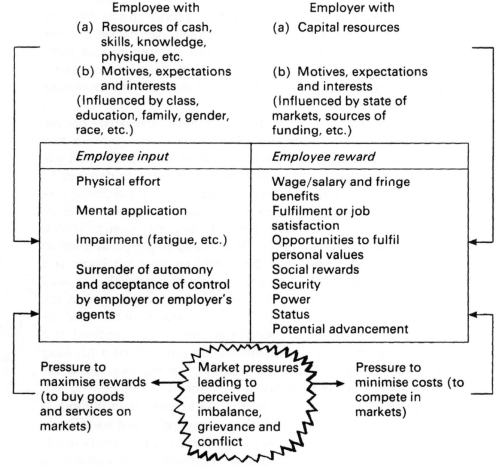

Employee with	Employer with
(a) Resources of cash, skills, knowledge, physique, etc.	(a) Capital resources
(b) Motives, expectations and interests (Influenced by class, education, family, gender, race, etc.)	(b) Motives, expectations and interests (Influenced by state of markets, sources of funding, etc.)

Employee input	*Employee reward*
Physical effort	Wage/salary and fringe benefits
Mental application	Fulfilment or job satisfaction
Impairment (fatigue, etc.)	Opportunities to fulfil personal values
Surrender of automony and acceptance of control by employer or employer's agents	Social rewards Security Power Status Potential advancement

Pressure to maximise rewards (to buy goods and services on markets) ← Market pressures leading to perceived imbalance, grievance and conflict → Pressure to minimise costs (to compete in markets)

Fig. 4.6 The implicit contract between employer and employee

behave in a certain way, can be seen as based upon the individual's reading of how the exchange relationship stands with the employer at that time.

Employees, when they first enter the organisation, take with them certain skills and aptitudes and various wants or expectations. All of these will be influenced by such factors as their gender, personality, social class, physical attributes and education. An agreement is then made with the employer, although only a very small part of this is explicit. The set of expectations which are established involve, on the employee's part, a willingness to exert a certain amount of effort, accept a certain amount of 'impairment' (tiredness, danger, etc.) and accept surrender of a degree of personal autonomy. In return a particular mix of rewards are expected, these potentially including cash, intrinsic satisfactions, security, power, status, opportunity to advance one's career or to fulfil personally meaningful purposes. The particular mix here depends on the specific circumstances which prevail as well as on the priorities of the individual concerned.

The basis of work motivation according to this model lies in the outcomes of a bargain between the employer and the employee. As long as the employer supplies what is expected by the employee, then the employee performs as the employer expects. This, of course is the basic principle of all employment relationships. But the practice is by no means so simple. And the main reason for this is that the contract is not one between equals. There is the basic inequality of the individual having limited resources whilst the corporate employer is likely to possess considerable resources. And this inequality is accompanied by an equally basic conflict of interests between the parties. The logic of the market context of the two parties is one which pushes the employer to keep down costs – including rewards to employees – yet pushes the employees (who have to buy goods on the market) to push up those same costs. The relative weakness of the individual employee (varying, however, with the scarcity of their skills or knowledge) leads to a tendency for individuals to come together in groups to defend or further their interests in workgroups, professional associations or trade unions.

These realities of economic conflicts of interest and of the tendency for oppositional groups to arise among employees is of considerable importance to the issues we are considering in this chapter. They remind us of a fact which, incredibly, is missing from much of the social scientific literature on motivation, leadership and job design: that what happens between employers and employees has a lot to do with power relationships and with conflicts and struggles. One of the most serious weaknesses of the psychology-based traditions of organisational social science is that it has worked on the assumption that motivation and leadership at work are somehow separable from 'industrial relations'.

My implicit contract model attempts to bring together motivational and industrial relations issues. This is done in the following way. The implicit contract between the employer and the employee (this being at the heart of the employee's orientation to work and hence their predisposition to act in a certain way) is seen as inherently fragile. Because each party has an interest in improving their side of the contract in a way which may disadvantage the other side, there is an ever-present danger that the contract will go out of balance. Whenever this occurs in a direction which is out of accord with the expectations of the employee, we have, in industrial relations terms, a 'grievance situation'. If the affected employees are industrially organised then a dispute is likely to follow.

When an industrial relations dispute occurs then we can expect some kind of formal negotiation to occur to resolve it. However, the typical type of negotiation between employers and employees is that which goes on everyday between managers and workers, whether or not there is a formal dispute and whether or not there are even any trade unions present. Given that human beings are political and economic animals as well as need-bearing creatures, it is sensible to see that managerial motivation efforts are as much about negotiating inputs and outputs as about 'meeting needs'. But, as the next processual approach which we are going to consider shows, negotiations at work are not just over material outcomes. They are also about the meanings of work itself. And effective motivators among managers can be seen as people who are especially skilled at ensuring that the meanings which are ultimately negotiated in the work setting are ones which encourage employee performance of the kind which suits managerial purposes.

The cultural and symbolic management approach

This approach to motivation and leadership takes us back to our discussion in Chapter 1 of 'management as magic' (pp. 30–2) and our review of the culture-excellence school in organisation theory in Chapter 3 (pp. 66–71). The basic assumption of approaches which I am bringing together under this present heading is that an essential feature of all human beings is a 'need for meaning' and that this is not met by the individual working out a set of meanings about the world for themselves. It is set by the individual taking from – and giving to – the culture in which they live. It is then assumed that the work organisation itself is a significant part of the individual's life world and that they will be more likely to perform in a way required by the organisation if organisational activities help 'create meanings' for participants. The organisation, to be effective, therefore needs to have an overall organisational culture of the kind discussed in Chapter 3 which can provide people with meanings which encourage them to perform appropriately.

Peters and Waterman (1982) state the 'need for meaning' view very strongly when they say we 'desperately need meaning in our lives and will sacrifice a great deal to institutions that will provide meaning for us'. They take up the observation of the psychoanalytical theorist, Bruno Bettelheim (1976), that we make great use of myths and fairy tales in shaping meanings in our lives and they point out how the 'excellent' companies which they studied were 'quite simply rich tapestries of anecdote myth and fairy tale'. The role of leadership is seen as of great importance in this. It is not just a question of dealing with big issues but also one of concern with minutiae: 'with the tricks of the pedagogue, the mentor, the linguist – the more successfully to become the value shaper, the exemplar, the maker of meanings'. These influential authors of the 1980s again go back to Philip Selznick (1957) who, decades ago, said:

The inbuilding of purpose is a challenge to creativity because it involves transforming men and groups from neutral, technical units into participants who have a particular stamp, sensitivity, and commitment. This is ultimately an educational process. It has been well said that the effective leader must

know the meaning and master the technique of the educator.
. . . The institutional leader . . . is primarily an expert in the
promotion and protection of values.

Louis Pondy (1978) has suggested that leadership can usefully be
seen as a 'language game'. The leader who possesses a dual capacity to both 'make sense of things *and* to put them into language
meaningful to large numbers of people' has 'enormous leverage'.
This accords with Karl Weick's (1979) view that the manager is
better seen as an evangelist than as an accountant: as one who has
to work at managing myths, symbols and images. And this is not
inconsistent with what has been observed by several writers on
accounting itself. Trevor Gambling (1977) has, for instance,
shown how the ritualistic aspect of accounting gives a protection
from uncertainty and gives people something to which they can
assent and hence be helped to keep going for the present. And
Michael Earl (1983) has discussed how the mythical aspect of
accounting can be seen as providing notions of what is legitimate
and acceptable and can therefore help 'secure commitment and
obedience to leadership and hierarchy'. This is all in the context
of the contribution made to explaining the world and its events.
    Jeffrey Pfeffer (1981) helps us keep in perspective this kind of
thinking by suggesting that organisational management or leadership operates at two levels. The first is the generally recognised
level at which substantive actions occur and results are brought
about. The second level, however, is the 'expressive or symbolic'
one at which the use of political language and symbolic action
helps to 'legitimate and rationalise organisational decisions and
policies'. Organisations can be seen as 'systems of shared meanings and beliefs' which are, in part, managed by the careful use
of language, symbolism and ritual. A considerable number of
ways of creating meanings are available to managers ranging from
that mentioned by T. J. Peters (1978) whereby leaders spend time
on an activity that is to be emphasised or defined as important, to
restructuring and devising new job or unit titles and even to
attending to the way the physical layout is designed. The implication for all this, says Pfeffer, is that managers need to be trained
in political, dramaturgical and language skills more than in
analytical and strictly quantitative skills.
    At first sight we see in this general perspective a retreat from

the achievement of the other third-wave views whereby the universalism of second-wave theories was replaced by a more careful attention to the specificities of the situation and of the particular people involved. Instead of generalisations about self-actualisation needs, it might be said, we now have an equally mystical stress on a general 'need for meaning'. I would argue that there is indeed a danger here. We have to recognise two things. First, that there may well be situations where people can find quite sufficient meaning for their lives in their activities outside work. This could be the case where the work was especially unskilled or where the employees belonged to particularly strong communities outside the workplace. It could also become a stronger likelihood if, in the future, a great deal of employment is part-time. If employment takes up only a minor part of one's week, in a time sense, it could more easily come to take up only a minor part of one's life in a symbolic or affiliation sense. And, second, we have to realise that there may be types of employment in which the employer prefers to keep some, if not all, employees at an arm's length. This point will be developed in the next chapter.

In spite of these reservations, the stress on meanings, symbols and cultures is important and necessary. I would argue that a general 'need for meaning' is, in fact, an essential feature of the human species and always needs to be taken into account in the employment context. I suggested earlier that the processual approach to understanding motivation, leadership and job design must have a balanced view of the general and the specific. Where I believe that the cultural approach complements the expectancy and orientations approaches is in its ability to prompt us to see that such things as 'expectations' and 'orientations' are in fact subject to modification by managements. In helping to define realities for employees, strong-culture organisations are influencing employee expectations and orientations to work. However, expectations, orientations and the perceived implicit contracts of particular individuals and groups will vary and will always be subject to the pressures arising in employer-employee conflicts of interest. These perspectives have to be used alongside each other then, and, if possible, integrated in the mind of the effective manager.

Effective motivation, leadership and job design?

The aspects of managerial work dealt with in the present chapter can never be considered in isolation. They have been separated out into one chapter of this book in recognition of the fact that they traditionally have been dealt with as an area, or a group of areas, in their own right – in 'Organisational Behaviour' textbooks for example. We have to recognise such traditions in order to go beyond them. And the direction in which I hope to push my readers is away from the tradition of seeing as separate the largely psychology-based materials dealt with in this chapter and the more sociologically oriented work covered in the previous one. That separation is well on its way to being undermined by the new tendency for thinkers in both of the traditions to recognise the role of 'culture' in organisations and management. 'Culture' is becoming an important bridging concept and I have left the 'motivational' aspects of it until the end of the present chapter so that it functions as a prompt to the reader now to connect what has been covered in this chapter back to the general conception of management with which Chapter 2 concluded (pp. 39–43) and back to the way that this was followed up at the end of Chapter 3 (pp. 81–5).

The content of the present chapter helps the manager with the set of 'people questions' which form part of the set of issues which, it was suggested at the end of the last chapter, underlie organisational and managerial effectiveness. Effective motivation, leadership and job design do not exist as such. They only exist insofar as effort is applied in these areas at the same time as attention is given to issues of strategy, structure and, of course, to issues of how the organisation is welded into a 'whole' by its overall culture.

Chapter 5

Employment strategy and the problems of managing people

The concept of employment strategy is an invaluable one which can enable us to bring together many of the ideas about the 'human' aspects of the organisation and management of work which have been looked at in previous chapters. It is a notion which helps us to pay attention to the general or the overall way in which an organisation deals with its employees. It has major theoretical value insofar as it can help us integrate – and see the relationships between – such things as organisational structures, organisational cultures, motivation, leadership styles, job design, recruitment, reward systems and so on. And it is valuable in the practical sphere in that it provides a starting point for organisational thinking about such things as 'employment', 'personnel', 'manpower', and 'industrial relations' policies.

I suggest that the emergence of the concept of 'employment strategy', or something like it, has signalled one of the more significant directions recently being followed by academic analysts. And I also suggest that a tendency to give more explicit attention to overall employment policies within employing organisations is something we will increasingly see as managements come to terms with the kinds of competitive, technological, and societal changes which are facing them. The present chapter will be concerned, first, with clarifying this valuable concept of employment strategy and noting how there are some basic variations in the types of strategy which can be followed. Second, it will consider previous attempts to understand the nature and variations of employment strategy followed by organisations, paying particular attention to the recently influential 'labour process' type of analysis which has done much to prompt attention to these important matters. Third, an attempt will be made to provide a theoretical understanding of the fundamental problems which underlie all employment strategies and practices.

The concept of employment strategy

The first thing that we have to say when considering any aspect of organisational strategies is that we are not, in implying that there is some overall direction in the activities of an organisation, adopting the rationalistic-mechanistic kind of model of organisations which we have rejected in our call for 'processual' approaches. To identify a strategy being followed by an organisation is not necessarily to imply that this is always a fully conscious and planned direction decided upon by the top managers or 'strategic planners' in the organisation which is then followed by the rest of the organisation. There are indeed conscious strategic decisions made by senior managements and these are perhaps usefully identified as 'policies'. But even these formal statements of strategic intent are, like the other aspects of strategy, best seen as emergent – as logical yet arising out of the interplay of actions and constraints which occur and apply across the organisation. The importance of recognising the 'logical incrementalism' of strategic behaviour was stressed earlier (Quinn, 1980; see above p. 76). We are suggesting, then, that we follow Henry Mintzberg (1978) in seeing strategy as a 'pattern in a stream of decisions'. Yet we must always be wary of the danger of imposing too much pattern on what we see going on.

The basic concept of organisational strategy used in this book has been a fairly simple one: it is *the general direction in which the management of an organisation 'pulls things together and along' in order to ensure long-term organisational survival.* To do this, use is made of finance, technologies, know-how and human effort but, as we have stressed, all this occurs within political and economic processes whereby the organisation has to fulfil the demands which are made on it by the range of constituencies upon whom it is dependent for resources (pp. 41, 80). And, at any given time, some constituencies are more 'strategic' than others in the sense that they present particularly strong threats to the organisation's future.

Taking this 'resource dependence' view as our starting point, we can suggest that *employment strategies are those general directions followed by organisations in the way they handle the problems created for their performance and long-term survival by the range of employee constituencies and other constituencies concerned with employees.* We mention 'other constituencies concerned with employees' in this definition in recognition of the fact that parties other than the employees themselves apply constraints on how the organisation relates to its employees. The state comes readily to mind here in the laws and regulations which it applies to employment matters. Also, trade unions, as external bodies, may be resource-dependent constituencies making demands different from those of internal union-organised groups of employees.

Although, later on, we will be noting the range of factors which influence the types of employment strategy which are followed, it will be suggested that *the basic factor influencing the type of employment strategy followed by any given organisation is the extent to which the management of an organisation perceive the various employee constituencies to be problematic in terms of long-term organisational survival.* And this leads us to make a fundamentally important point about employment strategies: because the degree to which employee constituencies are seen as problematic is relative to how problematic other parties are perceived to be, they can never be seen in isolation from the other elements of the organisation's overall strategy. Employment strategies have to be seen alongside financial, market and technological strategies, for example.

Employee constituencies are necessarily key ones in any organisation but they are only one group of constituencies among a constellation of others such as banks, shareholders, the state, customers or clients. And, as Batstone, Ferner and Terry (1983) stress, general corporate policies and strategies often contain built-in assumptions about labour relations, and decisions on such strategic issues as pricing, marketing, investment, product range and technology 'may imply, or amount to, labour strategies'. These authors note how research by both Winkler (1974) and Fidler (1981) suggests that many corporate board-level decisions 'embody an implicit labour strategy which defines labour as a cost to be minimised'. As they valuably point out, 'labour strategy cannot be identified merely by observation of those parts of management's organisation ostensibly to do with such matters'.

Sheila Rothwell (1984a), in her discussion of employment policies and strategies, suggests that we distinguish between their style and their content. She sees two main elements in the 'style' component of an organisation's employment strategy. The first involves the existence of a 'company credo' of the type identified by Peters and Waterman (1982; see above p. 69) as part of the corporate culture and the type of emphasis this puts on policies towards employees. As she says, these 'motherhood' type statements can be seen as largely meaningless propaganda. Yet the existence of a policy statement such as one about encouraging people to work as a team whilst, at the same time, encouraging them to be innovative and creative, can 'provide criteria against which to evaluate alternatives' not only in employment policy planning but in other policy areas such as choosing work systems and procedures. The second aspect of the style of an employment policy is what Rothwell calls the 'perceived role of the personnel function'. This is a matter of how influential and 'pro-active' the specialists in personnel management are within the organisation and will be our particular concern in the next chapter.

When it comes to the *content* of employment strategies, the present analysis is probably broader than most existing accounts of what is entailed. At the most detailed level it would include such matters as the general approach to office and shopfloor supervisory style or such a matter as whether employees 'clock in' and 'clock out' of work. At the most general level it would include the overall structure of the organisation: whether, for example, it is a centralised and functionally-based structure or a decentralised multi-divisional one. The reason that issues across this range are included here is that they involve *strategically relevant choices about the relationships which prevail between the employer and the employees.* Thus, both choices of supervisory style and of the degree of centralisation of decision-making structures imply something about the extent to which employees are to be seen as requiring close and direct management control or are to be seen as committed to the organisation in such a way that they will choose to pursue organisational objectives without being too specifically pointed in that direction.

There are similar implications with regard to the basic employer-employee relationship in many other issues which relate to the overall employment strategy: recruitment, terms and conditions, job design, rewards, promotions, redundancy, retirement, training, communications, consultation, participation and collective bargaining procedures, and welfare provisions. Despite the fact that, in all of these areas, there is a some degree of choice as to whether the employee is to be encouraged to be 'intimately and trustingly' attached to the organisation or 'distantly and calculatively' involved with it, we should not assume that the concept of employment strategy being developed here is one which sees every organisation as deciding on which side of this underlying divide it wants to come down *in every aspect of its relationship with its employees* or *in every area of the organisation*. But this is to look ahead. Before we deal with the question of what kind of theoretical generalisations are possible with regard to the choice of employment strategy, we need to look at some of the existing attempts to understand the variety of possibilities in the sphere of employment relations.

Four approaches to variations in employment strategy

The alternatives which exist or have existed in particular aspects of how employers relate to employees have been dealt with in a variety of different ways by writers approaching the issue from different perspectives and with different value-emphases. Four types of approach can be identified: the historical, the contingency, the labour process and the role-structure approach.

Historical approaches

These approaches to appreciating the different ways in which employers have chosen to manage their employees vary in the extent they are willing to generalise or to produce models of the possibilities rather than simply provide descriptions of changing practices. Here, we shall consider three examples of the latter kind of analysis. These are all produced by social scientists rather than by historians – some analysis of the finer-grain type produced by professional historians will nevertheless be drawn on in the next chapter when we consider these matters from a somewhat different angle.

Reinhard Bendix (1963), in his now classic historical and sociological analysis of changing managerial ideologies, concentrates on what we have identified as the 'style' aspects of employment strategy. He stresses the justificatory or legitimating functions of employment policies and philosophies, indicating how particular employment practices were justified by the beliefs to which they were attached. He observes that at the inception of industrialisation in England the way entrepreneurs justified their control over personnel was through a *traditional* ideology. This involved a paternalist theory of dependence in which the labouring classes were seen as children who owed obedience and deference to their superiors who, in turn, protected them against the vicissitudes of life. Later generations of employers found this diffuse and long-term commitment a burden, however, and, as markets and methods rapidly changed during the nineteenth century, they increasingly took up a *laissez-faire* approach. This treated labour as a commodity, the supply of which could be turned on and off as required. Social Darwinist ideas which were current at the time were used as a component of this managerial ideology. Bosses were to be obeyed because they were the fittest. They had survived in the economic jungle. Those who were employed, bossed and sacked had no grounds for complaint. Their position was the result of their own failure to take up the opportunities which were said to be as open to them as they had been to those who had managed to become employers.

Bendix suggests that laissez-faire employment philosophies and practices became less appropriate as enterprises became bigger and more complex, with fewer clearly visible single bosses. The ideology worked less well as unionisation became an increasingly significant factor in twentieth-century organisations. He argues that a *human-relations* ideology therefore emerged. This laid emphasis on human psychological needs and encouraged a perception of management as people who would help these needs be met in the workplace. The way the Hawthorne Studies (see above pp. 97–101) were reported and interpreted were important in this.

Charles Milton (1970) has produced an interesting account of the history of what he calls 'personnel philosophies' in the United States. His approach uses a finer mesh than Bendix's and he detects six personnel philosophies operating in different eras of American management history following the abandonment of what he calls 'pre-industrial' concepts of labour. It is valuable to look at these six approaches because they indicate the variety of ways in which different emphases within management thinking may be combined in different circumstances.

The first personnel philosophy observed by Milton is what he calls a *laissez-faire* one. This repudiated any employer responsibility for employee welfare. It justified leadership on the basis of superior hereditary endowment (demonstrated through the process of the survival of the fittest) and it treated labour as a commodity. Milton sees this eventually increasing employee dissatisfaction to an unacceptable level and being replaced by *paternalist* models of personnel philosophy. These had their heyday between 1900 and 1920 and saw leadership in the hands of benevolent autocrats who operated with a 'goodwill' concept of labour. Realising that labour could no longer be ignored or abused, docility, obedience and productiveness were encouraged by the seeking of stronger employee commitment through adding to direct financial rewards various indirect ones together with safer, more sanitary and more pleasant working conditions. Commitment and hence control came through gratitude. Leadership here stressed the rights of private property and was committed to protecting managerial prerogatives. The concept of labour was an impersonal one which was insensitive to employee needs and aspirations. Personnel policies were unthought-out and actions were unilateral and reactive.

New pressures came to bear on American employers in the 1930s, suggests Milton, and the result was a shift towards a more managerially conscious *technique* philosophy. Ownership rights were now seen as somewhat limited by the trusteeship responsibilities of managements. The labourer was now seen more as a unique individual whose characteristics needed to be matched to the job if productivity was to be achieved. Labour was not only an important resource which needed to be handled with care: workers were also consumers and this was a further pressure discouraging employers from offending them. Personnel policies now became more clearly formulated and sound personnel policies were seen as contributing to good public relations as well as to the ensuring of consistency and fairness within the enterprise. Personnel management was mechanistic and concentrated on setting up procedures and using formal techniques.

After 1940, Milton sees an increasing shift towards a *humanistic* philosophy. Within this, the management generally and the personnel managers particularly take into account increasingly influential social science thinking and, instead of relying on authority to achieve cooperation, they work towards developing an organisational environment 'conducive to providing each employee with an opportunity to gratify their economic, psychological and, to a lesser extent, social needs which permit their personal growth and development'. Out of this philosophy, Milton sees the future emergence of *total personality* models of personnel philosophy which appear to take further the 'participative' elements within the humanistic framework.

Milton's analysis of the changing approaches to the personnel aspects of management is an evolutionary one and he is at pains to argue that philosophies changed in reaction to pressures on managements rather than as the result of conscious and principled executive decision-making. This, he suggests, is indicated by the fact that the greatest changes occurred during the turbulent years of war, depression, rapid technological growth and major government intervention. Managements reacted to these pressures, he emphasises, primarily out of motives of employer self-interest. Nevertheless, Milton's view of the future is an optimistic one.

Blau and Schoenherr (1971), operating with a much briefer and more recent historical time-span, provide a picture which is much less rosy than Milton's, at least from the point of view of employees. This, however, may be a matter of value judgment as much as anything else. The trend that these two researchers point to as currently occurring is one in which employment strategies increasingly involve the subjecting of employees to *insidious controls*. They say,

> Slave drivers have gone out of fashion not because they were so cruel but because they were so inefficient. Men can be controlled much more effectively by tying their economic needs and interests to their performances on behalf of employers. ... The efforts of men can be controlled still far more efficiently than through wages alone by mobilising their professional commitments to the work they can do best and like to do most and by putting these highly motivated energies and skills at the disposal of the organisation.

Blau and Schoenherr argue that three forms of insidious control have become more common in contemporary organisations. First there is control through *expert power* whereby there is appeal to professional commitment. Second, there is control through *selective recruitment* whereby managements recruit only those people whom they feel sure will choose, through such things as a professional orientation, to comply with organisational priorities. And, third, there is control through *the allocation of resources* whereby the direction taken by the work done in an area of the organisation is not directly interfered with but is influenced by the central administrators through the encouragement which is given – or denied – by the way staff and other resources are allocated to that area. These controls are described as insidious because they are deceptive in that they encourage people to believe that they are conforming with some neutral situational logic rather than with the wishes of those in charge; because they are elusive in that accountability for harmful decisions is not possible; and because they are unresponsive in that they are not recognised as forms of control and are therefore immune to democratic constraints.

Contingency approaches

These are less concerned with noting historical trends in employment strategies than with examining how different approaches may be adopted to fit different circumstances. In fact, both the approaches of Bendix and Milton looked at above had an element in them which saw historical contingencies as influencing the general style of employment strategy as well as the particular practices which were seen as being appropriate to the circumstances applying at different times. Other approaches, however, give primacy of attention to the idea of 'fit' between employment policies and situational pressures in a way similar to that seen between circumstances and organisational structures (above p. 60) and circumstances and leadership styles (above p. 115).

Peterson and Tracy (1979) are good representatives of the contingency approach with their account of three basic types of 'human resource system models'. These three models first appeared at different historical times but may co-exist historically. The *traditional* human resource system is one where the managerial philosophy sees the achieving of productive efficiency and accomplishments of task goals as requiring the tight structuring and close supervision of the work of subordinates and the straightforward use of economic incentives as the primary motivators for work effort. This is not a historically redundant approach as is often implied in management textbooks. It is one which continues to be appropriate in circumstances where labour is cheap and plentiful and where technology permits the job to be broken down into very simple tasks. Labour can easily be treated as so many 'hired hands' since union or government pressure is unlikely to occur under such conditions. Consequently, no great care is needed in selecting and placing employees; training is simple and specific; discipline is a straightforward matter of ensuring regular attendance and obedience to work rules whilst industrial relations policy lays emphasis on the avoidance of union encroachment on managerial rights. Collective bargaining, if unavoidable, is restricted to basic issues of wages and work rules.

The *human relations* human resource system is based on human relations thinking (above pp. 97–101) and is appropriate, say Peterson and Tracy, where labour is less plentiful and where there is more union or government 'interference'. The human relations approach consequently encourages supervisors to be considerate towards subordinates. Selection processes are concerned with employees' attitudes as well as with their skills and aptitudes and employees are deployed in ways which encourage the existence of cohesive work groups. Good communications are greatly emphasised, as are fringe benefits and other welfare benefits which are supplied in order to gain employee loyalty. Industrial relations policy will aim either to keep the enterprise non-union or to foster cooperative relationships with unions – once they have to be accepted.

Human resources systems of personnel management are based on a management philosophy influenced by the democratic humanist type of thinking reviewed in the last chapter (pp. 101–16) and emphasise the management's responsibility for ensuring that work is organised so that the task needs are met at the same time as employees gain the satisfaction that they require at the level of intrinsic job satisfaction and 'self-actualisation' as well as at the financial and social level. The participative involvement of employees in certain aspects of decision-making is important here.

Peterson and Tracy see this system as appropriate to circumstances in which human skills are in high demand or are a critical factor in the success of the business. These conditions are most likely to arise where there is a turbulent and highly competitive economic environment or rapid technological change.

The contingency perspective on employment strategies, which is well represented by the Peterson and Tracy analysis, is valuable, when put alongside historical approaches, in that it begins to make some systematic and formal links between particular approaches to the management of employees and the prevailing circumstances. There is recognition of the part played by managerial philosophies and value preferences but this is seen as being interrelated with matters of expedience. As with the contingency approaches to organisational structuring (above, pp. 60-2), the virtues of contingency thinking as an antidote to 'one best way' organisational and managerial thought are rather compromised by weaknesses of the approach. Most significant here is that little is said of the *processes* whereby particular structures or policies are adopted to give the theoretical 'fit' between circumstance and procedures. The question of the role of managerial choice and the sectional or political implications of how particular employment strategies are adopted are left vague. Similar problems arise with the recently very influential labour process approach to these matters.

The labour process

This approach to questions of job design and employment strategy has its roots in a tradition of thinking about work and employment quite at odds with the more managerial approaches which, ironically, it has come to resemble in some ways. It derives from Karl Marx's analysis of capitalist exploitation of employees and has made a major impact on organisation theory, especially in Europe, through the strong interest shown in it by the more radical generation of younger sociologically inclined scholars who have taken an interest in employment and organisation practices. The very considerable contribution of what is often termed the 'labour process debate' is that it has firmly established the importance in organisational analysis of paying attention to the connection between how people are managed in the workplace and the overall political economy of the society in which this occurs. Employment practices within capitalist economies cannot be fully understood without considering the implications of capitalism itself for those practices, it is correctly stressed.

The labour process perspective concentrates upon workplace activity and what it calls 'labour processes'. The capitalist labour process is seen as one in which the interests of the capital-owning class are represented by managements whose basic task is to design, control and monitor work tasks and activities so as to ensure the effective extraction of surplus value from the labour activity of employees. The basic assumption is thus Marx's one of seeing capitalist employment as essentially exploitative in that it seeks to take from working people the 'value' which they create through their labour and which is properly their own. In managing the labour process to fulfil this function, managers are following the logic of the capitalist mode of production whereby the need for capital accumulation demands employers' constant attention to subjugating labour in order to extract enough from it to allow profitable survival in the stormy seas of the capitalist market economy.

It is widely recognised that Harry Braverman (1974) played a central role in encouraging this kind of analysis among organisation and employment theorists. In presenting his thesis that the pursuit of capitalist interests has led to a general trend towards deskilling, routinising and mechanising jobs across the employment spectrum, from manufacturing to retailing and from design to clerical work, Braverman awards managerial supremacy to the industrial engineers. These people apply the deskilling logic of scientific management or Taylorism to work tasks whilst the specialists in personnel management merely help them along. Generally, then,

> Work itself is organised according to Taylorian principles, while personnel departments and academics have busied themselves with the selection, training, manipulation, pacification, and adjustment of manpower to suit the work processes so organised.

Those concerned with 'human relations' are simply the 'maintenance crew for the human machinery', and, in this statement,

Braverman makes clear that he sees the kind of approach I described earlier as 'people as machines' (p. 96) as anything but a thing of the less-enlightened past. Taylorism is rampant in the later twentieth century and is aided and abetted by modern electronic techniques which are continually reducing the need for capitalist employers to depend on human skills and hence their need to reward them for their work in any but a minimal and straightforwardly economic way.

Braverman's book had a considerable impact in that it offered a wide range of examples of how jobs were being deskilled in many different parts of the overall labour market in a way which appeared to be accelerating the Taylorian initiatives of more than half a century before. The debate about Braverman's work which followed its publication has, to a large extent, featured criticisms of it from theorists similarly inspired by Marxist thinking but who wanted a more subtle, two-sided or 'dialectical' approach to understanding capitalist labour processes. These would give much greater recognition to the resistance offered to employers by organised labour. It was argued that managerial activity should be understood not as straightforwardly imposing upon employees the work tasks 'required by capital' but as engaging in a *competition for control* with employees, albeit in the same long-term interests of 'capital'.

The more developed or 'dialectical' versions of labour process theory allow for a more sophisticated view of employment strategies than does Braverman. Goldman and van Houten (1981), for instance, recognise the mixed and contradictory motives behind the growth of welfare and personnel management in the United States. They relate the growth of welfare measures and personnel management interventions to the recognition of some American employers in the early twentieth century that a 'heavy handed' approach to labour directed towards short-term profit might be ultimately less effective than an attempt to develop more subtle 'social controls' over labour. These would better facilitate long-term stability and growth. This corresponds with an attempt by Andrew Friedman (1977), a British labour-process theorist and researcher, to offer an analysis of labour processes which takes better account than does Braverman's of the extent to which some employees are more able than others to resist managerial controls.

Friedman emphasises the longer-term aspect of the capitalist profit motive and, most importantly, recognises that managerial treatment of behaviour *may vary according to the circumstances of its employment*. Working on the Marxian assumption that managements operate in the ultimate interests of long-term profitability, he offers an insight which is in some ways consistent with orthodox contingency thinking. He suggests that management may choose either a *direct-control* strategy which is largely in line with Taylorian deskilling policies or a *responsible-autonomy* strategy in which employees are allowed a degree of discretion and responsibility in their work. Given the capacity of some employees to oppose managements in certain circumstances, managements are often unable to risk introducing control techniques which might reduce worker goodwill. He goes on to argue that where workers are 'central' to long-term profitability (in that they have skills, knowledge or union power which renders their opposition dangerous) they have to be treated more carefully and given more responsible autonomy than when they are 'peripheral' or less critical to longer-term profitability and can be more directly controlled.

Although labour-process thinking focusses on workplace matters of job design and task control, the kind of analysis offered by Friedman has implications for employment strategies in a much wider sense. We can infer from it that a more 'sophisticated' range of selection, appraisal, training, reward and negotiating techniques are likely to be required with some types of employee than with others. And, in line with this, we can expect a greater formal presence of personnel management expertise in some sectors of employment than in others. This suggestion is also compatible with the analysis of Richard Edwards (1979).

Edwards suggests that the simple employee control strategies of early competitive capitalism were gradually found wanting as the trend towards modern monopoly capitalism developed. As class resistance towards 'simple' managerial controls grew and as the centralisation of capitalist organisation increased, various alternative approaches to control were experimented with. However, experiments with scientific management, welfare policies and company unionism were not successful according to Edwards's analysis of the activities of a selection of notable American companies. The shift, instead, was towards more 'structural' approaches to control in which there would be less dependence on the personal power of employers and managers and more on the effects of the physical and social structure of the enterprise. The first of these was a *technical control strategy* which depended on the discipline of assembly line and similar types of technology. However, as problems appeared with this approach, initiatives began to be made with the development of *bureaucratic control strategies.*

Bureaucratic control structures are said to involve the development of internal labour markets within organisations. There are career structures, and relatively high levels of job security are offered to privileged sections of the labour force. These function to gain the commitment of employees to employer purposes and encourage the kind of reasonably acceptable and predictable levels of performance required of many of the employees of the larger contemporary work organisation. Edwards's analysis is a historical one in that it is based on a Marxist view of how forms of capitalist domination have developed. But it also has elements of the contingency view, as had Friedman's analysis. Edwards notes that capitalist production has developed unevenly and that the three forms of control strategy (simple, technical and bureaucratic) exist at the same time. Simple control, for example, can be found in small businesses and 'core' sectors of the economy will use different strategies from 'peripheral' ones.

A valuable contribution of Edwards has been his attempt to connect the segmentation of labour markets in modern societies with the varying types of employee control strategy which are in use. Labour market theorists had for some time been pointing out the existence of 'dual labour markets' (Doeringer and Piore, 1971). This followed from the recognition of a tendency for there to be a *primary labour market* involving jobs with good working conditions and pay levels, opportunities for advancement and fair treatment at work and, especially, job security. This is contrasted with the *secondary labour market* which compares badly in all these respects and is particularly characterised by considerable instability and a high labour turnover rate. And, in best 'political economy' traditions (see above, p. 77), this is related to features of the structure of society: it is observed that the secondary labour force draws disproportionately on women, blacks, immigrants, unqualified teenagers, students seeking part-time work, disabled and handicapped people. In this way major social inequalities are connected with organisational and employment strategy practices.

Edwards builds on and expands this dual labour market approach to note that there is a particular labour market type associated with each of his three control strategies. Thus, corresponding to simple, technical and bureaucratic control strategies are the secondary labour market (including people in a range of lowly paid and insecure jobs like cleaning, portering and other casual service work), the subordinate primary labour market (including traditional unionised working class and clerical employees of 'core' firms) and the independent primary labour market (including professionals, managers, craft-workers and the like).

Labour process theory and the research which has been done by its advocates has been invaluable in stressing the connection between issues of class and power in society and the employment strategies followed in work organisations. In conjunction with historical and contingency approaches, it highlights the variety of employment strategies which both have existed historically and exist alongside each other in contemporary economies. But, most significantly, it has offered a *theoretical* analysis of employment strategies. It attempts to generalise about the factors which influence the adoption of one approach to employees rather than another. Nevertheless, the way this is done is less than satisfactory in that the basic Marxist preoccupation of most of these theorists with the role of capital-owning interests in bringing about employment initiatives tends to lead to an underestimation of ambiguities and contradictions inherent in all labour strategies and, especially, to an underestimation of the role played by managerial interests – as distinct from ownership ones – in making strategic choices.

Labour process theory tends to suffer from some of the basic problems of orthodox organisation and management theory. It comes very close at times to the over-rationalised conception of organisations criticised in Chapter 1 (p. 19) in its view of the employer as carefully, consciously and ruthlessly adopting policies which will produce profits and capital accumulation. This is not to say that, in capitalist societies, managerial decisions are not in some ultimate sense related to the profit criterion underpinning the economy. It is to say, however, that many particular decisions are made for a whole variety of reasons not immediately connected to concerns with profit – or even efficiency.

Motives which influence employment practices and which are rarely noted by labour-process theorists range from state-led concerns keeping unprofitable enterprises open to maintain employment levels to managements preserving jobs and practices which suit their own sectional interests or value preferences and to wealthy proprietors running enterprises to give them prestige or influence. To this has to be added all the realities of 'muddling through', the following of habitual practices and the ability of employers and managers alike to get things wrong! Not only do we need a theory which is flexible enough to allow for all this, we need one which gives more recognition to the tendency mentioned earlier (p. 135) whereby employment strategies emerge out of a process in which attention is given simultaneously, or perhaps more typically *first*, to issues of market, financial or technical strategy. Because theorists working with Marxist sentiments tend to be centrally concerned with issues of class conflict and economic exploitation they can too easily be led to exaggerate the extent to which employers and managers concentrate on and act pro-actively (rather than reactively) towards employment problems when making decisions.

Role-structure approaches

These approaches to understanding variations in aspects of employment practices are varied and not always explicitly directed to employment practices as such. In fact, I have created this category of ideas simply in order to pull together a wide range of ideas from organisation theorists and sociologists which relate to the fact that some basic variations exist in the kind of roles which are filled by organisational actors. The concepts made available to us here can be helpful when developing a model for analysing employment strategies which is intended to include considerations of organisational structures themselves as well as more obvious and traditional matters of personnel policy.

Amitai Etzioni (1961) focussed on the various types of compliance which can characterise the relationships between organisations and their members. He related three possible types of power which superordinates may apply to subordinates – coercive, remunerative and normative – to three possible types of involvement of members – alienative, calculative and moral. The three most likely combinations of these, he suggests, are *coercive* compliance in which coercive power is combined with alienative involvement, *utilitarian compliance* in which remunerative power is associated with calculative involvement, and *normative compliance* where normative power goes along with a moral type of involvement. In this latter case there are likely to be strongly shared values on both sides of the relationship together with a great deal of mutual commitment. And, in this framework, Etzioni is making the valuable point that how people relate to the organisations in which they are located is a two-sided matter: it combines the control strategy of the organisation's managers with what was discussed as the individual's 'orientation' in the last chapter (p. 122).

Robert Blauner (1964) stressed the role of technology in noting the ways in which different degrees of worker 'alienation' could be expected in different work organisations. In his famous 'inverted U curve of alienation' he claims that the typically high-autonomy roles of traditional craft industry (giving low alienation) were historically replaced by lower-autonomy/higher-alienation roles in machine-minding and assembly-line industries which will, in turn tend to be replaced by high-autonomy/low-alienation roles in the industries of the future where jobs will tend to be highly skilled, flexible and concerned with problem-solving within the automated plant.

Alvin Gouldner's (1964) classical contribution to questioning the idea of there being just one overall type of organisational structure concentrated on managerial attempts to gain compliance with rules. He distinguishes between punishment-centred, representative and mock bureaucracies and very usefully shows, in his study of a gypsum plant, that managements may fluctuate in their adherence to different modes of controlling employees. A management can well vary its style from one in which it is 'indulgent' towards minor rule infringements in a spirit of 'give and take' with the workers and a regime in which it strictly imposes rules and procedures in a much more unilateral approach to control and achieving output.

David Hickson (1966) was able to pull together a considerable number of ideas of theorists ranging from sociologists like Gouldner, to organisations writers like Burns and Stalker (above p. 61), with their mechanistic and organic structures, and managerial writers like Douglas McGregor (above p. 110), with his Theories X and Y, to argue that there was a convergence developing within organisation theory. He argued that, throughout organisation and management theory, there is a tendency to reduce structural variation to a single aspect of role expectations. This is the specificity (or precision) of role prescription and its obverse, the range of legitimate discretion.

The importance of the distinction between prescribed elements in organisational roles and discretionary elements had been most clearly stated by Elliot Jaques (1956) when he put forward his 'timespan of discretion' approach to establishing how different jobs might be seen to be fairly rewarded. He suggested that any given job can be broken down into the elements that are fixed or prescribed and the elements which are left up to the employee's own judgment or discretion. The higher the degree of the latter the more people would see it as reasonable for a relatively higher level of reward to be given, said Jaques.

Alan Fox (1974) took up Jaques's concepts and uses them to a very different purpose to that envisaged by Jaques. He suggests that there are two basic 'work role patterns' in contemporary organisations. The first he labels the *low-discretion syndrome* which involves highly prescribed low-discretion roles which have, as their key feature, an implicit assumption that their occupants cannot be trusted by their superordinates to deliver, of their own volition, a performance which fully accords with managerial goals or values. Taylorian job design fits in here. The second work-role pattern makes up the *high-discretion syndrome* in which role occupants are expected to be highly committed in a calling or to either the 'organisational' goals or values. These people are trusted and, in Etzioni's terms, they are 'morally involved' in the organisation.

The distinctive contribution of Fox is that he goes beyond noting the existence of these two types of role to look at the social and 'industrial relations' implications of their being applied. He focusses on what he calls 'institutionalised trust relations' which are embodied in the structural arrangements of the organisation (and are hence not to be confused with matters of 'personal trust' between individuals). He suggests that contemporary organisations suffer from a 'low-trust syndrome' which results from the fact that at senior levels they employ people in high-discretion roles, thereby implying that they are trusted, whilst the people in the bulk of the manual and other routine jobs are given low-discretion tasks and are effectively branded as not to be trusted. From this follows what Fox calls 'low-trust industrial relations' with all its implications of confrontation, win-lose bargaining and distortions of communication and understanding. Fox looks at employment strategies such as human relations or job enrichment initiatives which attempt to ameliorate this but he insists that the problems here have to be considered on a societal level.

Ouchi and Jaeger (1978) have made a distinctive contribution to the consideration of employment strategies in that they, like Fox, see an important relationship between the ways in which people are employed in organisations and how those people relate to the society in which they live. In a way reminiscent of the writings of Elton Mayo on the problems of modern societies, these writers suggest that organisations in America are beginning to develop new approaches to employment as part of a response to the allegedly increasing social anomie of a society in which there is a less and less effective contribution being made to 'social bonding' by institutions such as family, church and community. Having observed that modifications of Japanese employment strategies were being successfully applied by some Japanese companies in America, these writers note that, although Americans do not appear to want old-style paternalism, they do 'favour a work organisation that provides affiliative ties, stability and job security'.

Ouchi and Jaeger (1978) and Ouchi (1981) see a trend away from what they call Type A, or traditional American, organisations in which employment relations are 'limited, contractual and ... partially inclusive' towards Type Z structures. Where Type A is 'hierarchical', Type Z involves a 'clan' type of control characterised by long-term employment, relatively slow advancement and performance evaluation, less specialised career paths, implicit qualitative evaluation, consensual decision-making and a 'holistic' concern for employees and their family. This still retains an emphasis on individual responsibility. It does not go the whole way towards the Japanese or Type J organisation, which emphasises collective responsibility and life-time employment.

Tensions and contradictions in the employment of people

Our main argument in this chapter is that employment strategies, whether they are consciously thought out or not, are necessarily followed by those running work organisations to deal with the fundamental problems which arise from the fact that organisations *use* employees. To employ and manage people is to have to deal with a whole series of rather fundamental tensions and contradictions. Management, in fact, is very much a two-sided phenomenon. On the one hand it is an initiating and directing component of the organisational 'system' whilst, on the other hand, much of its activity – and a large part of its membership – is far more involved with keeping that system in working order, or even in existence, than it is with the production of goods and services as such. Employment strategies are caught up in both of these aspects of management and to fully understand what they involve and how they vary we need to look closely at the contradictions and tensions involved in employing people.

The modern employing organisation is *a social and technical arrangement in which a number of people come together on a basis of contractual exchange in a relationship where the actions of some are directed by others towards the achievement of certain specified tasks.* To achieve the overall purposes of the organisation – or more accurately those of its controllers – it *uses people.* But the very principle of organisational employment and its concept of exchange means that those people who are used also *use the organisation* to achieve purposes of their own. This occurs at all levels and has been especially stressed in the organisational analyses of Tom Burns (see above p. 71). In effect, organisations serve many more purposes than simply producing the goods and services which, at first sight, give them their purposiveness. They can provide profits for some and careers for others. Wages, salaries, opportunities for meeting people, job satisfactions, power, status and meanings are all sought by people to different degrees and in varying combinations.

Essentially, employees are problematic within organisations

because, in return for being partially 'used', they seek to 'make use of' the employing organisation in a whole range of potentially conflicting ways. Multiple-directed competitions are inevitable and, to more fully understand why this is so and how these tensions manifest themselves, we can consider the problematic nature of the use of people as labour resources at three analytical levels. These are, first, at the level of human nature, second, at the level of social interaction and, third, at the level of the overall political economy of the society in which the organisation is located.

Problems at the level of human nature

These have to be discussed very carefully. There is a very considerable danger in talking of 'human nature' when considering social behaviour, patterns and structures. This is the danger of 'reductionism' whereby problems which arise out of the way social life is organised are 'reduced' to alleged qualities of human individuals. Thus, for example, we see industrial relations conflicts being explained in terms of 'envy' or wars being explained in terms of some basic human quality of 'aggression'. There may well be such factors at work in these situations but to analyse any industrial or international conflict solely in terms of such factors at the expense of considering the nature of the relations between the two sides is to miss various crucial factors. A strike, for instance, cannot be separated from the economic relations between employer and employees affected or from the bargaining procedures and the set of socially developed expectations which prevail in the circumstances of the dispute.

There is also a problem with the concept of human nature itself – at least in the commonsense way in which it is often used. I refer here to the tendency for commentators on 'human nature' to pick on some feature of human beings – selfishness or aggressiveness, say – and to argue that this is what basically characterises them. Thus we get statements like those which suggest that you could not have a peaceful society because people are 'basically aggressive' or an egalitarian and just society because people are 'basically selfish'. One objection to this kind of thinking is that it is dreadfully and pessimistically deterministic. Our 'human nature' totally compromises our capacity for social, political – and indeed managerial – choices. But the more fundamental problem with this kind of thinking is that, through a tendency to set up one-sided caricatures of humanness, it totally fails to appreciate the essentially paradoxical nature of what it is to be human. Human beings are *both* aggressive and pacific, selfish and altruistic, kind and cruel, individualistic and social and so on and so on.

In a sense, we all have *dual natures* and, to make sensible decisions in politics, social policy or organisational management, we have to take this fact into account. The secret of effective human organisation at any level, from that of international relations to that of work organisations and work groups, is one of coming to terms with an often contradictory mixture of human characteristics, wants, values and needs. People do indeed have a tendency to come into conflict with others. But they also have a tendency to cooperate. People do want to look after their own personal interests and needs. But there is plenty of evidence of a human willingness to care about and act thoughtfully towards others.

There are, then, certain basic contradictions in the individual characteristics of human beings. Anyone involved in the organisation or management of people has, therefore, to seek ways in which both sides of that whole range of dualisms (selfishness and altruism, inclination to cooperate and inclination to conflict, etc.) can be taken into account in devising patterns of relationships. Recognition of this is of far more value than attempting to work on the basis of a list of universal human needs like those discussed in the previous chapter (esp. p. 106), whether or not these are arranged in a hierarchy. It is also wiser to think in this way than to orient oneself towards some mystical ideal in which everybody is either to be 'self-actualised' (in the managerial-humanist conception) or 'non-alienated' (in the critical-Marxian conception).

Certain key characteristics of the human species derive from the infinitely more complex way in which humans relate their thoughts to their actions compared with other species. The human animal is to be distinguished from other species by its ability to reason, its ability to evaluate and its capacity to think constantly in terms of alternatives. There is always the likelihood that humans will ask 'why should this be?' or 'cannot things be otherwise?'. This means that those managing the work efforts of others cannot expect every instruction given and every procedure laid down to be happily and willingly followed by every individual on every occasion. Far from it! However – and here we come to the paradox of the situation which has to be coped with – we can no more expect people to work effectively towards managerial purposes if they are left totally free to decide for themselves what to do and how to do it.

There is a basic tendency in the human species which is in direct contradiction to the above inclination. This is the tendency for people to seek predictability and the comfort of taken-for-granted assumptions about the world and their circumstances. This in part relates to the fact that human beings need to be able to look to their culture to help them with the 'problem of meaning' (see above p. 129). Individuals, on their own, are unable to make meaningful the potentially chaotic world in which they have to exist and therefore have, to a considerable extent, to rely on the meanings that are made available to them in the social world of which they are a part (Berger and Luckman, 1971). Also, our humanness is such that, as much as we might want to be independent and autonomous, we simply could not cope psychologically with a permanent engagement in critical questioning, analysing of alternatives and the working out of the full implications of every action.

We all want freedom but too much freedom would terrify us to death – literally in the final analysis. And, in addition to this, we simply would not have the cognitive capacity to cope with all the relevant information and all the calculations which would need to be done with regard to every decision if we were left to do things on our own. Our rationality is 'bounded' and we necessarily resign ourselves to living with a certain degree of ambiguity and with accepting the compromises that follow from the realities of unclear criteria, inadequate knowledge and the vagaries of chance and unintended consequence.

The inference to be drawn from this consideration of humanness is that employment practices and the employment strategies which underlie them have to cope with this general human 'duality' and have to be sensitive to the particular balance of the two sides of human nature which apply to the particular people being employed in the particular circumstances of the particular organisation. They also have to be aware that these problems are never, in any final sense, 'solved'. There is always possible that tendency referred to by Max Weber as the 'paradox of consequences' (above p. 53). Purposive actions in the sphere of human relations often have unintended consequences. And this can occur with reference to these 'human nature' issues as readily as it can to problems at the other levels. For example, a management may decide that it is not sufficiently taking into account that part of its employees' 'nature' whereby they might apply their own personal judgments in their work rather than simply follow instructions. In McGregor's terms the management would be deciding to follow Theory Y assumptions instead of Theory X ones (above p. 110). However, we can readily imagine a management going too far the other way and leaving employees with so little guidance on how to perform that they begin to react against a situation which affords them too little predictability and an insufficient amount of that security which can follow from a degree of taken-for-grantedness.

This general need to think in terms of the dualities of human nature provides a further example of that essential ability to achieve 'balance' which was referred to in our examination of the nature of managerial work in the last part of Chapter 2. However, employment problems deriving from these features of human individuals cannot be seen in isolation. How people actually behave is a function of their group involvements as well their species nature. The human animal is a social animal and, to consider the implications of this for our present interests, we move to our next level of analysis.

Problems at the level of social interaction

These are problems which arise for organisers and managers as a result of the tendency of human beings to form themselves into groups. There are two main types of factor behind this. First, there are the psychological factors such as the need for human association, affiliation and the 'meanings' to be derived from belonging to a collectivity. Second, there are the social and political factors relating to the universal tendency of human individuals to join with others in order to defend or further their material interests. In practice these two types of factor come together. People tend to associate with others with whom they have common interests (family, club, party, union, professional groupings or whatever) and they tend to derive their identities, meanings and social satisfactions from the same sources.

When people are first employed they bring into the organisation a variety of affiliations which will influence their orientations to work. These may be family, ethnic, class, craft, religious or any number of other memberships which influence their personal priorities and their willingness or reluctance to cooperate with other people at work. All this has to be coped with managerially, but such problems are greatly added to by the tendency of people to form numerous coalitions, once within the organisation, to defend or further their interests as employees. Here we have the whole range of activities to which employers have to respond, such as unionisation, professionalisation and the forming of informal workgroups, cliques and cabals.

Dealing with problems of the existence of a multiplicity of interest groups, coalitions and constituencies, whether these be recognised as industrial relations issues, politicking or just group management issues, is a considerable one, given that a key job of a management is to *integrate* the various parts of the organisation to achieve a level of overall cooperation. However, we here come up against our notion of contradictory tendencies and the paradox of consequences again. The great irony here is that many of the potentially divisive or disintegrative groupings come about as a result of the management's own initiatives in organisational design. Every time the management initiate an extra piece of division of labour or 'differentiation', they create for themselves a further problem of integration and another 'constituency' whose resource demands they will have to meet. So, here again, we see the importance of the 'balancing' principle in managerial work. In this case we have the tasks of balancing integration and differentiation and of handling internal resource dependencies which are referred to in the concept of management developed in Chapter 2.

Problems at the level of the political economy of society

These have traditionally been given too little attention in discussions of management, organisation and employment relations.

The recent radical and sociological contributions have played an important role in drawing attention to the fact that what goes on in work organisations simply cannot be well understood without relating them to the structures, priorities and values of the society and culture which surrounds them. Also, the increasingly recognised need for organising and employing interests to look more closely at their 'environments' has helped to make the point that what goes on in employment and what goes on in society, economy and politics are closely interlinked.

The problems with much of the radical material on organisation and employment issues – the Labour Process writers looked at earlier being a good example – is that they give priority to issues of political economy at the expense of considering issues at the two levels we have just considered. Marxian writers are very prone to put down to 'capitalism' problems which may well have more to do with general tendencies of human beings anywhere or at any time than with the particular economic system within which they occur. However, once we have established the general issues which are likely to arise in any kind of organised work operation, regardless of the type of society in which it occurs and relating to problems at the level of human nature and at the level of social interaction, we have to recognise that the ways in which any of these manifest themselves is very much a matter of the type of society in which that work goes on.

From a survey of human history we can see that there exists a variety of possible ways in which work and economy can be organised. People may work predominantly on the land or in industry, people may be largely self-employed or they may work for others, people may work in their homes or they may 'go out to work', and people may choose their own working methods or they may follow the instructions laid down for them by others. It is important, therefore, to note that the industrial capitalist mode of economic organisation, which we so easily take for granted, is merely one form which people have happened to develop. And it has to be understood as such.

To understand the problems which arise in the work setting we have to appreciate the basic features and consequent difficulties of the kind of social order of which they are a part. At the centre of the industrial capitalist order – in which all the phenomena with which this book is concerned occur – is the institution of *the* employment and rational organisation of free labour*. And, as would be the case with any other central principle of societal organisation, this has its particular and essential problems. The essential problems with which we are concerned here, because they have to be met in part by the employment strategies of industrial capitalist organisations, turn on the difficulty of balancing the aspects of 'control' of human beings which are implicit in the ideas of 'employment' and of 'rational organisation' with the expectations of freedom or autonomy implied in the notion of free labour. To help us draw out the implications of this kind of contradiction we must first examine more closely the three key institutional elements from which it follows: those of free labour, employment and rational organisation.

The concept of free labour within industrial capitalism is not a concept which implies that people necessarily have complete and actual freedom of choice about where or how they work. What we are recognising is the institution of *formally free labour*: an arrangement to be distinguished from ones like slavery or serfdom in which people are *formally tied* in some way with regard to how they labour. A free labour arrangement is one in which, in principle, each person is allowed to choose their way of making a living. The principle of choice has profound economic implications in the potential that is offered for flexibility and innovation in the work sphere.

Economies are very much 'opened up' if they develop free or 'open' labour markets. But the implications are no less significant socially and politically: the principle that individuals are free to work in whatever way they feel enables them to meet their own priorities or interests cannot but encourage a belief in the validity of the principle of individual liberty, autonomy and self-advancement in every other sphere of social and political life. We will return to this but we must first note the close tie which exists between the idea of free labour and that of employment.

The concept of employment within industrial capitalism here implies something different from the everyday use of the term as synonymous with working or 'being in work'. It sees employment as a distinctive kind of work arrangement which developed with the emergence of capitalist market-oriented societies. It grew in importance as people became increasingly free from feudal or other land-based ties and came more and more to 'work for'

Feature	Implications for management		
		Positive	Negative
Employment	Most people 'work for' an employer to whom they sell their capacity to work on a market basis	Employee acceptance of control bought and assured through employment contract	Employees encouraged to be constantly aware of possibility of improving rewards elsewhere. Calculative attitudes encouraged: commitment made problematic
Rational organisation	Tasks and work forms calculatingly designed by employers on basis of a logic of efficiency	Efficient use and control of labour assured through careful selection of best systms and procedures available	Employees made aware of their use as 'means' ('cogs in machines'). Challenge to control encouraged. Control and commitment made problematic
Free labor	Employees formally fee to choose what work they do and for whom	Availability of a mobile and motivated work force	Employees encouraged to 'think for themselves'. Personal autonomy encouraged. Control made problematic

Fig. 5.1 Managerial implications of key features of industrial capitalist work arrangements

someone or, to put it less colloquially, to sell their labour-power on the market. We thus see two key groups of economic actors emerging with the growth of industrial capitalism: employers and employees. The developing logic of this was one in which the human capacity to work became a resource or a commodity to be bought and sold. And this logic is also one of potential unfreedom or exploitation because, implicit in the idea of the selling of any commodity is the idea that the seller is surrendering to the purchaser the rights of control over that commodity. The implications of this, like the implications of the free labour idea, are considerable. But, before considering why this is so, we have to bring into the picture the notion of rational organisation.

The concept of the rational organisation of work under industrial capitalism does not suggest that modern work is organised in a way which is intrinsically more sensible or reasonable than in previous times. I am referring to what Max Weber called *formal rationality*: an approach to making decisions about how to proceed in any area of human activity which involves the constant and calculated choosing of appropriate means to achieve any given end. Formal rationality does not replace irrationality or stupidity but tends to replace 'traditionalism'. This is the relatively less reflective type of thinking about how to proceed which depends heavily on considering how things have been done in the past. The characteristically modern dependence on rational organisation and its associated institutions of bureaucracy, science-based technology, accountancy and the rest are associated with a general style of thought based on *calculation*. And, as we shall now see, this – like the other two dimensions of the employment and rational organisation of free labour – involve contradictory tendencies which have to be coped with.

The organising of work on the basis of employing people and paying them a monetary reward provides a prime example of a contradictory tendency within industrial capitalist societies. Rewarding employees for the work they do clearly encourages appropriate performance and helps achieve the purposes for which the people were employed. Success here is dependent on employees being enthusiastic about earning money and – for the incentive effect to be significant – being concerned to earn more than the basic kind of subsistence level of return which has satisfied populations in traditional societies. A logic of financial gain on the part of the employees is thus an inherent part of an employment system. But there is also an equivalent logic operating among the employers, a logic which involves the treating of rewards to employees as *costs* which are to be kept down.

Wage employment systems, we can see, contain two elements which are in contradiction with each other: one whereby cooperation between employer and employee is fostered through the operation of an economic contract and the other whereby conflict is engendered through the logic which makes the reward to one group the cost to the other. Hence we see a fundamental tension underlying our economic arrangements. It is a tension deriving from a structure which has as an inherent feature a conflict of economic interests. The structure can be highly economically effective, but only as long as the tension is controlled – the basic conflict 'managed' in some way. Here again is a task for the employment strategies of employing organisations.

The employment contract in the modern economy is by no means one between equal parties. History shows that the basic existing pattern has its roots in the efforts of human interest groups who sought to develop a profitable and advantaged role for themselves in a changing society (Watson, 1980a). However, the way they chose to set up this role was one which meant that, from the start, they were creating conditions in which the people they were employing would be unlikely to leave unchallenged their carrying out of that role and their taking of their preferred level of profit. When working people were divided and scattered among domestic producing units the entrepreneurs who 'put out' work to them were unlikely to face a great deal of concerted challenge. But once people were brought together under one factory or office roof, the employer control that was made possible was also immediately compromised by the opportunity created for workers to perceive a common interest and to act collectively to improve their lot. The potential for what came to take the form of trade union challenge is thus built into the system. So, of course, is the potential for other groupings to form. And it was this tendency that Karl Marx saw as creating some of the potential for an ultimate uniting of all working people into a revolutionary class which would bring down the whole system. Whether or not this potential is a real one, there are clearly some major tensions here to be managed.

The institution of free labour also has its 'double-edged' aspects from the point of view of economic controlling interests. The employment contract formally involves no long-term or extra-economic obligations on either party. In principle, either side can withdraw when it suits them not to continue with the arrangement. And both a causal factor behind the growth of this institution and a reflection of its growth is the *individualism* with which it is associated. A relatively high degree of emphasis on the individual as opposed to the social collectivity or community has long distinguished English culture from other European cultures and can be seen as an important factor in the emergence of Britain as the first industrial nation (Macfarlane, 1978). The notion of the independent and self-responsible worker (in contrast to the traditional and 'tied' peasant) fits closely with the idea of a mobile and flexible labour force which, in turn, is congruent with the interests of employers who do not so much want a loyal and life-long working community as a tractable labour force whose numbers and deployment can easily be changed as adjustments are made to changing technologies, markets and administrative practices. However, the independent-mindedness, the concern for personal self-interest and the desire for liberty which is an inherent part of modern 'possessive individualism' (Macpherson, 1962) inevitably compromises the tractability or malleability of the labour force.

To foster the idea of the citizen as an independent, free and mobile economic actor was inevitably to encourage citizen demands for *rights* with regard to many issues, including ones of how their society was run. The historical working-out of this has seen not only a growth in the ways employees have resisted the power of employers to control them at their whim in the workplace, it has also seen the spread of the franchise and the associated granting by the state of concessions to employee interests. In this way, limits have increasingly been put on to employers' freedom to manage as they might prefer. This is continuing dynamic force because the individualistic and democratic ethos of modern culture ensures the continued debating of the basis of patterns of inequality between individuals, whether this be to do with material inequalities or with matters of racial and sexual inequality. And employment strategies are affected by all this insofar as they have to pay close heed to state, and especially legislative, pressures on employer behaviour.

The division of labour aspect of 'rational' work organisation has led to a number of contradictory tendencies within the economic organisation of modern societies. The splitting down of formerly integrated craft-based work into partially or non-skilled tasks has been a central strategy of managements ever since Adam Smith's celebration of its alleged efficiency in the eighteenth century (see above p. 91). Not only can more work be turned out under these arrangements, but less skilled workers are easier to train, quicker to replace and cheaper to pay. Furthermore, the removal from the producers themselves of the decisions of how the work is to be done guarantees a role for managerial staff. However, there are clearly counter-productive elements in this which can lead to low-quality work, inflexibility and intransigence in a way which was recognised long before the terms 'job enrichment' and 'the quality of working life' were invented. Questions of balance and employment strategy choice are again raised.

A further problem arising out of the prevailing patterns of the division of labour is the tendency for them to encourage divisive 'them and us' attitudes. The division of employees into groups who carry out work tasks and groups who conceive and supervise tasks too easily becomes a source of resentment and tends to make distant from each other people who were initially intended to work together. This distance is further increased by the use of superior status and pay levels to 'motivate' those involved in the expert or administrative roles. The tendency for the low-trust syndrome recognised by Alan Fox is especially significant here (above p. 152).

The managements of employing organisations, then, are caught up in an enormous range of issues, tensions and contradictions arising at individual, group and societal levels of human behaviour. They have got to come to terms with the dual aspects of 'human nature' together with how these are influenced by the expectations, values and priorities encouraged in the type of society and economy in which they live. And, on top of this, they have to cope with the way these problems tend to manifest themselves through the tendency of people to form coalitions to further and defend what they see as their interests and wants. Employment practices have to handle all these problems whilst coping too with the irony that they may often make worse the very problems with which they are dealing. They have to come to terms with the basic problem of the institution of employment: that people are to be used as means to ends which are not their own whilst people – because they are people and citizens and not automatons – will have ends of their own which do not necessarily coincide with those of the employer.

Employment strategies: choice and variation

In the introduction to the notion of employment strategy early in the present chapter it was suggested that there may be a pattern of choice underlying the strategies adopted by organisations. This amounted to whether employees are encouraged to be 'intimately and trustingly' attached to the organisation or 'distantly and calculatively' involved with it. Such a dichotomy of logical possibilities was implicit in many of the existing analyses of variations in employment philosophy and practices discussed above, in spite of the fact that the actual number of possible patterns is shown to be far greater than two.

The argument to be put here is that there is a considerable range of possible patterns of employment strategy, but that underlying the choices that are made in each of the aspects of what adds up to the employment strategy is a tendency for there to be stress on either *employee control* or *employee commitment*. This is similar to the choice of 'direct control' or 'responsible autonomy' approaches identified by Andrew Friedman (above, p. 146). But the similarity is only partial. Whereas Friedman stresses the decision of a management to apply either one or the other of these two approaches to any group of employees, I would see the possibility of an employer mixing control-oriented practices in some aspects of the employment relationship with a given group with commitment-oriented practices in other aspects. It is thus possible that close-control employment practices of a Taylorian kind are applied to certain employees in the sphere of job design whilst welfare measures and communication practices (employee club facilities, house newspaper and so on) which encourage commitment are also provided. However, in spite of this recognition that there is not a simple either/or choice to be made about employment strategy, there is a general pattern behind practices which is usefully seen as amounting to a general control-orientation or a general commitment-orientation.

The most useful way to proceed in examining choice of employment practice, I suggest, is to look first at general tendencies for strategies to be oriented one way or the other and only then to consider the actual mixes of pattern which may be adopted in practice.

Every management has continually to tackle two interlinked problems with regard to its employees. First, there is the *problem of control*. This arises because managements need to have control over employees both to achieve tasks and to justify their own existence. Yet, at the same time, they become aware that to exert too much control or to exert it in too obvious a way may cause a reaction among employees resulting in challenges to control and potentially to the loss of it. Second, there is the *problem of commitment* which exists because management needs a degree of employee commitment in order to keep the organisation reasonably stable, to keep recruitment and training costs down, and to encourage employees to take the kind of initiatives felt to be appropriate to the technology being used and the task being performed. But, at the same time, to create too high a level of employee commitment could lead, in some circumstances, to labour inflexibility or over-conservativeness (cf. Salancik, 1977).

The historical, contingency, labour-process and role-structural approaches to variations in employment practices reviewed earlier mostly recognised that the approach to handling what I have called the twin problems of control and commitment may vary according to circumstances. Yet, among all these approaches, there is no single sufficiently general or inclusive model which suggests which direction may be followed in handling these problems in the light of particular circumstances. I suggest that we can make the following generalisation: *the employment strategy of any organisation will be the outcome of managerial choices which are influenced by, first, the micropolitical and value preferences of the dominant management constituency and, second, the extent to which this key coalition perceives varying contingent factors as making employee constituencies relatively problematic or unproblematic to organisational survival and performance.* In resource dependence theory terms this is a matter of how 'strategic' the employee constituencies are perceived to be.

Figure 5.2 represents the model which follows from this generalisation. It is a model which draws on and adds to the processual kinds of model of organisational structuring discussed in the third wave of theories covered in Chapter 3. It shows the interest-based and value-oriented preferences or orientations of the managers themselves as *mediating* the range of labour market, technological, state and organisational contingencies which push and pull the organisation towards a particular approach to various employee constituencies (groupings within the workforce).

The model recognises that strategic choices are made in organisations by those managerial interests or 'dominant coalition' within the management in the light of both their own preferences and the structural contingencies which are relevant (Child, 1972, and above p. 75). The contingencies listed here mean that we would expect, for example, that an employer would be more likely to perceive as problematic a labour force, or a part of it, which was large, male, white, skilled, unionised, expensive, aspiring and difficult to replace than if it is small, female, black, unskilled, non-union, cheap, unambitious and in plentiful supply. In practice, of course, several of these factors overlap and even amount to the same thing (technical complexity and skill level, for example) whilst others may cross-cut each other. A minority-race or female workforce may be made much more problematic than they had previously been, for example, as a result of a change in equal opportunity legislation imposed by the state.

However, the employing managers may not choose to take these traditional criteria as automatically suggesting that the workforce is 'problematic' or otherwise. For example the managers, or an owner-manager, may hold to a philosophy which sees employees as a key constituency to be treated carefully regardless of whether, at first sight, they appear to create particular pressures on management. A management with unskilled and non-unionised workers might, for example, take a very strongly Theory Y-oriented view of people which implies that workers of any calibre or bargaining power are worth 'cultivating' in order to produce an organisation with a high morale and an especially healthy long-term future. In fact this tends to be the view encouraged by the culture-excellence school of organisation theory (above

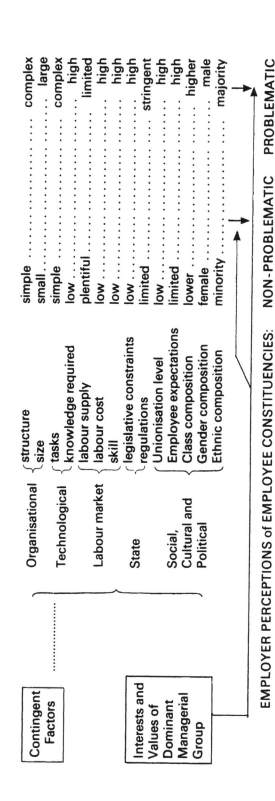

Fig. 5.2 Factors influencing choice of employment strategy

p. 66). In this view, the effectiveness of any organisation is increased by employees being treated as important. However, it is most unlikely that the contingent factors listed are ever going to be completely ignored. What, in effect, is different about the kind of management considered here is that they take a particularly employee-centred view of resource dependencies. But the cost and other pressures arising from the existence of all the other constituencies will force the costs of 'involving' such workers to be kept within limits.

The influence of the management as a factor (or a constituency itself) is not limited to matters of philosophy, ideology and values within this present model. We have to remember that certain employment strategies may suit the career interests of different managerial groupings differently. For example, there is the research evidence of Michael Poole and his colleagues (1981) that personnel and industrial relations managers tend to favour participative reforms and not to be hostile to trade unions, whereas the bulk of other managers appear to be hostile both to such reforms and to unions. This could be a matter of the values of the people occupying these different roles. But it is equally likely to be connected with the fact that more participatory and collective-bargaining-based employment strategies tend to enhance the power and career opportunities of personnel specialists whilst they tend to inhibit other managers who, these authors suggest, are concerned about 'control' in terms of having 'freedom to perform their own jobs unconstrained by intervention from the state, trade unions and other pressure groups'. This means that the extent to which there are people within the dominant managerial coalition who are interested in 'personnel' type careers is likely to influence the way employee constituencies are perceived.

The final comment needing to be made about our model of how employment strategies are adopted relates to the possibility that the overall employment strategy of an employing organisation may be to treat different parts of that organisation differently – in effect to apply different employment strategies to different segments of the organisation. These might be seen as 'sub-strategies'. And such an approach has traditionally been the case with regard to different hierarchical levels where, typically, 'staff' constituencies are seen as more strategic and hence as to be treated differently from 'works' constituencies. But it can happen in other ways. An organisation with both manufacturing interests and retailing outlets, for example, may recognise that the more unionised factory-based workforce is best treated differently from the less-organised shop-based workforce. Not only might employment procedures (hiring, firing, consultative, promotional, etc.) vary between the two, but the former might well have a more developed personnel management structure associated with it than the latter. This is something we will return to in the final chapter.

The next two chapters take up two major aspects of the employment strategies of contemporary organisations. Chapter 6 will look at various aspects of personnel management practice and Chapter 7 will review a whole range of trends and current directions in employment practices in areas ranging from job redesign and new technology to industrial relations policies, state involvement and the adoption of new patterns of organisation structuring.

Chapter 6

The employment specialists: personnel management

Employment strategies represent one component of the overall strategy or direction adopted by an organisation's controllers to deal with the range of constituences whose demands have to be met to make possible the organisation's long-term survival. They exist alongside financial, marketing, technological and various other strategies. And, although each of these strategies is concerned with a number of the constituencies inside and outside the organisation, some strategies are more clearly concerned with particular types of constituency than others. This would clearly be the case with finance or marketing strategies where specialists with a competence for handling particular constituencies and their associated problems are likely to emerge. And in the same way that organisations of some size and a developed division of labour may appoint finance specialists to deal with financial constituencies, marketing specialists to deal with customer constituencies and public relations specialists to deal with such constituencies as pressure groups and the 'media', so may employers appoint personnel specialists to deal with problems connected with employee constituencies.

Personnel management is an activity which both derives from and contributes to the employment strategy of the organisation. It is to be understood as *that component of the management of an organisation which specialises in dealing with the problems which emerge from the fact that organisations employ human beings*. This involves all the problems discussed in the last chapter and not least the fact that organisations *use* employees who, in turn, *make use of* the organisation. In this chapter we will look at the factors leading to the development of personnel management, both in its early and more recent forms, and at the range of difficulties which arise in the practice of personnel management within organisations. Underlying the practice of personnel management is the fact that personnel managers not only deal with the ambiguities and tensions involved in employing assertive, independent-minded and self-interested people in modern complex societies, but that they themselves become embroiled in a whole lot of tensions and ambiguities of their own within the organisations which employ them. The extent of this is such that problems arise even when one looks for definitions of personnel management.

Definitions and insecurities

In Chapter 2 (pp. 25–7) it was suggested that people in managerial careers suffer from a number of status and other insecurities. It was earlier suggested that the problems for those specialising in dealing with people might be even greater (p. 16). In fact, we find personnel specialists having to look two ways at once in their work. And this is reflected in the definitions offered by those who have written texts for personnel people.

Management generally is an activity very much concerned with establishing its legitimacy and, especially with justifying its authority over the managed. And the nearer we get in managerial thinking to issues which are overtly to do with human beings, the more important this becomes. We would therefore expect personnel management texts to colour managerial work to make it look acceptable to employees. There is thus a pressure to portray personnel management as *caring* for employees. However, there is a further legitimacy problem in this area: that of persuading other managers that personnel management is an important and not a peripheral activity. They have to be persuaded that it is hard-headed and not unduly soft-hearted. There is thus a second pressure which tends to counteract the first: a pressure to portray personnel management as involved in *controlling* employees. This is represented in Fig. 6.1.

With these dual pressures in mind we can go on to look at some definitions of personnel management. This not only helps us develop our understanding of the field of activity but reveals the kind of balancing and judicious image-management exercise

To meet employee expectations must be seen to	To meet managerial expectations must be seen to
Be concerned with employee welfare	Be concerned with the efficiency of labour utilisation
Maintain justice in the way staff are treated	Ensure that staff interests are subservient to those of organisational effectiveness
Care for the workforce	Control the workforce

Fig. 6.1   Dual pressures on the personnel function

which is as essential to the work of the practitioner as it is to the writers of texts.

A particularly judicious definition is offered by the writer of a British text, Michael Armstrong (1984):

> Personnel management is concerned with obtaining, organising and motivating the human resources required by the enterprise; with developing an organisation climate and management style which will promote effective effort and cooperation and trust between all the people working in it; and with helping the enterprise to meet all its legal obligations and its social responsibilities towards its employees with regard to the conditions of work and quality of life provided for them.

The caring and controlling elements of the work are both recognised here with the emphasis on the latter very carefully put into soft focus. The organisation is portrayed as a cooperative system very much concerned with trust, obligation, and responsibility. There is no mention of ownership, of profit, of industrial conflict and, whilst the obtaining, organising and motivating of employees is mentioned, the equally likely concern with *dispensing with* people is somehow forgotten. Nevertheless, we have here a good example of the kind of ideal with which those trained in personnel management are currently imbued.

The extent to which formal definitions can easily become ideological exercises is effectively illustrated by the definition offered in one of the editions of the influential American text by Pigors and Myers (1969), which begins: 'since management aims at getting effective results *with people*, personnel administration is a basic management function or activity permeating all levels of management in any organisation.' The authors go on to describe personnel administration as

> organising and treating individuals at work so that they will get the greatest possible realisation of their intrinsic abilities, thus attaining maximum efficiency for themselves and their group, and thereby giving the enterprise of which they are a part its determining competitive advantage and its optimum results.

There are a whole lot of questionable assumptions here about the connections between employee satisfaction and employee performance (as discussed in our previous chapter) and our stance of constructive scepticism soon begins to shade into cynicism when we ask ourselves just how credible or realistic is this implicit image of the employing organisation as a kind of fun camp which, by maximising the fulfilment of its participants, gets as its inevitable by-product some kind of economic results! The focus on ultimate managerial purposes is made softer than ever with the use of the words 'optimum results'.

One of the most quoted British conceptions of personnel management is the formal definition produced by the Institute of Personnel Management as part of its Jubilee Statement in 1963 (IPM, 1963). Again, we see the characteristic concern with balancing care and control, characterised here as 'justice' and 'efficiency', neither of which, it is claimed, can be pursued successfully without the other. Personnel management, it is said,

> seeks to bring together and develop into an effective organisation the men and women who make up an enterprise, enabling each to make his own best contribution to its success both as an individual and as a member of a working group. It seeks to provide fair terms and conditions of employment, and satisfying work for those employed.

This statement, with all its suspect philanthropic emphasis has been widely cited and taught although Peter Anthony notes that more recent publications from the IPM appear to be abandoning the kind of ambivalence manifested here (1977). He notes a recent starker formulation which suggests that personnel management is concerned with 'how the efforts of the people who make up the enterprise can be organised and developed in order to attain the highest levels of efficiency, adaptability and productivity'.

We are here getting to a more realistic description of what happens. However, to point up the justificatory overtones and comforting mystifications of much of what we have examined here, let us look at a definition which provides a contrast:

> Personnel management is concerned with assisting those who run work organisations to meet their purposes through the obtaining of the work efforts of human beings, the exploitation of those efforts and the dispensing with of those efforts when they are no longer required. Concern may be shown with human welfare, justice or satisfactions but only insofar as this is necessary for controlling interests to be met and, then, always at least cost.

This definition has not appeared in any personnel management textbook, nor would it be likely to appear in any official management policy statement or training manual. Clearly, it is loaded. Indeed, it neglects the extent to which many personnel managers sincerely care for their employees and genuinely want to see people happy and fulfilled at work. But I would ask whether this invented 'alternative' definition is any less realistic a characterisation of what goes on than the formulations with which I designed it to contrast.

The truth of the situation is that there is a deep ambivalence within personnel management which in part can be seen, as George Thomason (1981) puts it, 'as having developed from two diverse origins, the one paternalistically oriented towards the welfare of employees and the other rationally derived from the corporate need to control'. As a consequence of this ambivalence it is possible to see a managerial action as serving either type of end – or both. Thomason gives the example of the setting up of a joint consultation committee which could be done either to improve communications generally for the benefit of all concerned or, alternatively, to discourage employee initiatives like unionisation.

Any given managerial activity has to be analysed in terms of the mixture of motives, interests and ambiguities which permeate all work organisations, I suggest. Official accounts of what happens in personnel management – and unofficial accounts too – all have to be treated sceptically. An illustration of the problem here can be taken from some of my own research. A personnel manager was asked to explain why his company operated a closed-shop policy (only union members allowed to work in a certain department). The answer was as follows:

PERSONNEL MANAGER: Well, it depends on whether I am speaking anonymously or not. For the record: we operate a closed shop policy here because we sympathise with the right of our employees in these departments, as skilled and valued workers, to choose with whom they are or are not to work.

INTERVIEWER: And off the record?

PERSONNEL MANAGER: We adopted the policy when the union members got increasingly awkward about working with the one or two non-members who were in those departments. We never knew, when we were dealing with the shop steward, whether he was speaking for everybody or just for the majority. It suits us now though; we know exactly where we are and we know that the stewards can police our agreements across the board.

Personnel management: tasks and functions

There is an element of personnel management in the work of most managers, whatever their formal designation might be. There are also, of course, specialists in personnel management. At this stage it is useful to look at those activities which are usually seen as part of personnel management in the more general sense and to consider their function within the employing organisation before going on to look at the specialist roles which exist to take a lead in carrying out these functions. Personnel management covers the following task areas:

Information and records: maintaining a profile of the labour force characteristics and various indicators of activities, such as labour turnover and stability indexes, numbers of disputes, disciplinary actions and so on. All this is used to inform managerial decision-making generally as well as to aid processes of manpower planning, training, industrial relations and the completion of government and other returns. Information may also be used to check the compliance with various legal requirements (with regard to ethnic or sex discrimination laws for example).

Manpower planning and control: the relating of future staffing requirements to both internal and external sources of supply and the control of how existing personnel are deployed across the organisation.

Selection and recruitment: the obtaining of appropriate staff to fill jobs.

Training and employee development: analysing training requirements, both organisational and individual, and devising programmes to meet them.

Industrial relations: the range of consultations, communications and negotiations which occur with organised labour over whatever conditions or details of employment have become subject to group bargaining.

Wages and salaries: the fixing of levels of pay and other rewards and the administration of these.

Employee services: the administration and monitoring of health, safety and welfare policies. Under this heading may be a diversity of items ranging from canteens and sports facilities to pensions, insurance schemes and company cars.

To make sense of these personnel management tasks and activities it is important to recognise that personnel management functions within the organisation at two levels. It is often seen as only playing a part at the first of these – at the surface level. But to appreciate the full significance of the work we must stress the deeper level at which it operates.

At the first or surface level, personnel management is involved in *supplying and maintaining staff*. It *supplies* the organisation of which it is a part with the personnel required to carry out the tasks which have to be fulfilled for the organisation to achieve whatever purposes constitute its controllers' policies. It then *maintains* this staff by monitoring performances in certain ways and setting up training programmes, bargaining procedures, motivating devices, allocation and replacement mechanisms, and so on, to keep the performance of this staff up to required levels as circumstances change.

At the second or deeper level, personnel management is involved in *managing conflicts and tensions*. Through many of the above activities as well as through a range of informal and unofficial activities, the personnel management element can be seen as coping with the tensions and conflicts which inevitably arise in work organisations as a result of what we might call the central problem of modern work organisations: the problem that organising involves the use of the efforts of human beings who all have their own uses which they wish to make of the organisation which they join. Personnel management is caught up in the series of problems which we saw in the previous chapter as making the employee constituencies essentially problematic (pp. 153–66).

No human social arrangements or structures can be trouble-free, predictable or easily manageable whilst such a thing as human individuality exists. And this is even less likely in a society and culture which stresses liberty, freedom and democracy. Human beings in work organisations, both individually and within various coalitions, will set out to meet their own purposes, values and interests within the work setting. Ensuring that this does not lead to total failure in meeting organisational purposes is a central personnel management role. Large amounts of managerial effort are thus put into handling conflicts between the organisational controllers and various employee groups, to avoiding clashes between different groups of employees, to resolving conflicts between short-term and long-term goals, to persuading employees to seek rewards from their work which are closely tied to successful task performance, to avoiding too much ambiguity in what is required to task performance, to disciplining or dispensing with staff whose activities are problematic or no longer required.

This involvement in fundamental conflicts and contradictions is common to all of those engaged in such work, and especially to those who specialise in personnel work in a formal sense. Personnel management not only deals with the utilising and controlling of people as labour resources it also copes with the unintended consequences of such practices – as shown in Fig. 6.2. And this

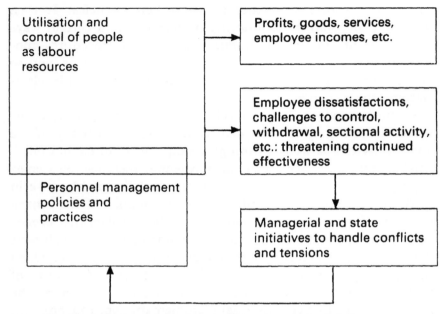

Fig. 6.2 Personnel management involvement in both labour utilisation and the handling of its unintended consequences

engagement with tensions and contradictions frequently puts those who specialise in personnel matters in situations of considerable ambiguity.

Personnel management and ambiguity

As was stressed in the first chapter (p. 22), all organising or managerial work is involved in ambiguity. And what makes organising activity generally confusing and ambiguous is that it is involved with human beings and all that follows from this. It should not be surprising, therefore, that writers such as Karen Legge (1978), Shaun Tyson (1980) and myself (1977) who have studied the activities of personnel specialists should stress the extent of the ambiguity which surrounds that work. The specialist personnel function is especially and centrally involved with the human element of work organisations and, inevitably therefore, gets very mixed up in the general ambiguities and contradictions of organisational life. This comes out in a number of ways.

The first ambiguity is that considered earlier with regard to whether the main role of the personnel department is a caring or a controlling one. In practice, personnel managers are often looked to to represent the employee point of view in the organisation or to see that the employees are sufficiently well cared for. Yet, ultimately, they are expected to control or manipulate the labour force. This tension between the co-existing care and control function in part relates to the twin historical roots of the occupation in philanthropic and control concerns and leads personnel managers frequently to wonder, as Karen Legge (1979) puts it, whether to emphasise the 'personnel' or the 'management' aspects of their functions. To watch a personnel manager operating over a period of time is to go through a process of constantly wondering whether one is seeing the wielding of an iron fist in a velvet glove or a velvet fist in an iron glove! To do personnel work is to find oneself regularly switching from a tough to a tender mode of operation and frequently being amazed that one is at times operating in the two modes simultaneously. One may, for example, find oneself conscientiously and caringly counselling an older employee about the desirability of their taking an early retirement at the same time as one knows that one is expected to cut labour costs in that person's employing department and reduce the general levels of jobs available to people.

A second area of ambiguity for the personnel specialist is that regarding the nature of their authority. It is common, if not practically universal, for the official position to be one in which the personnel specialist is merely an adviser to other managers; advising them on whom to recruit, how to discipline an employee, what to offer a union negotiator, how to train staff, and so on. Yet the personnel department's rationale of maintaining consistency, avoiding conflicts between groups or between employer and employees, and of ensuring at least apparent compliance with legal requirements, means that this advice simply has to be taken on very many occasions. There is thus frequent ambiguity as to whether recommendations from personnel departments are in fact recommendations or are orders disguised as advice.

The third ambiguity closely relates to the second and applies to the expertise component of the personnel manager's authority. The personnel manager is meant to be the expert in personnel management whilst personnel management is 'something that all managers do! Thus, if the personnel manager stresses too heavily his or her specialist expertise, the other managers may well push all personnel decisions towards the personnel department, with the effect that the department becomes overloaded. But this is not all: the line managers are also likely to lose touch with their own staff and are rendered less effective by this in the same way that the personnel department is made less effective by its becoming overloaded. If, on the other hand, the personnel manager lays no claim to specialised knowledge or expertise, they may end up being ignored by other managers, if not by the staff generally.

The fourth area of ambiguity relates to the question of just what this 'effectiveness' of a personnel department might be, or rather, what might be the criteria of successful performance. This is not just a problem arising from the fact that personnel work is often a matter of dealing with the unique, the subjective and the intangible, none of which is measurable. There is also the awkward problem that successful personnel management tends to lead to a situation in which few personnel problems, whether they be union disputes, staff shortages or low morale, appear to disturb the smooth operation of the enterprise. The effect of this, ironically, is that the personnel department's existence may be little noticed. And what follows from this is that the personnel department may be left out of certain decisions, with the further effect that it becomes less able to act successfully in avoiding personnel problems.

A fifth area of ambiguity is the very general one which results from the fact that the expectations, orientations and wants of the employee constituencies, with which the personnel function is especially concerned, are frequently unclear and the information about these which the personnel specialists must collect to carry out their functions will inevitably be inadequate and ambiguous. Frequently it will be biased or twisted in the process of transmision through the many third parties, in management and unions, who act as information channels and 'gatekeepers' at the same time as possessing interests of their own which will colour the information they transmit.

The sixth area of ambiguity is probably for some the most troubling of all. Attempts are typically made in the personnel field to bring order into the potential chaos which follows from all these other ambiguities and contradictions by the setting up of various personnel procedures, systems or techniques. All of these have potential for coping with uncertainty and controlling ambiguity. However, the very systems or procedures which are established to bring order or certainty to managing can also develop into sources of further disorder or uncertainty. We are back here to the dreaded 'paradox of consequences' (above p. 53). Thus, for example, a new wage structure may bring order into the bargaining activity of an organisation. But it will also create particular expectations among individuals and groups which can become major constraints on organisational changes which may be subsequently required. All personnel procedures contain the seeds of their own destruction. This is because they involve the human element: groups and individuals who bring their own values, interests and aspirations to bear on any activity with which they become involved. Management has constantly to monitor and modify personnel systems and procedures to avoid too high a degree of entrenchment and inflexibility as people establish a personal or sectional stake in the pattern which is set up, thus compromising the effectiveness of the procedure as a means of fulfilling managerial purposes which do not coincide with those of employees.

Does all this mean that personnel systems and procedures are pointless? No: it means, first, that there is no such thing as the *right* technique or system and, second, that whatever procedures are introduced will frequently have to be modified, adjusted or replaced as their internal contradictions break through. The impossibility of operating any kind of mechanical personnel management is stressed by John Henstridge (1975), who points out that when we look at what actually happens in personnel work, as opposed to what the traditional theorists suggests, we find a succession of reasons given by practitioners as to

> why procedures and policies have been initiated, altered, adjusted, dropped, made more flexible. 'We tried this, but it didn't work . . .'; 'we had to think of something to deal with that . . .'; 'we do it this way here because . . .'; 'we had trouble with the unions, so . . .'.

As this commentator goes on to say, speaking from the heart as a former personnel manager we suspect, every personnel manager 'finds himself "forced", "pressurised" into developing a unique, contingent approach to the problems of his particular patch.'

To echo some points about management generally made in Chapter 2 we might say that, although personnel managers have various control systems and autopilots to give them some help in piloting their departments, they nevertheless spend a great deal of their time 'flying by the seat of their pants'. Not only this, but it would appear that they frequently have to get out of their seat and redesign and reconstruct parts of the craft in which they are flying!

The ambiguity, tension, conflict and unpredictability of much personnel management work is clearly likely to put considerable stress on those engaged in such work. But when we come to look closely at the experiences of people in such work, we come across yet another ambiguity or paradox. In my research (Watson, 1977) into personnel specialists' reported sources of satisfaction and dissatisfaction in their work, it was observed that many of the things that people complained of – the unpredictability of people, the lack of clear authority, the need constantly to be alert and always to have to persuade and cajole people – were often referred to again when people talked of what they liked about their work. Ironically, the source of satisfactions and the source of dissatisfactions came down to the same thing: dealing with the human element. Human relationships here, as in any other social sphere, can be an agony or a delight. What we see is an ambivalence about personnel work in one of the stricter meanings of that word: ambivalence in the sense of simultaneously harbouring feelings of love and hate.

A corresponding recognition of ambivalence within personnel management is suggested by Strauss and Sayles (1980). They say that the work is 'inherently frustrating', especially since most problems are never fully solved and those that are solved are succeeded by new ones. They argue that such work is among the most demanding to be found in society but that those who take on dealing with 'contradictory employee wants and demands, with inconsistent and ever-changing governmental constraints, and with the inevitable politics of any human organisation' can find such work exciting, fulfilling and challenging – and also well-paid. In inviting people to engage in personnel management careers, they promise: 'you need never fear that people will dull your senses or your spirits: be assured, you will never have a dull moment.'

The origins of the personnel specialism

Our emphasis so far has been very much a 'functional' one. The stress has been on what contribution both general and specialised personnel management makes to the functioning of the modern work organisation. What, however, is not explained is how there comes to be the phenomenon of the specialist personnel department in such organisations. The existence of any social institution is never explained by pointing to the function it has within the social system of which it is a part. Functions have to be recognised to understand any particular social institution but they have to be related to the human purposes and activities which provide that particular way of handling a functional requirement rather than another. Accordingly, I suggest that we have to recognise three basic factors behind the emergence of personnel management as a specialist activity in contemporary societies.

The first set of factors are those which have been dealt with at length already in the present chapter and in the previous chapter's examination of the factors underlying the wider phenomenon of the employment strategy. These are the conflicts, tensions, and contradictions which are inherent in the employment of human beings as resources within industrial capitalist systems of work organisation. All of these problems provide a rationale for a separate and specialist personnel department to act as an integrator, arbitrator and maintainer of consistency within the organisation.

The second set of factors are those relating to the general trend of task specialisation or developing division of labour which has occurred over the years of the present century with the growth in the scale of work organisations. There is a logic of efficiency behind the gathering together of all personnel records in one place, for instance, just as there is in asking one person to do all the sick visiting. A similar logic justifies all the job advertisements for an organisation being placed by the same official and the efficiency of training being increased by organising courses in a central setting so as to avoid duplication of training efforts across departments. Most of these matters are ones of keeping down

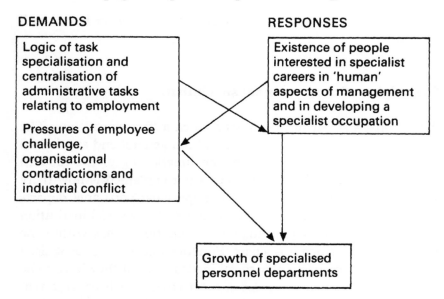

Fig. 6.3 *Structural and 'careerist' factors in the growth of personnel departments*

administrative costs and enabling administrative systems to work more smoothly but, underlying this, is the overall logic of employers being concerned to find more efficient ways of using labour.

The above two sets of factors are, in a sense, the 'demand' side of the equation. They relate to pressures within organisations which invite a personnel management response. The third set of factors behind the growth of personnel departments is on the 'supply' side. The growth of such departments has to be understood in part as a consequence of people putting themselves forward as experts in personnel work who can meet these 'demands'. This means that we must take into account the 'empire-building' efforts of personnel managers, the self-conscious career-seeking activities of individual specialists and the whole range of activities of occupational associations like the Institute of Personnel Management in Britain, who set out to establish the need for the employment of experts in personnel and then to supply and accredit individuals who allegedly possess the requisite skills and knowledge to meet these needs.

The spread of specialised personnel departments is as much an outcome of organisational politics and career or occupational advancement as it is a matter of system needs. In the language of organisation theory: personnel departments do not emerge simply as a result of there being certain 'contingent' factors which demand them. They emerge because the relevant contingencies are perceived by particular social actors and interest groups as opportunities for careers, incomes and influence if they offer themselves as the necessary experts who can deal with them. And personnel management has been the specialism within the managerial world which has most enthusiastically embraced the notion of professionalism as an aid to gaining recognition and influence to succeed in these terms. But this, as we shall now see, is a double-edged sword when it comes to fighting for the personnel occupation's cause.

Management, personnel management and professionalism

The idea of the profession as a special kind of prestigious occupation is a peculiarly British and American one. It can best be understood as part of a strategy devised in the nineteenth century by the members of several prestigious occupations like law, medicine and university teaching to maintain for themselves a role in the general division of labour which kept them apart from the increasingly dominant principles of commercialisation and bureaucratisation. The original and essential aim of the professional was to avoid being employed by an employer or managed by a manager.

The professional's expertise and the ethical implications of its application are such, they claim, that the control of the occupation must stay in the hands of the experts themselves. A pure profession is an occupation whose members possess a high degree of expertise, belong to an occupational association which oversees their training and performance and which licenses them to apply that expertise, and provide an expert service to clients in return for a fee. Their emphasis is on altruistic service to the community rather than on profit: the fee is the means which enables them to practise and not an end in itself. They are paid to be able to work rather than work in order to be paid. Most important of all, however, the professionals are accountable to themselves (although ultimately to the community via the mandate which they have from the state) rather than to any employer.

The autonomy which is at the heart of this ideology of professionalism – together with the high level of reward and prestige which accompanies it – is something to which many occupations have aspired and it has encouraged many occupational groupings to imitate the traditional professions of law and medicine by following a strategy of professionalisation. An occupation following this strategy lays claim to esoteric competence, the quality of which it says must be maintained for the sake of client and society. It therefore seeks for its licensed members the exclusive right to do work in its sphere of competence whilst controlling who enters the work, how they are trained, how they perform and how this performance is checked and evaluated.

At first sight, the potential for managerial staffs to follow this professionalising strategy is completely absent: their fundamental *raison d'être* is as the agents of employers. They are senior employees acting not on behalf of the community or a fee-paying client but to meet the purposes of those at the top of the bureaucratic hierarchy who pay their salaries. Not only this, but many managers are employed in commercial organisations in which service is a means to profit rather than an end in itself. Nevertheless, managerial groups – like many others who are no less unlike the lawyers and medical practitioners who inspire them – have taken up the professionalisation theme, to the extent that their circumstances have allowed them. And, within the management world, the personnel management occupation has found its situation the most conducive to attempts at some kind of professionalisation.

The ideals of professionalism were in the minds of British personnel specialists from the start, largely because the earliest full-time practitioners were social improvers motivated by altruism and imported into the industrial commercial world by various philanthropically inclined employers who wished to go some way towards humanising their enterprises. The motives of the early welfare workers who are generally seen as the founders of the personnel management occupation reflected in part the service ethic of the professional class from which they often came. In *The Personnel Managers* (1977), I traced in detail the way these professional interests played a part in the history of British personnel management. They helped the welfare workers insist on their autonomy from the paternalist employers with whom they were closely identified within the 'welfare movement'; they provided an organisational focus for the eventual coming together of the welfare workers with the labour and staff managers who form a later and different strand of the personnel management movement, and they provided a way of legitimating a claim to occupational expertise through the overseeing of training, examinations and technical publications. Making all this possible was the occupational association which, after many changes of name, finally became the Institute of Personnel Management in 1946.

Is personnel management a profession, then? In one sense it is not and cannot be, since the original idea of professionalism was one associated with occupations intent on keeping themselves free from employer control and keeping to a minimum any mediation between themselves and the clients who paid them a fee for services directly rendered. In another sense, it is a profession since it has taken on certain features of those occupations which established the idea of the professional association as a focus for occupational training and as a representer of the interests of its members in a way analogous to the approach of the (originally) more working-class trade union. This latter aspect of professionalism is of great importance: it reminds us that professionalisation is an occupational *strategy*. It is a way in which the members of an occupational group pursue their own common interests – using as a legitimating device a claim to be providing a service to the community. This is not to say that so-called professional groups do not provide a service to the community. But a degree of scepticism about the extent to which such claims are valid must operate, given the self-interested motives which accompany altruistic motives in every would-be profession. Peter Anthony (1977) has brought to the analysis of personnel management such a degree of scepticism.

Peter Anthony accepts that the original welfare workers did have a 'genuine welfare interest in their "clients", the workers'. He notes that nowadays, however, the remaining welfare workers tend to be despised by the personnel managers who have largely succeeded them. The genuine altruism of the older welfare worker does not fit with the currently typical devotion to the pursuit of efficiency, profit and survival. Yet, paradoxically, says Anthony, 'while personnel managers have excluded the genuinely professional elements found in their progenitors they have embarked on a ceaseless quest for their own "professionalisation", almost entirely in order to enhance their status in the eyes of other managers.' Because they do not adhere to the service ideal in which the client's interests are put before personal or commercial profit, personnel managers have been 'in continuous retreat from the position of close proximity to real professionalism which they once occupied'. The welfarism which still exists is not an end in itself, it is a means by which personnel managers make their 'own contribution to business efficiency', and thereby further their own careers.

Although the status and credibility associated with possession of the professional label had been attractive to personnel management specialists, they have also realised the danger that a claim to superior expertise can distance them from the line managers with whom they so importantly need to work closely. As Anthony and Crichton (1969) said, 'the history of the personnel specialists as a group is the history of a struggle for status to become full members of the management team.' To push too hard their membership of the professional community of personnel managers at large, to stress too much their adherence to professional ethics or to indulge in too much of the mystique of professionalism would be to risk their fellowship with other managers, to question their loyalty to the organisation and to raise doubt about their pragmatism and practicality. Professionalism can smack too much of the theoretical, the academic and the tender-hearted for many of the managerial fraternity.

My own research suggests that many personnel specialists are doubtful about the programme which the Institute of Personnel Management has followed in its pursuit of professional status (Watson, 1977). Particular doubts are held about the principle of examination-based qualifications as an indicator of suitability for holding a personnel management identity. It appeared that they resolved the possible contradiction here by redefining the word 'professional' to mean simply 'competent' or 'good at the job'. And the research also suggested that those who belonged to the professional body did so for highly pragmatic reasons. Member-

ship of the institute was useful insofar as it indicated the possession of some basic knowledge of the work and because it gave the
member access to the various publications, information and services which would enable them to do a better job for their employer, and hence assist their career.

The personnel managers are professionals when it suits them
and part of the organisation when it does not. They are experts
when it is helpful to claim expertise and they are just one of the
general team when it does not. And other branches of management have shown similar ambivalence to the idea of professionalism. But a number of commentators have suggested that the
fact that British managers are at all interested in the conceits of
professionalism is a matter for serious concern. To Alistair Mant
(1979), the interest in professionalism is another illustration of
the tendency of management generally to set itself apart from the
rest of the workforce, with whom they need to be closely involved.
And Peter Lawrence (1980) implies that the much lower level of
managerial professionalism in West Germany may be a factor in
the greater effectiveness of German management compared to the
British. It frees them from an excessive concern with the status
of 'management' as a special group and from the 'inanity of
arms-length management'. Fores and Glover (1978), in a similar
vein, are scornful of what they see as 'the professional bandwag-
gon'. They believe that the professional's idea of a reliance on a
body of formal scientific knowledge is misguided. Personal expertise and an 'immeasurable quality known as flair' are more
important than 'management science' and the first loyalty of managers cannot be to the community in which they operate. To act
in this way, say Fores and Glover, would lead to 'bad performance and bad civics'.

The mentioning here of one international difference in how
managerial work is viewed brings to our attention the fact that,
although there may be common patterns to organisational and
personnel management activities within industrial capitalist
societies, there are also variations. But international comparisons
can offer us more than this insight. They are also useful in showing how the development of employment strategies together with
the formal personnel management component of these is a complex mixture of positive initiatives and reactive accommodations
to historical and societal contingencies. A brief consideration of

the different ways in which personnel management has developed in Britain and Japan brings this out effectively.

Expedience and choice in personnel management: Britain and Japan

Sidney Pollard (1979) observes that one of the most significant departures in the British industrialisation process was the setting up of Arkwright's water-powered cotton mill at Cromford in Derbyshire. The approach taken towards labour here was a traditional one, reproducing exactly 'the practices of the better eighteenth century Tory squire'. Pollard suggests that Britain was standing at a critical parting of the ways at this stage. He speculates that there was a choice to make: whether to industrialise further in line with the traditions of the eighteenth century or, alternatively, to set out to coerce the labour force through the use of terror. It was this latter policy which was followed and the employment strategies of the first half of the nineteenth century were characterised by employer rejection of traditional values, the embracing of the laissez-faire doctrine and powerful resistance to the idea that shorter hours, higher pay, better working conditions and so on, might be the key to greater efficiency. Historians have often puzzled over why the value of such reforms took so long to be recognised by employers.

Various explanations have been offered of the ruthlessness of labour management – or employment strategies as we are calling them here – in the early nineteenth century. For example, it has been pointed out that the increasing use of machinery meant that human beings could easily be treated as mere adjuncts to machines whose morale was unimportant. The fear which each employer had of increasing their own labour costs, so giving at least a short-term advantage to a competitor, is also suggested as a factor. Pollard adds to these explanations one which is more fundamental. He claims that the employers came increasingly to believe that industry could not be operated under the old traditions of 'the relative independence, willing collaboration and self-respect of the labouring classes'. Instead, they decided that industry required 'totally new mental attitudes and habits of work' and that these could only be achieved by the destruction of the old ones. The idea was to develop a kind of discipline which would dehumanise workers, undermine their dignity and put them through a 'phase of disorientation and anomie in order to build afresh with new suitably tailored human material'.

During this especially repressive early nineteenth-century period, sight was not lost of the paternalist alternative and, towards the middle of the century, certain facets of it began to be revived. The advantages of gaining a more positive kind of commitment from the labour force were increasingly recognised as the possibility of trade union challenge grew as the state, the church and social reformers became increasingly concerned about the moral and physical state of the new urban proletariat. Most significantly perhaps, it was realised that reforms paid. And the early unions played a part in this in showing that employer enlightenment was as profitable as it was charitable.

Pollard comments that the newer approach, which reached its high point in the hosiery schemes of the 1860s, in Port Sunlight in 1888 and in Bournville in 1885, was never fully realised in practice. In the same way that the laissez-faire approach had always been limited by memories of the earlier traditionalism, so these new more enlightened approaches were inhibited by the ways in which workers remembered the earlier harshness and remained suspicious and untrusting. This view is supported by a reading of Patrick Joyce's (1980) rigorous and detailed study of factory life in the north of England in the later Victorian period. He writes of the 'new paternalism' of this period and questions traditional historical interpretations of this by arguing that the new paternalism did not so much represent a logical opposite of the laissez-faire which preceded it as a logical outcome of it. The new paternalist practice 'developed within the matrix of strongly held laissez-faire notions of what the relations of employer and worker should be'.

The newer paternalism was a paying proposition with its fairly primitive use of a mixture of carrot and stick approaches. And, as Joyce emphasises, the paternalist innovations of works dinners, treats, trips, libraries, canteens, lectures, gymnasia, burial societies and the rest were by no means 'the pure milk of benevolence'. Their role as an antidote to trade unionism was as important as the religious and charitable motives which also informed them. Joyce helpfully illustrates the ambiguity which existed between paternalism and laissez-faire. He notes, for example, that Crossley's spent vast sums of money on the town of Halifax yet insisted that the Crossley Institute and the works canteen were as far as possible paid for out of the pockets of the operatives. Even more revealing – and this is said to be typical of larger firms – the Institute and the Provident fund which was set up were in part paid for out of the fines imposed on the workforce. Joyce also notes that in the public utterances of employers there was still the laissez-faire oriented claim that they were *employers* with *employees*. Yet, in practice, in the everyday life of the enterprise, the paternalist-oriented terms of *master* and *man* continued to be widely used.

We can say that the nineteenth-century history of British labour management is one in which both laissez-faire, with its uncompromising insistence on labour being a manipulable resource, and paternalism, with a warmer and more patronising emphasis, were tried. What is important to us today is to realise that the two emphases are living parts of the present. As Pollard says, 'we have developed what is essentially a compromise between the two systems which carries on its back the burden of the history of both.'

The modern era, I suggest, is best seen as starting in the late nineteenth century as labour management, incorporating its twin roots of laissez-faire and paternalism, began to become bureaucratised. The spread of the joint stock company, the increase in size of enterprises, the accelerated use of technology, the eclipse of internal contracting systems, the slow but sure spread of formalised work-study methods and rationalised incentive schemes and, above all, the growth of strata of both generalist and specialist managerial employees all played their part in this area. These initiatives are to be understood not simply as unilateral choices of business interests but as developments which involved a coming to terms with a desire to continue to control labour in the face of a recalcitrant labour force and a state increasingly requiring capital work together with labour. It is in this context that specialised personnel management departments emerged and haltingly grew. Many of the ambiguities and contradictions which inform the operation of these, and which we looked at earlier, relate to the fact that the British personnel department is a bureaucratic embodiment of the two-faced approach to labour which

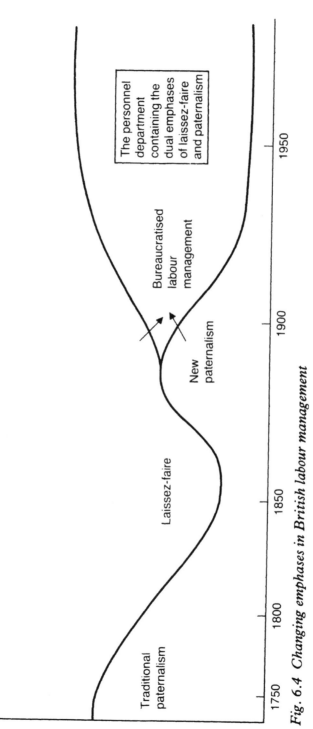

Fig. 6.4 Changing emphases in British labour management

the nineteenth century developed and with which the twentieth century has to live.

Figure 6.4 attempts to represent in simple form the historical background to the situation of the modern specialised personnel function in Britain. This is a situation in which the personnel department has to contain within itself the dual emphases which it has inherited: the laissez-faire emphasis which treats labour merely as a manipulable means to the employer's end and the paternalist emphasis which modifies the harshness of this with a desire to encourage a greater social commitment of employer and employee to each other.

The type of personnel management which typifies the large Japanese employer is quite different from the British type in some important ways. The most significant difference is that Japanese personnel management is more central to general corporate management. This has been stressed by Keith Thurley and his colleagues (1980) who see the specialised personnel presence in the Japanese corporation as a functional device which enables the headquarters to make and implement decisions on such matters as appointments and promotions. This contrasts with the British situation in which the personnel management specialists are formally restricted to an advisory role in which they assist the management proper in its control and deployment of personnel. This is explained as deriving from the pattern of British industrialisation in which there was no conscious theory of management or body of personnel management knowledge. Hence personnel management as such grew as a *movement* within industry 'attacking the neglect of the human factor that so characterised the industrial revolution in Britain'.

In terms of the underlying thesis I am presenting, I would argue that the formalised British personnel management has tended to play a compensatory or continually reactive role in the handling of the various tensions which are inherent in industrial capitalist employment systems. In contrast, the Japanese paid close attention to the problem of the labour force from a relatively early stage of their industrialisation process.

The employment policies of the large Japanese corporations with their emphasis on lifetime employment (shusin koyo), rewards based on length of service (nenko joretsu) and a level of company involvement in the lives of employees fitting with an ideology of corporate paternalism or industrial familism, are often seen as aspects of the way Japan's industrialisation spontaneously grew out of the pattern of traditional social relationships of pre-industrial Japan. Instead of this, I would argue that modern Japanese personnel philosophies in the larger companies are the outcomes of the conscious attempts made by Japanese employers to deal with the tensions and conflicts associated with the large-scale employment of paid labour which was becoming central to the Japanese industrialisation process by the early decades of the twentieth century. These philosophies and practices were a carefully judged mixture from the personnel and industrial relations experiences and innovations of European and American companies.

The paternalism of modern Japanese corporations was not a feature of the earliest stage of Japanese industrialisation. This was very much a state-initiated process introduced after the Meija restoration of 1868 to help Japan achieve parity with western economics. However, the officials of these new enterprises, the *shoku-in*, were typically former samurai who were given the traditional status of their class. This was reflected in their being salaried, their being given life-time job tenure and their being provided with accommodation. Elements of these policies later spread to the manual labour forces only as employers found themselves faced with major labour supply difficulties, especially after the acceleration in industrialisation associated with the First World War. Not only were employers faced with growing labour unrest and militancy, they experienced severe problems of labour shortage and labour turnover, especially among the increasingly crucial skilled workers.

The need to attract, train and keep skilled labour was clearly a factor encouraging employers to develop a higher degree of commitment between themselves and their employers. But another major influence on the manner and the extent to which they did this was the particular form taken by worker resistance. Unionisation was developing under the leadership of the *oyakata* or labour contractors who were resisting managerial attempts to wrest from them control over work processes. As Craig Littler (1982) has emphasised, the status and legitimacy of these oyakata, combined with their near monopoly of technical expertise, meant that the managements could not cast them aside in their attempts to increase and centralise their control over the labour process. The alternative was to incorporate them. And this involved giving them the privileges which had previously been the monopoly of the shoku-in class. The followers, the *kotaka*, were granted their share of the new privileges, in proportion to the length of time they had been attached to the oyakata. Here was the basis of the seniority or nenko joretsu system which is of great importance today. The phenomenon of the company union, which also plays a significant stabilising role in modern Japan, can be seen too as having its roots in the way the oyakata-led groupings of workers were incorporated into the growing Japanese corporations.

In the interwar years, Japanese managements looked closely at personnel management innovations occurring abroad. Works councils were modelled on some of those observed in Britain and America. There was an expansion of welfare programmes in heavy industry where, at the instigation of senior managers, industrial relations sections had been established in factories and central offices by the late 1920s. E. Daito (1979) describes these measures as the practical responses which large-scale industry made to the situations which they faced and he suggests that they also deliberately 'adopted the ideology of the traditional family system as an integrating principle of their policies'. The ideology of company familism concurrently played two roles according to Daito: first, it protected the managerial prerogative from the protests of employees and from outside hostile forces and, second, it demanded of employees 'a single-minded devotion to the family business'. In this way the Japanese approach to employment deals with the two central problems of *control* and *commitment* through one coherent system of personnel management.

Both Britain and Japan are industrial capitalist societies and both employ free labour which is organised on the principles of formal rationality. The two economies are of the same basic type but yet there are significant differences in the kinds of employment strategies which are followed – at least in the bigger corporations. Japanese employment strategies, including the role given to the personnel department, is more coherent and consistent than has typically been the case in Britain. Employment strategies are also much more clearly a central part of the overall corporate style. British personnel management is perhaps more constrained by the ambiguities which it inherits from a more confused and a less deliberately and consciously managed past.

The personnel department: size and influence

In the previous chapter, it was argued that the nature of the formal personnel management presence in an organisation would, like the other aspects of the overall employment strategy, be determined by the interaction of two sets of factors. The first of these were the political and value-based choices of the dominant managerial group and the second were the organisational, technological, labour market, labour force and societal contingencies which prevailed. Depending on whether the employee constituencies (the labour force) was seen as relatively problematic or non-problematic to the organisation's future performance and survival, the personnel department would be more or less well-developed. The contingent factors tending to encourage a view of the labour force as more or less problematic did not directly or automatically affect the nature of the personnel department: as always, contingent factors are mediated by the personal, political and career interests of the human actors involved. A 'problematic' workforce presents opportunities for people to make careers for themselves in personnel management, rather necessarily bringing about the growth of such a specialism.

It was a recognition of this situation that led Albert Cherns (1972) to point out to British personnel managers that 'leadership' in an organisation passes to those who are involved in coping with the organisation's source of maximum uncertainty. He suggested that during various periods in postwar Britain engineers have given such leadership, followed by accountants and then by marketing experts. He goes on to ask: 'What next? We are already seeing that the interface between the organisation and society is becoming turbulent. Personnel managers fasten your seat belts!' However, the possibilities are not as straightforward as this might imply. The personnel managers have to prove themselves before they will be looked to in this way. And this is clearly recognised in Karen Legge's (1978) discussion of the factors which influence the amount of power which personnel managers are likely to achieve to implement the policies they see as appropriate. She sees two types of factor operating. First, there are three 'organisational factors': the organisation's dominant ideology, the areas of contextual uncertainty it defines as being of crucial importance to resolve, and how it defines, measures and evaluates success. Second, there are four 'individual factors': the manager's level of expertise, their right of access to those who have to be influenced or from whom information has to be elicited, their ability to establish credibility with such people and the resource power their position commands.

An important contingent factor which encouraged the growth of personnel departments in Britain is often said to be that of trade union power. In his review of what he sees as a fairly dramatic increase in specialist representation of the personnel function at board level, Keith Thurley (1981) suggests that the emphasis is firmly on industrial relations. And this is supported by the evidence of the major study of industrial relations in British manufacturing industry carried out at Warwick University in the later 1970s. The researchers took the presence of a member of senior management with sole responsibility for personnel management as an indicator of the relative status of personnel management within the management hierarchy. And, on the basis of statistical analysis, Beaumont and Deaton (1980) claim to show that this is associated with the presence and exertion of 'trade union power'. The researchers do make the point, however, that this is not an automatic response but one influenced by bargaining between managers about what is to be done.

William Brown (1981), in his discussion of the same findings, also stresses that this is not a simple reaction. The combination of contingency factors (constraints) and managerial initiative-taking (choice) which occurs here is clearly suggested by Brown's comment on the data to the effect that the appointment of specialist managers does not just arise in response to collective bargaining pressure but also 'from the overall size of the firm, from a certain preference for managerial division of labour which may be greater with overseas ownership, and, above all, from the decision to conduct bargaining within the company at a higher level than the individual establishment'.

This same material has been re-examined by Eric Batstone (1984) who interprets it somewhat differently. He argues that increasing specialist attention to industrial relations issues in the decade following the Donovan Report (HMSO, 1968) can be seen as resulting from four different types of factor. First, there is the 'reformist rationale'; second, there is 'union pressure'; third, there is 'external pressure' such as legislation or national incomes policies, and, fourth, there is the 'organisational rationale' whereby growing personnel specialisation can be seen as equivalent to the parallel increase in accounting – as a reflection of attempts to integrate organisations through an increased division of labour following the wave of mergers which occurred in the late 1960s. Although it is recognised that all of these may intermingle, Batstone sees the organisational rationale as the most important factor influencing the growth of personnel management.

To see whether there has been any reversal in the fortunes of personnel departments in the different circumstances of the 1980s, we can look at the evidence of the follow-up of the Warwick survey carried out by Eric Batstone (1984) in 1983. This showed that there has been no statistically significant change in the number of plants which had personnel specialists at establishment or board levels. Although there was some decline in the number of plants where a personnel function exists above the level of the establishment, it is interesting to note that half of the 1983 respondents say that the personnel function has become more important. Only 5 per cent reported a decrease and these were cases where there has been a dramatic decrease in the labour force and where there were especially acute economic difficulties.

Managers and personnel managers

Although we can gain a useful impression of general patterns of personnel management involvement in organisations from large-scale studies of the type we have been considering, more qualitative studies and the evidence of numerous management speeches and articles suggests that what goes on within the organisations is altogether more complex and less peaceful than might appear from the wider picture. The significance of the issues which arise here is indicated by the way the respondents in my study of personnel managers (Watson, 1977) answered a question about what they felt was the biggest difficulty faced by personnel managers generally. The overwhelming pattern of the responses indicates that personnel managers see their non-personnel managerial colleagues as providing their greatest problems. Where the personnel department was not well-developed, the personnel practitioner was constantly faced with overcoming the low status of the function and with establishing its credibility. But where the personnel department was well-established, personnel people frequently complained of other managers 'dumping' personnel problems on them and leaving them in the difficult situation of handling issues on their own which they could only really effectively handle in cooperation with the managers of the area concerned. Criticisms also came from the other side of the relationship, however.

The evidence of Ritzer and Trice (1969) and Foulkes (1975) in the United States shows that managers tend to see personnel managers as defensive, passive, reactive, conservative people who are not business or risk-oriented and who play little part in business decisions or influencing management generally. Karen Legge's (1978) British evidence also shows a tendency for personnel departments to be seen as 'out of touch', especially by middle and junior line managers. This corresponds with Kingsley Manning's (1983) comments on what he sees as a widespread apathy towards personnel management. There is a lack of the sort of analytic and creative thinking which has been demonstrated in the fields of finance and marketing, it is argued.

The sense of insecurity engendered in personnel specialists by these kinds of attack have frequently been added to by comments directed their way by a series of management gurus, trade-union leaders and eminent managers. Time and again, for instance, articles, speeches, lectures and books by and for personnel managers have referred to the comments by the arch guru of the management world, Peter Drucker. He suggested in 1961 that the personnel department was merely a hodge podge of activities, 'a collection of incidental techniques without much internal cohesion'. Drucker questioned the very existence of the personnel department, grievously wounding generations of aspiring personnel specialists with his accusation that they have a view of management as 'partly a file clerk's job, partly a house-keeping job, partly a social worker's job and partly fire-fighting to head off union trouble or to settle it'. Since this is not how Drucker –

to whom all managerial heads must bow – sees management, personnel work is being denied the legitimacy of the master's approval.

One of the most eminent British managers of the 1980s, John Harvey-Jones (1982), whilst Chairman of ICI, revealed that he has not been impressed by the people whom he has seen working in personnel departments he has known. He accuses them of being more ready to draw on their knowledge of management theory to advise others than to use it to put their own house in order. And Michael Edwardes, addressing the annual conference of the Institute of Personnel Management in 1984, expressed concern about those who had 'moved into personnel management to avoid the rat race of line management'. He pointed to the 'soft line on pay and overmanning which sometimes comes from the personnel area' and he suggests that a 'good chief executive' would welcome a 'more robust approach from the personnel function'.

Additional blows to the confidence of the personnel specialists have been added by various researchers. J. B. Miner (1976), for instance, reported that American personnel managers showed a lack of assertiveness which is so pervasive that it appeared to be 'a defining characteristic of the field'. And, whilst Miner was implying that personnel managers lack a 'motivation to manage', Michael Poole (1973) was citing his British evidence showing the tendency for both managers and union representatives to bypass personnel offices in the carrying out of plant industrial relations. And the trade union leader, Clive Jenkins (1973), had reported that the personnel manager is a sort of buffer or conduit between the trade union side and 'those with the real power to authorize settlements'. Jenkins suspected that personnel staff were simply being used as part of a managerial delaying tactic whereby the personnel specialist would continually refer matters to higher authorities.

The achievement of general managerial acceptance of personnel managers seems always to be beyond their grasp. Evidence presented by J. T. Akinmayowa (1980) suggests that sales, production and finance managers have a less impressive view of the part played by personnel managers in achieving corporate goals than do personnel managers themselves. And a contrasting type of concern is expressed by an eminent company chairman, Peter

Prior (1981), who suggested that to make the personnel department too central is to see a usurping of the leadership function of top management. And who should this manager quote to frighten his audience of personnel managers but Peter Drucker, who is reported to have alleged that 'anybody who has a personnel department mismanages people'. It must seem to those within personnel management who agonise over their occupation's role that they cannot win. If personnel specialists are not passive administrative nobodies who pursue their social work, go-between and fire-fighting vocations with little care for business decisions and leadership then they are clever and ambitious power-seekers who want to run work organisations as a kind of self-indulgent personnel playground.

Why is personnel management caught up in this 'double bind'? On the one hand it can be seen as trapped in a vicious circle, condemning it to perpetual marginality. And, on the other hand, it can be seen as creating conflict with other managers through the power it can wield over them. The vicious circle view was put by Clive Jenkins (1973) who said that 'a vicious circle has been created whereby the brighter managers steer clear of the personnel function because of a lack of status, and, in consequence, the personnel department remains in low status because of its relative lack of talent.' Michael Poole (1973) argued similarly, suggesting that it was personnel departments' lack of authority to handle industrial relations problems that lowered their status and hence made it more difficult to attract 'first rate staff'. Karen Legge (1978), however, sees the vicious circle as starting at the point where personnel departments are left out of the managerial planning process. This causes human resource problems which are left to or 'dumped on' a very busy personnel department who can only cope through crisis management. This leads to a poor general perception of the personnel department who are therefore left out of the managerial planning process. The circle has been completed.

Crucial to all of these problems within the relationships of personnel and other managers is the line-staff principle of organisational design whereby the line department, who are directly involved in producing the goods or services with which the organisation is concerned, are *serviced* by the staff departments such as personnel. The role of the staff departments is formally a secondary one and this means that they do not have authority over the line. Their influence is meant to be felt only through the advice they give to the line. The logic of this is clear: if, say, a production manager needs new staff, he should be able to turn to the personnel department to find them. But, since the production manager has to deal with that person once recruited, it is quite reasonable that he should make the decision as to whom is finally selected. The personnel officer's findings from selection procedures and aptitude tests can only be used to advise that manager. They should not be used to justify the imposition of particular staff on a manager.

The flaw in the logic of the personnel department's advisory role soon becomes apparent, however, if we go a little further with our example. What if the production manager's choice raises the possibility of the organisation's being charged with illegal discriminatory practice? What if the recruit is a member of the 'wrong' trade union and their appointment is likely to trigger a dispute? In an ideal world of calm reflection and fraternal co-operation the line manager would take personnel advice on such matters and avoid the problems. But in a real world of rivalries and varying departmental priorities the firmness and persistence of the type of guiding advice which personnel departments give soon begins to resemble dictatorial intrusion to some managers. And resentment frequently follows.

The ultimate rationale of the personnel department is one of keeping the organisation as a whole going on a long-term basis through maintaining the staffing resource and coping with the conflicts and contradictions which arise wherever and whenever people are employed. But this longer-term or more *strategic* emphasis and the necessity of constantly keeping in mind the state of the organisation as a *whole* can clash with the more specific short-term and sectional priorities of managers who are less concerned with what is ultimately the organisation's most problematic aspect: its human element. In the modern work organisation where employee problems are not simply matters of personal relationships but ones bringing in legislative constraints, trade union pressures, national wage policies, labour market problems and so on, the human problems of work organisation often hit the ordinary manager in the form of some intervention from the personnel department. The personnel department becomes a constant constraint on how managers manage their own staff. There is thus an ongoing cause of conflict between personnel managers and others. The conflict is structural as well as interpersonal and Fig. 6.5 illustrates this.

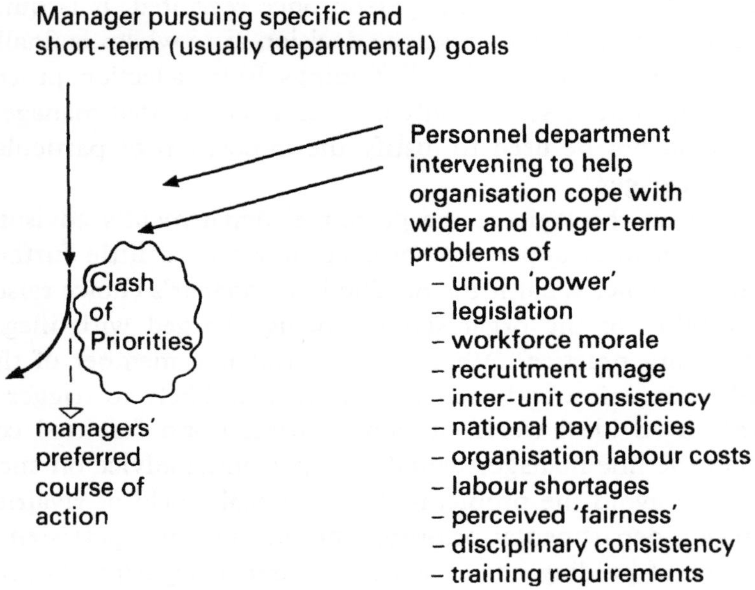

Manager pursuing specific and
short-term (usually departmental) goals

Personnel department
intervening to help
organisation cope with
wider and longer-term
problems of
- union 'power'
- legislation
- workforce morale
- recruitment image
- inter-unit consistency
- national pay policies
- organisation labour costs
- labour shortages
- perceived 'fairness'
- disciplinary consistency
- training requirements

Clash
of
Priorities

managers'
preferred
course of
action

Fig. 6.5 The personnel department mediating problems which constrain managerial activity

The personnel department is always likely to be marginal within the organisation in one way or another. And, in addition to the danger of isolation from peers, is the possibility of the personnel department – however significant a presence it may have – being kept at an arm's length by the very senior management. On the basis of a study of company directors, Jack Winkler (1974), for instance, suggested that directors liked to keep themselves above personnel and industrial relations problems. To do this provided the directors with a defence mechanism and a 'double repository for blame' when labour problems arose: 'not just the recalcitrant workers, but the subordinates to whom he delegated the task of keeping quiet'. But, in contrast to this, we see complaints such as that expressed in the magazine *Chief Executive* in which Derek Hollier (1979) reports various views which see 'top men' relying too much on their personnel departments. Personnel departments are the 'growing barriers' and are leading to a situation in which top people are getting their involvement with staff by proxy. This, it is felt, is likely to exacerbate problems between managers and managed. There are echoes here of the point made earlier by Peter Prior. Once again, where the personnel department is not being accused of being weak and therefore ineffective, it is being accused of being strong and ineffective!

Paradox and ambiguity pervade personnel management but this does not necessarily mean that the job is an impossible one. Shaun Tyson (1980) goes as far as saying that personnel managers, rather than complaining about the ambiguities of their position, should welcome and *exploit* it. And a typical way in which this occurs, I suggest, is when personnel managers use their advisory role as something of a façade: beneath the cloak of their act a counsellor has the firm intention of getting managers to do exactly what it is that the personnel manager wants done. The secret lies in making the manager feel that the decision is their own rather than anything imposed by the personnel department. But to be able to handle ambiguity in this way requires a high level of social skills.

My own research strongly suggests that the personal qualities of personnel people are greatly stressed in practice. Personnel management involves a lot of art (see above p. 28)! And this is supported by the research of Guest and Horwood (1981) which found that among the personnel managers studied the criteria for success in personnel management most heavily stressed were ones relating to personality attributes. This outweighed both background and professional training. The possession of appropriate social skills like 'being approachable' or being 'able to communicate' were emphasised to an outstanding degree. And that this is recognised in a clear and public way is implied by the wording of a prospectus for a major Institute of Personnel Management conference which, in encouraging people to attend the session on 'building the credibility of the personnel function' said:

Personnel managers constantly sell ideas. Whether an idea is accepted often depends less on its intrinsic merits than on the skill and credibility of the seller. To be effective, the

> personnel department must win the respect of line
> management and this requires a high degree of personal skill
> on the part of certain key individuals.

The research evidence suggests that personnel managers fly much further and higher by using the seat of their pants than by relying on the instruments with which they can be equipped through professional training and the acquisition of social science knowledge. In the 1960s, Tom Lupton (1964) advocated a role for personnel managers as applied social scientists who would gain integration into the management team in recognition of their 'diagnostic skills' and problem-solving capacity. Alan Fox (1966) went so far as to suggest that failure to take on this kind of role would mean personnel management risking relegation to permanent inferior status. This type of social-science-based problem-solving capacity as the basis for personnel management credibility has continued to be advocated by, for example, Karen Legge (1978) who sees an ability to apply the ideas of the contingency approach to organisation theory as a possible key to success. But Legge's advocacy is firmly rooted in a clear perception of the realities of life in the personnel department: the key to power and effectiveness lies not just in being able to 'solve problems' but to recognise and define key contingencies which no one else can handle and to deploy whatever micropolitical and interactive skills might be needed.

A clear picture of the ways in which personnel specialists operate less as professional experts and more as micropoliticians 'mediating contingencies' and negotiating their own credibility is given by the study by Fred Goldner (1970) of industrial relations managers in an American organisation. Goldner observes that organisations do not like to 'leave to chance' any activities which may make a difference to the organisation but which may involve uncertainty. It is therefore 'advantageous to an individual's career' to find such activities 'if they are not already apparent'. The labour relations specialists studied were clearly managing their careers by exploiting the uncertainties created by the activities of trade unions. Their nominal antagonists were the source of their internal power. The union could be used as a threat in arguments with production managers who were frequently told that it was the personnel men who 'knew the bigger picture' and who had to be heeded if the very necessary uniform industrial relations pattern was to be maintained.

Goldner observed that the personalities of the industrial relations men were very important and he notes the range of micropolitical tactics which they used. This involved a strong emphasis on salesmanship and persuasion with a constant willingness to talk of precedents which must be avoided ('using history as a tactic'). The marginality of their position was exploited in various ways to enhance their power: they controlled knowledge and insisted that agreements had to be interpreted by themselves; they bypassed normal hierarchical channels of authority and communications, and they helped to construct the measurement system by which they were evaluated. This closely compares with my own investigation of this area (Watson, 1977) in which we see the importance of 'persuading people', cultivating contacts, planting ideas in the minds of others as well as using threats and even a degree of 'blackmail' where appropriate!

It is quite possible to argue that this kind of behaviour is by no means unique to personnel managers. And one reason that this is true is that most managerial work contains an element of personnel work. But, in the end, all management is beset with ambiguities, conflicts of priority and interest and the sheer bloody-minded tendency of all organisational arrangements to go wrong. All organisations are confronted by that paradox whereby the means which are chosen to meet efficiently the required standards of performance do not necessarily lead to that performance since the 'means' involve human beings who have goals of their own – goals which may not coincide with those of the people managing them. To cope with this, as was implied in Chapter 2, all managers need to be scientists, artists, politicians and magicians!

Chapter 7

Emerging policies, practices and possibilities

The major concern of this book is with ideas, theories and perspectives. The emphasis has been on understanding rather than on practice itself as I have presented and reviewed some of the major contributions of social scientific thinking which can inform managerial work, all the time trying to bring out and encourage certain trends and new directions within this thinking. But what has shaped the ways in which this material has been organised, interpreted and synthesised has not been a desk-bound academic desire to achieve intellectual and conceptual coherence for its own sake. Rather, the intention has been to bring out of existing and developing thinking ideas which are, first, in tune with the real world rather than with an idealised one and, second, in tune with trends and directions which we can perceive being followed in the employing organisations of the late 1980s. The concern with ideas, then, is a concern conditioned by an interest in practice. The point of research and theorising is to *inform practice*.

To meet this criterion of being 'realistic' about organisational life, there has been a stress on those ideas which encourage a view of managing and organising less as a matter of rationalistic, neutral decision-making within a machine-like and unambiguously goal-oriented system and more as a matter of coping with ambiguity, paradox, conflict of interest in a context of demanding and ever-shifting coalitions and constituencies. This is seen to be done by managers through the use of political, social, symbolic, as well as analytical, skills and sensitivities. And to comply with the principle of being in tune with trends in practice, there has been a heavy emphasis on the notions of organisational and managerial effectiveness and the importance to this of a strategic emphasis in managerial thinking and effort which judges all decisions and actions in terms of their contribution to the long-term performance and survival of the organisation as a whole. Within this, particular emphasis has been put on the idea of employment strategy. This is used as an idea which links the whole range of 'behavioural' and employment policies and practices to the overall strategic concerns of the organisation.

The general stress in this work on strategic thinking and on the need overtly to consider just what it is that constitutes 'effectiveness' gives us our most important point of connection between theoretical trends and the directions being followed in the world of managerial practice.

The circumstances of an increasing proportion of employing organisations in the modern world are such that they have to take more seriously and treat more explicitly than ever before questions of long-term survival in a challenging and competitive environment. Managers in all employment sectors are having to ask themselves how they can manage their organisations more effectively in order to ensure future health and survival. I have argued that effectiveness and survival is ultimately a matter of organisational managers minimally complying with the requirements of all those constituencies which supply the organisation with the material, behavioural and symbolic resources upon which it depends. And the pressures on many organisations – be they large, small, public or private – are increasing, whether they come from the state, from investors, customers, employees, competitors or public opinion. Demands and competitive pressures, together with an increasing awareness of the potential of new technologies and of such contextual matters as a growing level of unemployment and a state stress on private ownership, individualism and the primacy of the market, have all led employers to recognise the need for close self-examination and a searching review of established practices.

Inevitably central to the rethinking which has been occurring has been examination of employment practices themselves and, increasingly, consideration of how they add up to a general employment strategy which, in turn, contributes to the overall direction of corporate policy. To cope with the pressures of an increasingly difficult environment, managements find themselves seeking predictability and tighter control over circumstances whilst, at the same time and for the same reasons, recognising the need for adaptability and flexibility. The key question for those considering their organisation's employment strategy is therefore one of achieving an appropriate balance between the level of direct managerial control which will enable them to steer the ship through troubled waters and tricky passages and a degree of flexibility in their relationships with the crew which will, on the one hand, allow them to modify the crew as circumstances demand and, on the other hand, encourage certain key crew members to think for themselves and take initiatives without waiting for orders when faced with either crisis or the challenge of a technically complex piece of seamanship. *Vital to effective management in the future will be a clarity of ends and direction combined with a flexibility in the means and practices used to get there.*

The brief review of emerging policies and practices in management, organisation and employment with which this final chapter will be concerned is not an attempt at futurology. What will in fact occur in the world of work will be in part an outcome of choices which have already been made but, more significantly, it will be a result of choices which have yet to be made. My selection of trends, tendencies and possibilities is therefore based on what choices are already being made together with a consideration of what choices might be made in the future if managers do follow the general directions being suggested by the kind of applied social scientific thinking which we have been reviewing. Managers may or they may not follow that general approach to achieving effectiveness summarised earlier whereby practice is based on answers to three types of question: strategic questions, structural questions and people questions (pp. 81-5). They may or they may not devise clear employment strategies which fit with technological, market and other strategies and which attempt to balance meeting the need for predictability and control with a need for flexibility in the practices and devices which they adopt.

My analysis will be based on the assumption that managers will choose to move in these directions. However, I am not assuming this because I see managers as suddenly becoming willing to adopt the ideas of social and behavioural scientists in a way they have shown little tendency to do in the past. Instead, I am working on this kind of assumption because I believe that ideas emerging from managerial and organisational research and theorising are such that they fit better than they have before with the realities, concerns and emphases of managerial and organisational practitioners. At the heart of this coming together is my hoped-for recognition of the common rootedness of successful theorising and successful practice in what I described in the first chapter as *critical commonsense*. And it is this, I am daring to assume, that can see managerial practice and applied academic thinking coming to follow similar directions. They can now be mutually supporting in a way not seen before.

A number of key areas of organisational and employment practice will now be examined to see what generalisations can be risked about emerging and possible patterns. This review will be based on a mixture of conceptual thinking, derived from what has put forward in the main body of the book, with a consideration of what research evidence is available on emerging patterns. But, before each of these aspects of *organisational level* behaviour is considered, we have to give some thought to the issue of the societal context in which these organisations function and the role in this of choices and actions *at the level of the state*.

State involvement and context

It is not possible to forecast what kind of policies will be followed by the state in the future. The election to office of political parties with distinctive economic and employment policies involves that kind of choice which has yet to be made. But what can be argued, on the grounds of both historical precedent and conceptual analysis, is that there will be considerable state involvement in the matters we are concerned with here, regardless of the particular rhetoric or specific policy decisions of elected governments and local authorities.

Any review of British personnel management over recent decades will indicate the considerable influence of government legislation and income policies over what has occurred. In the theoretical framework developed in Chapter 5 (pp. 166–71), legislation was recognised as one of the contingent factors influencing organisational employment strategy and the role of personnel specialists. I would argue that we can view the passing of labour legislation by governments and the growing importance of formalised personnel management in the 1960s and 1970s as part of the same overall process whereby problems of societal and macro-economic tensions are dealt with. This view is illustrated in Fig. 6.2 (p. 180) where state and managerial initiatives are shown as jointly handling the unintended consequences of the way labour is utilised in any industrial capitalist economy. The state often acts ahead of employers and uses legislation as a prompting mechanism to get them to play their part in containing problems which arise at the wider level of the national employment pattern.

The state tends to be ahead of individual employers largely because it is at the national level that many of the tensions inherent in the industrial capitalist employment system (pp. 158–66) become most clear. This may be as a result of worries about the level of inflation, the level of unemployment or the overall level of output. It may be the result of public worry about industrial disputes or it may be the outcome of pressures put on governments by groupings of employers, or by the labour movement. Alternatively, it may be a consequence of pressures and concerns about the justice of the way particular ethnic, age or gender groups are treated in the economic and labour sector.

To understand the role of the state in the sphere of employment we need some basic theory of the state. The state is most usefully seen as a set of institutions which include the government, parliament, civil service, educational and welfare apparatuses, police, military and judiciary. The state operates to maintain the overall social, political and economic system of which it is a part. It modifies or reforms that system to deal with tensions or conflicts which arise within it but, fundamentally, it strives to retain the integrity of that system. In societies of the type we are concerned with here this is a democratic industrial capitalist system. And, as Colin Crouch points out (1979), it is the pursuit of stability which is the clue to the ultimate motivation of state action in such societies and 'most of the time this is best served by securing the interests of the existing mode of production, because it is on that that prosperity seems to rest, and in a liberal democracy prosperity is usually crucial to social stability.'

As I argued at length in Chapter 5, the industrial capitalist type of economy has within it major tensions which have to be managed. The consequence of this is that ideological perspectives which see the involvement of the state in economic matters as state *interference* miss the point entirely. Although there is a valid and important debate about the appropriate level and nature of state involvement in the economy which will continue, there can be no doubt that state actions of a very significant kind are an inherent component of modern democratic societies. The state can only be seen as 'interfering' with the running of the economy in the same way that the bus driver can be understood to be 'interfering' with the operation of the bus whose throttle, brakes and steering wheel he or she manipulates.

An invaluable help in understanding the particular British context in which the state has involved itself in employment matters is Keith Middlemas's (1979) historical analysis of politics in industrial society. He argues that, earlier than in any other industrial country, British governments began to make the avoidance of crises their first priority. Throughout the twentieth century the state has increasingly practised the 'art of public management', extending its power to 'assess, educate, bargain with, appease or constrain the demands of the electorate'. Compromises were used to avoid crises in sensitive areas like wages and conditions, public order, immigration, unemployment and the position of women. The avoidance of a Hobbesian 'natural anarchy of competing wills' was achieved, not through the use of authority (there being a general decline of faith and deference here), but by the 'alternate gratification and cancelling out of the desires of large, well-organised, collective groups'. These groups were primarily those representing employers and employees.

Middlemas uses the term 'industrial politics' to refer to the fundamental instabilities which have been discussed here as underlying industrial capitalist societies. He suggests that in Britain the 'line of greatest social conflict, like the earthquake fault between continental plates, lay through industrial politics'. Employers' groups and the trade unions came, by the mid-1960s, to be treated almost like 'realms of the state'. This did not lead to what is often termed the 'corporate state' (which implies a complete cooptation of capital and labour into the state apparatus with market forces and class conflicts being overcome in a fully 'managed' economy). Instead, it led to a pattern of 'corporate bias': something like the bias in a wood in the game of bowls - a tendency to run to one side.

Following the Second World War, the state of equilibrium associated with the pattern of corporate bias became dependent on the state guaranteeing certain basic conditions: in particular, full employment, rising living standards and stable prices. And it was the first of these three which has increasingly been abandoned since the early 1970s. Middlemas suggests that this can be related to the tendency of both major political parties to move away from 'consensus' politics which appeared in the 1960s when 'party primacy' began to assert itself and the system of corporate bias, like an overloaded electrical circuit 'began to blow fuses'. The 1980s have seen a government operating with a powerful anti-corporatist rhetoric whilst still playing a major role in the steering of the economy and the labour practices which occur within it. In one sense, an ideologically based devotion to non-interference and the leaving to market forces of business and employment trends is, paradoxically, a decidedly powerful form of intervention. But the state policies followed through most of the 1980s have been significantly interventionist in many more ways than this.

This can be brought out very effectively – and in a way which indicates that similar underlying patterns are likely to be followed in the future – by adopting Alan Fox's (1979) notion of the four 'intensified search processes' which have been followed by successive governments of varying ideological stance in recent years to 'avert the political threat of continued economic failure'.

The first search area has been that for an effective incomes policy – whether or not the government of the time was willing to accept the formal label of 'incomes policy'. The search has seen initiatives ranging from the Prices and Incomes Act of 1966 through to the 'social contract' of the late 1970s and the government's guidelines and limits on public sector pay through most of the 1980s – limits which it has risked considerable disruption to maintain. The centrality of the level of incomes to national economic policy is such that no elected government is likely to abandon a significant interest in levels of remuneration, in either the absolute or the relative sense – especially in the public sector where the state itself is the employer.

The second search area has been one which resulted from mounting pressure to 'do something about the unions'. This saw the setting up of a Royal Commission on Trade Unions and Employers' Associations which reported in 1968, the ill-fated Labour government White Paper *In Place of Strife* (proposing compulsory strike balloting, 'cooling off periods', fines, etc.) and the Conservatives' Industrial Relations Act in the early 1970s. After a period in the later 1970s when legislation was introduced which tended to favour trade union interests, the 1980s have seen a series of laws which have not only restricted closed shop agreements and picketing practices, required secret ballots prior to strikes but have intervened in the internal practices of the trade unions themselves with regard to the appointment of officials and the maintenance of a political fund.

Different approaches to trade unions may be favoured by different governments in the future but we need to recognise the limits that are likely to be put on this by the evidence suggesting the general public popularity of many of these measures, even among people who belong to trade unions themselves (Worcester, 1984). The massive 'investment' of state resources made by the Conservative government to allow the National Coal Board to defeat the National Union of Mineworkers in the dispute of 1984–5 and their willingness actually to ban union membership in one large government establishment (the General Communications Headquarters at Cheltenham) may or may not be repeated. But the unwillingness, or the inability, of the potential opposition to these policies to prevent their being carried out is likely to encourage future government reluctance to allowing organised labour too great an opportunity to constrain the state's freedom to manoeuvre in its attempt to maintain overall national stability.

The third search area has been for ways of making good some of the deficiencies in the achievements of collective bargaining by 'enlarging the basic floor of individual employment rights'. The point of this, Fox suggested, was to make more amenable to orderly joint regulation 'issues which were manifestly becoming more contentious'. The legislative sequence which began with the Contracts of Employment Act of 1963 included the Redundancy Payments, Race Relations, Equal Pay, Sex Discrimination and Employment Protection Acts. The search also saw the establishment of Industrial Tribunals and the establishing of ACAS (the Advisory, Conciliation and Arbitration Service) which was put on a statutory basis in 1975 and was charged not only with helping to resolve disputes through conciliation and arbitration but with extending and reforming collective bargaining machinery in order to improve industrial relations. This function continues to exist and, although the governments of Margaret Thatcher have not been enthusiastic participants in this kind of search (as is seen, among other things, in their policy of weakening Wages Councils), they have trodden carefully in areas of discriminatory behaviour and would claim to be increasing individual 'rights' at work in moves like those restricting closed shops – even though it may be debated whether such measures improve industrial relations as such.

The fourth search is that for ways of mobilising and conserving labour resources through measures as varied as the passing of the Industrial Training and Health and Safety at Work Acts to the establishing of the Manpower Services Commission and the upgrading of technological education through the setting up of the Polytechnics and the encouraging of management education through the developing of prestigious Business Schools. The 1980s have seen a massive and increasing allocation by the state of resources to the Manpower Services Commission with the stated intention of training a workforce for the future. Whether one accepts that these measures function in this way or one sees them as an attempt to contain public revulsion at record levels of youth unemployment, it does support my general thesis that the state is, and will continue to be, caught up in a major involvement in labour and employment matters.

From government policies on matters directly relating to employment issues to policies on welfare provision, economic management, international affairs, the encouragement of technological innovation and education, there will inevitably continue to be a central and significant role played by the state in the context in which employing organisations will operate in the future. And insofar as state policy, through its sensitivity to the ballot box and to mid-term public and pressure-group opinion, reflects the wishes and preferences of the population at large so will the social values and choices of the members of society formally constrain the options of those managing employing organisations. Prime ministers will continue to perform, in part, as 'personnel director to the nation' as Winifred Marks (1978) put it in her review of government employment policies in the 1970s. She notes that the adoption of such a role was often against a declared intention not to interfere with workplace practices. Laissez-faire policies, suggested Marks, 'proved incompatible with effective government'. This, I suggest, will continue to be the case.

Personnel and employment practices

Although, for the reasons which have been suggested above, state and general social and political pressures on employing organisations are likely to continue, there is nevertheless a likelihood that managements in both the public and the private sectors will increasingly rather than decreasingly be given freedom to take those initiatives which will enable them to cope with a rapidly changing domestic and international context. Policies of privatising and 'liberalising' public enterprises may not be continued by future governments but it is unlikely that the state, whichever political grouping controls it, will adopt tight centralist control policies which would impair the ability of either state-owned or private organisations to react to changing circumstances. The increasingly recognised need for organisations to achieve a balance between predictability and flexibility will mean that few managements will, in the future, find themselves securely cushioned against environmental pressures.

Managers will need increasingly to consider the effectiveness of their policies and practices in terms of long-term survival. And the employment or 'behavioural' sphere will inevitably be central to this. Already, the concern with effectiveness among managers has been reflected in the interest which has been shown in studies which attempt to bring out the distinctiveness of those organisations which are viewed as outstanding in the terms of business performance. The best-selling status of the *In Search of Excellence* study (Peters and Waterman, 1982) is significant here. As we have seen (pp. 68–71), this suggests that the quality of the relationship between the organisation and its employees is at the heart of the features which distinguish the excellent companies. We should note, however, that the focus of the 'culture' of these companies is not on employee relations for their own sake. The stress on new styles of leadership and team-building is a stress that continually focusses attention on issues of *customer* satisfaction. Good employee relations are seen as a means to good customer relations and hence to healthy business performance and survival. They are not an end in themselves.

Another influential study of relatively effective business organisations is Rosabeth Kanter's (1983) *The Change Masters*. This stresses the importance of organisational adaptability in the light of a claim that world events – ranging from the rise of the oil powers to increased international competition and the problems of inflation – have disturbed the smooth working of corporate machines and threaten to overwhelm them. Organisations will need to 'rely on more and more of their people to make decisions on matters for which a routine response may not exist'. Part of the study attempts to compare 47 companies which were identified by an expert panel of 65 personnel directors as having the most progressive and forward-thinking human resource policies, with 47 companies which were not so nominated. The financial performance of these firms was compared over a twenty-year period and it is concluded that the companies with reputations for progressive human-resource practices were significantly better in long-term profitability and financial growth than their counterparts.

It is possible that the association between progressive personnel policies and business success seen in the Kanter study is the outcome of better performance leading to greater willingness to give time and resources to staffing issues rather than the other way round. But other parts of the study are interpreted by Kanter as showing that these practices were indeed encouraging innovation and hence effectiveness rather than following from them. The employment practices are not seen in isolation, however. They are combined in the more effective organisations with structures and cultures which Kanter describes as *integrative*. This is in contrast to the more conventional – and less innovative and effective – *segmentalist* organisations where actions, events and problems are 'compartmentalised' with 'each piece kept isolated from the others'. Successful organisations, suggests Kanter, have a close understanding of how 'the microchanges introduced by individual innovators relate to macrochanges or strategic reorientations'. This clearly corresponds with the emphasis made towards the end of Chapter 3 (pp. 81–5) on how managerial effectiveness is a matter of regularly relating small-scale detail to overall strategic questions.

The importance of the combination of a highly integrated organisation with the giving of scope to individual initiative which comes out of the American studies is also revealed in Goldsmith and Clutterbuck's (1984) comparison of British 'excellent' and not-so-excellent companies. The organisations with the 'winning streak' are characterised as having exceptionally clear definitions of aims and a determination to pursue these obsessively on the basis of a high level of loyalty and commitment among employees. In the same way that Kanter emphasises the contribution to business success of 'participative' styles of management, these British authors note the emphasis on 'involvement' of employees in the more effective organisations.

Generally, the studies of relatively high-performance business organisations seem to be suggesting that a vital ingredient of their success is the existence of a strong and clear culture in which individual employees 'think for themselves' but in a way which accords with corporate purposes. Participative styles are not, as Kanter points out, appropriate because they somehow improve 'the quality of working life' or even because they help 'motivation'. They are appropriate because they encourage innovation. In this way they make good business sense and we might say that, whatever rhetoric might accompany the following of such styles, these policies have little to do with philanthropy or managerial liberalism as such. They are simply one mode of managing the human aspect of organisations which helps make effective organisations which have to cope with the pressures of life in the latter part of the twentieth century.

The evidence supporting the relevance of apparently enlightened employment strategies to organisational effectiveness is not only to be found in best-selling studies of famous and outstanding business corporations. We can find a similar message in a quite different and relatively more modest type of investigation which was done to find out how different incentive or bonus payment schemes introduced in 63 British organisations contributed to organisational performance. The original theoretical position of Angela Bowey and her team (1982) was firmly in the tradition of contingency thinking (see above, pp. 60–3). That is, they were attempting to discover a pattern of 'fit' between particular types of incentive scheme and particular sets of organisational characteristics. However, the study was unable to find such a pattern. It did find that the circumstances of the organisations explained some of the variations in success *but these were almost irrespective of the type of payment system adopted*. The factors which appeared to be most relevant to the success of whichever scheme was adopted were, in fact, social and behavioural ones.

The most important factor recognised by three investigators was the extent of consultation about the scheme which had occurred prior to its introduction. This, we can fairly safely say, had little to do with the kind of wishful thinking of social scientists which was discussed in Chapter 1 (pp. 13) whereby 'findings' are made which accord with pre-existing ethical preferences. These results were, as the researchers make explicit, neither what they were looking for nor what they expected. And we can interpret these findings as fitting the general argument developed in Chapter 5 where it was suggested that any specific facet of employment or personnel policy has to be located within the overall employment strategy of the organisation. In this case of payment systems, it was not the particularities of the scheme adopted which made a difference to organisational effectiveness. It was how the implementing of the scheme fitted into the more general way in which the managements related to their employees. Where there had been a high level of consultation there was not only an increase in output but also an improvement in the quality of the products, a demonstration of more positive attitudes towards work and a greater willingness to accept subsequent manpower reductions.

Our mention here of manpower reductions in the context of discussing employment strategies which are in many ways 'employee-centred' is significant. The employment strategy cannot exist for its own sake. It has to be a component of the more general strategy of the organisation and thus, in simple terms, has to 'pay its way'. It has to contribute to the long-term survival of the organisation, something that is forcefully brought out in John Hunt's (1984) challenging discussion of 'the shifting focus' of the personnel management function.

Hunt envisages a future of continuing high levels of unemployment in which 'survival and adaptation will be traded off against unemployment as politically viable alternatives' which, in turn, means that 'tougher "hands on" survival management will mean tougher "hands on" personnel management'. Personnel managers will therefore become highly involved in 'exiting' employees, whether through redundancy, early retirement, or need for career change. Selection and appraisal processes will become very rigorous, especially for the managers themselves, who will be a small, highly pressured elite, and rewards generally will be much more closely related to performance. But all of this will occur within a highly integrated overall corporate process: instead of designing such practices as reward structures or training sessions in isolation, personnel managers will need to

> evolve and integrate the organisation's culture; to relate personnel practices to beliefs, to link each and every process of the recruitment, induction, training, appraisal, rewarding of employees to an overall set of articulated beliefs of that organisation.

In all this we can see an abandoning of the old 'either/or' terms in which personnel policies have traditionally been conceived – the choice either to 'care for' *or* 'control' the workforce, for instance. If there is the move we are envisaging here towards personnel management basing itself increasingly on what Shaun Tyson (1985) calls 'the business manager model' and less on the 'systems/reactive' and 'administrative/support' model, then we can expect to see a mixture of a ruthless attention to getting the best possible return out of those employed with what Goldsmith and Clutterbuck call a high level of 'integrity' in their relations with these employees. And if this seems like asking for the impossible from those designing employment strategies then perhaps we can see the point of Hunt's claim that management is more about vision and magic than science (cf. above pp. 30–2). Similarly, we can understand better the characteristics put at the top of his list of requirements of the personnel manager in the future by Gordon Lippit: a high tolerance for ambiguity and complexity, a strong sense of self and identity and 'a low need for public approbation and positive feedback' (Tugwell, 1984). Not surprisingly, the list continues with mention of a need for high conceptual skills and an ability to be comfortable with conflict!

Organisational shapes and staffing patterns

The type of general employment strategies and practices we have been envisaging for future organisations is very well characterised, in Peters and Waterman's terms, as being both 'loose' and 'tight'. The need for predictability and control is met at the same time as flexibility is achieved through at least some, if not all, employees being given space to innovate and take initiatives. The same principle is likely to apply to what Chapter 5 saw as a particular dimension of employment strategy: the ways in which organisations will be patterned. And closely associated with this is the way the workforce itself will be structured. First, however, we will look at organisational shapes.

The basic proposition we can state here is that the concern to balance predictability with flexibility and an ability to innovate will encourage organisations to favour 'decentralised' structures which retain a degree of strong 'centralisation' in some key respects.

Survey evidence suggests the popularity among key organisational decision-makers of decentralisation policies. A Henley College survey of 35 senior British business executives from large employers (*Personnel Management*, 1984) highlighted this trend and quoted one personnel director's statement that their objective of 'operating in devolved structures is to make profit centres autonomous, decisions local, relationships personal . . .'. A survey by the Institute of Personnel Management (Evans and Cowling, 1985), which looked at 50 private and public sector organisations found that a high proportion had undergone restructuring and rationalisation with a view to cutting employment costs, increasing productivity and, in the private sector cases, being more competitive in both home and overseas markets. And the major theme emerging from the organisational changes was 'a shift towards greater decentralisation of decision-making and to some extent a revival of the view that "small is beautiful" '. Many of the organisations studied reported that they had discovered shortcomings in the results of their policies during the 1970s of centralising decision-making based on the development of large and powerful corporate functions.

Generally, when both practitioners and writers distinguish between centralised and decentralised organisations, they have in mind the difference between a 'functional' structure in which the main grouping of managerial efforts is in terms of functions like production, personnel, sales and so on and a 'divisional' structure in which the organisation is broken down into relatively autonomous chunks based on some geographical, product or service logic. Each division is likely to have its own functional structure, although some of these will more closely be tied into the overall organisation's 'centre' than others. Finance or perhaps management development would be strong possibilities here. The decentralised structure is implemented in the hope of overcoming the tendency of large centralised structures to become slow and bureaucratic as significant decisions are regularly pushed upwards. Communications is believed to be generally slowed down in this way with the decision-makers at the 'centre' becoming remote from issues arising in the various workplaces and from markets or public service clients.

The renewed British interest in decentralisation is, in a sense, a revival of an old idea. The principles behind divisionalisation policies were brought out by Alfred Chandler (see above, p. 75) after having been championed in the United States by Alfred Sloan of General Motors in the 1920s and Ralph Cordiner of the General Electric Company in the 1950s. Such structures are, as Richard Vancil (1979) points out, now 'pervasive' in America. But Vancil's study very clearly brings out the fact that decentralisation is not simply a matter of restructuring into divisions or 'profit centres' and seeing effectiveness increase. A whole shift of management style is required. As Sloan himself realised, there are contradictions involved in this kind of structure and, as Vancil puts it, you are deliberately designing 'ambiguity' into the structure. In effect there has simultaneously to be both decentralisation and centralisation. Although you may indulge in the former, without the latter there is no organisation! Thus Sloan himself (1964) put as his main thesis the statement that 'good management rests on a reconciliation of centralisation and decentralisation, or "decentralisation with coordinated control"'.

Sloan's key principle brings us back to the 'loose-tight' notion and we can see the recently fashionable stress on organisational cultures as drawing attention to these as a qualitative feature of an organisation that can give 'centralisation within decentralisation'. Among the writers of the culture-excellence school (Ch. 3, pp. 66–71) we can see this perhaps most clearly in the analysis by Pascale and Athos (1982) of the Japanese Matsushita corporation where a strongly divisionalised organisation is held tightly together through a centralised emphasis on management development and deployment. Deal and Kennedy (1982), in their culture-oriented look at future structures, talk of 'atomized' organisations where small, task-focussed work units are bonded through 'strong cultural bonds' like molecules into a 'strong corporate whole'. Computer links will play an important role in this bonding.

Deal and Kennedy see in these trends a taking-up of the 'small is beautiful' theme which, they say, serves the needs of 'both business and people'. And they see the trend manifesting itself in other ways. They see 'clues' to the future in the increasing popularity of franchising operations, divestitures and spin-offs. A study by Kudla and McInish (1984) in the United States confirms this trend and argues that business managers have reacted to the merger fever of the 1960s and 1970s by seeing greater advantages in its opposite. Especially important here is the 'spin-off', a type of divestiture which leads to a large company splitting off part of its operation as a separate business. A similar trend, of growing importance in Britain, it is that towards the 'management buy-out' – a policy of allowing former company employees to buy and run as owner-managers that which they previously only managed (Wright & Coyne, 1985).

The leaders of the culture-excellence school, Peters and Waterman (1982), see the future application of their loose-tight principle as involving organisations resting on three pillars. The first is *stability* which will be achieved by there being a simple basic underlying form (usually a divisional structure) combined with a set of 'dominating values' or 'superordinate goals' and minimal or simplified 'interfaces'. The second pillar of *entrepreneurship* will be achieved by the 'chunking' of organisations into 'small is beautiful' units, 'cabals' and other problem-solving and implementation groups. And the third pillar, *habit-breaking*, will involve a willingness to indulge in regular reorganisation and experimentation. As divisions get big and bureaucratic they will be hived off into new ones.

A corresponding argument is put forward by Sethi, Namiki and Swanson (1984) as part of their alternative to the uncritical western adoption of Japanese management practices. They oppose the adopting of group-based systems which seek to gain employee loyalty to the organisation. Instead, they advocate a modifying of current organisational structures and practices away from bureaucratic and hierarchical approaches to 'more individualistic and less adversarial models'. They argue that managing the new type of 'high discretion employee' needs a 'more collegial style, where informed consent of the governed would become increasingly important'. This would be achieved through a 'cell-organisation' approach involving what they call a 'decentralised-centralisation' type of organisation structure. This is achieved with a system of values, or corporate culture, appropriate both to the environment and the values of individual employees. Interestingly, the British Empire is given as a major historical example of this phenomenon of decentralised-centralisation. Loose-tight organisation has a grand pedigree it would appear!

In what has been said here, and in this whole chapter so far, there has been a leaning towards what might be seen as 'universalistic' organisation or management thinking – something approaching the one-best-way philosophies which have been so heavily questioned (see Ch. 3, pp. 60–3). This is not completely inappropriate, insofar as there will always be a set of general propositions about managing and organising – at least for a given time and social order – which exist alongside principles which vary with organisational circumstances or 'contingencies' (above p. 60). And having made some general statements about overall trends in future employment strategies and organisational structures we now have to balance this with a recognition of the ways in which employers are likely increasingly to locate their employees in different groups which they treat differently. These may be groups which are, in effect, treated with different 'employment sub-strategies'.

In Chapter 5 it was argued that there is a range of contingent factors which contribute to how 'problematic or non-problematic' a management perceives its workforce and hence influence the type of employment strategy which is adopted (pp. 166–70, esp Fig. 5.2). But it was also argued that these contingencies, which make some employee groups more 'central' to long-term effectiveness than others, can also lead to different approaches being applied to different sections of the workforce. Totally consistent with this model is the very important research and analysis carried out by the Institute of Manpower Studies (1984) of some key common themes underlying the employment plans of British companies.

These investigators recognise among employers a perceived need to achieve a permanent reduction in labour cost, a wariness about overcommitment in terms of employment and investment, a desire to be able to respond quickly to technological changes (in products and working methods) and a belief that pressures towards reduced working hours should be met through new approaches to restructuring working time. Employers therefore wish to achieve three types of flexibility through their employment strategies: *functional flexibility* whereby people can easily be deployed between tasks and activities, *numerical flexibility* whereby the 'headcount' can be readily expanded or reduced in line with changes in demand, and *financial flexibility* whereby labour costs can always be kept to a minimum (mainly through control of relativities rather than overall pushing down of wages) and rewards kept closely in line with the work being done (through assessment-based pay systems rather than traditional rate-for-the-job structures).

The study suggests that a new employment model is emerging. This is based on a key core-periphery split. Organisations will maintain a *core group* of permanently employed staff of a 'primary labour group' type (see above pp. 147–8). These will have long-term careers within the organisation's internal labour market on a single-status basis (abolishing old works-staff distinctions). They will be skilled workers, managers, designers, technical sales staff and the like but will accept, in return for their security, an acceptance of functional flexibility – a willingness to abandon craft and discipline demarcations and to be prepared for retraining and career shifts. A *first peripheral group* of 'secondary labour market' type will also consist of full-time employees but their security and career potential will be far less. These will be in clerical, assembly, supervisory or testing jobs which can more readily be filled from external labour markets. Numerical and financial flexibility is achieved here through this closer tie to external labour markets.

To give additional numerical and functional flexibility there will be a *second peripheral group* of part-timers, people on short-term contracts or job-sharing and public-subsidy trainees. Finally, specialised tasks, sometimes highly skilled ones like systems analysis and sometimes simple ones like cleaning, can be 'put out' through using agency temporaries, sub-contracting or outsourcing through such practices as 'teleworking' or 'networking', whereby people working from home link into the organisation via information technology systems.

All these changes have considerable implications for the whole future of society as well as for employing organisations. Organisational effectiveness is likely to increase in the middle to long term. But, because these labour market issues closely relate to patterns of class, gender and ethnic divisions in society, we must recognise that organisational effectiveness in the very long term will be dependent on a degree of social and cultural change which will prevent these employment practices so increasing social divisiveness and conflict that the organisations will no longer be able to function within a split and rancorous society. These are issues which will inevitably become important at the state level discussed earlier. But they will have to be handled by those running work organisations as well as by politicians. And the same can be said about the impact of the new microelectronic technologies which are only just beginning to show the impact that they can make.

The implications of new information technologies

In many ways it would be wise to be sceptical about the frequent and common talk of 'revolutions' in the ways in which we use technology. For decades a 'computer' or 'automation' revolution has been talked of and no major impact on society has been visible. However, it is becoming clear that the latest trends in the application of microelectronic technology can potentially have a very major impact indeed in the quantity and quality of employment that is going to be available. The current developments in electronics, using ever smaller and more compact micro-processor 'chips' in place of the older valves, transistors and printed circuits are not essentially 'new'. They are refinements of the computer phenomenon which has been with us for more than a generation. But it is their potential impact which justifies the epithet 'new'. And this follows from the emerging degree of cheapness, speed, reliability, smallness and, above all, breadth of application which is being achieved.

The breadth of application of 'new' microelectronics not only means a whole new and developed range of goods ranging from 'chip-controlled' kettles to chip-controlled door-locks and motor-car engines, it means an automating or partial-automating of tasks across all sectors of employment. In manufacturing there are robots and other computer-controlled machine tools and processes as well as the use of computers in designing, draughting and work progressing. In the service sector there are applications in fields as diverse as retailing – where barcoded products are not only priced by computer at the 'point of sale' but are stock-controlled and monitored by the electronic system – to financial institutions where innovations ranging from cash dispensers and electronic funds transfer are taking place, to medicine where 'expert systems' can help in patient diagnosis. And in the world of administration and office work there are extensive applications ranging from word-processing and information storage to electronic mail and computerised data analysis and selection.

Despite the fact that the degree of automation of both physical and mental work within these various areas can radically change jobs, the greatest impact is likely to come from the integrating of what have previously been treated as separate sectors. Through the electronic networks which will connect-up future organisations and link together their component parts, learning, research, design, manufacturing, administration, product and service-delivery will be connected up in a way which can not only abolish existing distinctions between office and factory, works and staff, service-delivery and administration but even blur those between home and work – with electronic 'outworking' – and, in many areas, managers and workers. The degree to which coordination, information monitoring and processing can be assisted by machines means that a large proportion of existing management roles can disappear.

Whilst it is important and necessary to try to envisage what might and can occur to employment with the spread of new technology, it is also wise to keep our feet firmly on the ground and balance speculation with attention to evidence about what is occurring at present. The limited evidence that we have leads us to conclude that on the *quantity* and distribution of employment there has been, as yet, little discernible effect. And on the issue of the *quality* of work with new technology, the evidence suggests that we have an important degree of choice with regard to how we proceed. Let us briefly consider the quantity issue first.

The main problem that faces us in considering the impact that technological innovations have had so far on the numbers and distribution of jobs is that a great deal of workforce restructuring has occurred for reasons largely unconnected with technical change. When organisations are generally 'rationalising', 'slimming' and 'streamlining' it becomes very difficult indeed to detect what degree of job loss and change can be attributed to technology. Also, the picture is complicated by the fact that in the early stages of a technical change there could occur a temporary increase in employment levels. This might be brought about by organisations maintaining older systems alongside the new whilst the new systems are 'run in' and have their teething problems dealt with. I suggest that this effect is especially likely in office systems where shrewd office managers frequently maintain their manual or paper-based clerical systems until such time as they decide they can 'trust the computers' not to lose or corrupt vital data.

In spite of these problems, we do have the attempt by the Policy Studies Institute to quantify the extent of job loss brought about by new technology (Northcott and Rogers, 1982). This suggested that in the first two years of the decade only 5 per cent of the job losses occurring in manufacturing could be attributed to technical change. However, the study also shows how limited the use of microprocessor technology was by this stage in Britain. It may be some time yet before the full impact occurs, and how great this will be will, of course, depend on the extent to which British organisations innovate technically. But since survival for many of them will depend on such innovation, the effect will inevitably be considerable. However many new jobs may be created by new technology making possible new products and services, we must recognise that the labour-saving implications of technologies whose rationale is to automate both mental and physical work are so considerable that the effect is bound to be a major one.

But what about the impact of new technology on those who will be working with it? In Chapter 5 (pp. 143-9) we encountered an influential type of analysis which suggested that the logic of the 'labour process' in capitalist societies is one in which we can expect employers to use any opportunity to down-grade and de-skill the work of employees in order to make them more easily controllable and exploitable. On this reckoning, we would expect to see technical change widely bringing about the reduction of work experience to machine-minding and machine-feeding. The Taylorian dream of management experts taking all choice and discretion away from workers and into their own orbit is made possible. And, indeed, we must take this possibility seriously. To have a relatively limited workforce who can be cheaply employed, easily trained, readily recruited or dispensed with and who have little bargaining power or 'industrial muscle' can significantly meet the central requirement of future organisations to have a *flexible* workforce. However, what we are considering here is only one aspect of the type of labour force flexibility discussed earlier.

The other aspect of workforce flexibility considered earlier was that whereby employees are encouraged to be willing to think for themselves or take initiatives to cope either with crises or technical problems. This requirement would tend to lead employers to avoid using new technology to deskill and down-grade jobs. In practice, of course, we can expect there to be a mixture of employment sub-strategies, in accordance with the trends discussed in the previous section. However, there is still a variety of possible ways in which jobs can be affected, as some important research evidence shows.

A number of studies of computerised numerical control machines (CNC machines) - a key machine-tool development in engineering - have been carried out and show that the way these are introduced and the associated jobs designed can lead to *either* an enhancement or a down-grading of the work of the people involved (Jones, 1982; Rosenbrock, 1982; Wilkinson, 1983). It is possible, on the one hand, to remove from the workers most of their control over the machining process, putting the programming, for instance, entirely in the hands of specialists located away from the workshop. Alternatively, managements in some circumstances may choose to involve the engineering workers in the implementation of the new system and, to some degree, to retrain and reskill them so that they play a part in programming their 'own machines'. Case studies collected by Boddy and Buchanan (1985) show that such choices exist across a range of industries. New technology decisions, say these researchers, can either 'distance' employees from their tasks, so limiting the contribution they can make, or they can bring about 'complementarity' between the employee and their job. This, they say, enables full use to be made of both technical capabilities and human skills.

Despite the existence of this kind of choice of strategy in the introduction of new technology, we have to note from our knowledge of organisation theory that managerial choices are always made in a context of 'contingent' pressures. Again we must consider the set of contingent factors discussed in Chapter 5 (pp. 166–71) as influencing managerial choices of employment strategy. And an important study by John Child and his colleagues (1984) shows how the combination of both the contingent type of factor and the management values factor represented in our earlier model are brought to bear on cases of microelectronic technical innovation in service industries. Considerable variation was noted in the way new technology altered the quality of the work being done by different groups in hospitals, banking and retailing.

As these authors say, a management may believe in 'the value of enlisting workers' commitment to managerial objectives' and it may desire to 'develop human capital'. Both of these would discourage a job 'degradation' policy. But so would a technically contingent factor such as a need for workers to have sufficient skill to cope with work processes which are 'variable and uncertain'. And there is also the crucial political type of contingency whereby some workers are more able than others to *resist* degradation. This can arise from the workers' being collectively organised, from their scarcity value on the labour market or from their key position in the production process. But there may also be ideological factors here too. Consumer preferences for personal service may, for example, justify the preservation of employee discretion and, very importantly, the members of some occupations may be able to sustain claims that they have an exclusive right to conduct certain activities 'according to their expert discretion' – even with work that can be automated.

The hypertension clinic consultant studied provides a strong example of the possibility of employee discretion's being maintained. This individual's professional status and his care to maintain control over the introduction and use of automation protected his job from the possible downgrading which could have occurred. Other workers, such as laboratory technicians, bank cashiers and retail staff, who were less involved in the selection, development and application of new technologies, were, on the other hand, observed to have lost elements of skill and control.

The future for the quality of work experience with new technology is, then, to some extent open. However, with electronically assisted control and coordination, there is the potential for organisational processes to occur at a speed hardly envisaged before. And, if this is combined with the increasing flexibility of reprogrammable manufacturing and administrative systems, we can see that electronics provide the technological basis for the overall future type of organisation which we have been considering throughout this chapter: one which combines an emphasis on control and predictability with an emphasis on flexibility in order to respond effectively to a challenging environment. We saw, in the previous section, how this might be combined with structural and employment patterns to give 'human flexibility' in future organisations. And we now move on to consider trends in one aspect of employment behaviour in Britain which has frequently been seen as a major source of inflexibility: employment or 'industrial' relations.

Industrial relations

A number of developments which have occurred in the 1980s could well lead us to expect employers to be overcoming the trade union limits which have been put on their 'managerial prerogative' by adopting an aggressive or 'macho' style of industrial relations which is aimed at crushing collective employee representation. The high and increasing levels of unemployment could encourage this expectation as could the effects of government legislation on industrial relations and trade unions. Similarly, falling memberships of unions and the relatively weak position of the Labour party, together with a growing confidence among managers about their 'right to manage', could be expected to invite a concerted employer challenge to organised labour. However, we can apply the same principles which we applied to the issue of deskilling under new technology to the area of industrial relations. It suggests that the picture is by no means as straightforward as might be expected.

A major attack on the trade unions and an undermining of the influence of employee representatives in workplaces could clearly help managers achieve the first of the two types of employment flexibility we have been examining. The size and cost of the labour force can much more quickly be adjusted, for instance, if there is no need to get involved in collective bargaining or be in any danger of being collectively challenged over payments, working arrangements or manning levels. But to attack those institutions which employees have built up over many years as a defence against employer exploitation (whether pragmatically as a kind of insurance policy or as an expression of principled democratic representation) is to invite such a level of distrust and resentment as to preclude the second kind of flexibility – that whereby employees are willing to take initiatives which help the employer and to work enthusiastically and cooperatively to cope with changing circumstances. Inevitably, there will be certain organisational circumstances in which employers will be happy to take this kind of risk to gain the first type of flexibility. But there will be other situations in which employers will be reluctant either to invite resentment by attacking collective organisation or to lose the important channel of communication which the union system can provide.

What approach would our conceptual analysis lead us to expect organisations to take to industrial relations in the future, then? Given that many organisations will wish to maintain both types of flexibility, we can expect to see them maintaining relationships with trade unions where they exist and, at least with their core workers, combining the union channel of contact with employees with other direct and often 'consultative' means of relating. Unions will be respected but 'kept in their place': the management-union or 'industrial relations' relationship being only one facet of management-employee or 'employee relations' contact. Where possible, employers will encourage trends towards single-union representation or, at least, to works-committee type arrangements where different union groups put their being employed by the same organisation before their being members of particular unions.

Away from the core or primary groups of employees, we can expect to see somewhat different approaches to trade unions. Because the first of our two types of flexibility is often more important here than the second, we can expect there to be a greater willingness to risk antagonistic relationships with organised labour. Two types of strategy are possible. The first is one in which union representation is systematically resisted or, if inevitable, is minimised. The second is one where more-or-less arms-length bargaining with trade union representatives becomes a central feature of generally arms-length relations with employees. The management do deals with union representatives who are left to pass them on to their members.

This general analysis does not mean that trade union representation, even if kept within limits that suit managements, is going to be welcome in all future employing organisations. Those organisations which have in the past resisted unionisation through the use of 'sophisticated paternalist' employment strategies (Fox, 1974) – in which employees are taught that the benefits they enjoy are better than those which unionisation could achieve – are likely to continue with this policy. And it may well be adopted by newer organisations, especially those in the advanced technology sector. But, in spite of the fact that such policies do seem to be favoured by many of the, largely American-owned, high-tech companies which have opened plants in places like Scotland's 'silicon glen', it is instructive to note the policies tending to be adopted by Japanese companies establishing themselves in Britain. These are organisations which we would expect, from their highly authoritarian attitudes and involvement with 'company unions' at home in Japan, to be very resistant to British trade unions. However, they appear to favour bargaining relationships with single but established trade unions, albeit keeping the union link as only one dimension of their general employment relations policy. This is directly in line with what I am suggesting will be a fairly typical future pattern of employment relations between employers and 'core' staff.

Brown and Sisson (1984), in their review of future possibilities in British industrial relations, foresee a similar pattern to that envisaged here. They note that even the most aggressive companies have begun to see the need for a much greater degree of employee commitment if international competition is going to be matched. They therefore expect there to be 'much more emphasis on individual personnel policies and a considerable increase in the use of quality circles, briefing groups, business and company councils and the like'. This, Brown and Sisson argue, will generally be accompanied by continuing relationships with trade unions. There will not be a move towards a highly formal or 'constitutional' type of bargaining but a maintenance of the British tradition of 'informality'.

The research evidence which we have of emerging industrial or employment relations trends supports this type of analysis. The major studies of industrial relations developments which had occurred in the 1970s (the Warwick survey, Brown, 1981; and the DE/PSI/SSRC survey, Daniel and Millward, 1983) showed a growth of workplace union activity and the acceptance by managements of increased shop steward arrangements, closed shops, check-off facilities and agreed procedures to deal with issues ranging from pay and conditions to grievance handling. But, very significantly, the latter study (which covered public and private sectors) noted an increase in joint consultative committees, alongside the more developed management-union arrangements. It was found that the number of Works Consultative Councils which had been introduced since a similar 1973 survey outnumbered those which had ceased by a 9:1 ratio. This is significant, because it marks a change of direction. The previous pattern had been one in which *consultative* arrangements had been declining as *bargaining* arrangements increased their scope.

Eric Batstone's (1984) follow-up to the large Warwick survey of industrial relations in manufacturing shows that, in spite of all the factors which might lead us to expect otherwise, there has been no major attempt in the 1980s to reduce union influence. Such strategies had been followed in about a fifth of the plants surveyed, but these were cases where there were especially acute economic difficulties and where shop steward organisation was particularly strong. And, in these cases, the policy appears to have been one of reducing shop steward influence down to the level of what is normal elsewhere rather than attempting to remove it. The most widely reported change in organisations' approach to employee relations was one towards attempts to increase employee involvement. This was mentioned in 47 per cent of cases. And the policy does not appear to be associated with attempts to reduce general union influence. In accordance with my employment strategy model (pp. 166–71) however, it is associated with relatively high labour costs and a relatively well-developed personnel function. The manifestations of this 'consultative' trend include systems of employee reports, briefing groups, quality circles and autonomous workgroups.

A further study of large manufacturing organisations in Britain, carried out in 1984 (Edwards, 1985), shows concerted attempts by managements to make major changes to working practices. But these are clearly aimed primarily at increasing efficiency rather than at reducing trade union activity as such. Instead, there is clear evidence of a growing interest in joint consultation. Consultative committees existed in 78 per cent of establishments and 20 per cent of the organisations having them had introduced them over the previous three years. The impact of this should not be exaggerated and neither should the evidence of this survey that nearly two-thirds of the chief executives surveyed described their overall policy or 'philosophy' of labour relations in terms reflecting a desire to achieve employee commitment. Nevertheless, we should perhaps note that these responses came not from personnel managers but from the top general managers of the organisations, where there has been less of a tradition of talking in such terms.

Generally, it would appear that employment strategies, at least in the especially competition-prone private sector, are very much secondary components of wider organisational strategies. An attitude friendly to or hostile to trade unions or an attitude for or against employee involvement is more dependent on what is perceived to be most appropriate for efficiency and effectiveness of the whole organisation rather than a matter of basic principle or a sign of a 'macho' need to celebrate managerial dominance. Such an impression is gained from both these broad surveys of industrial relations practice and from more specific studies such as those on the introduction of new technologies. Sheila Rothwell (1984b), for example, noted from her study that, although non-unionised companies tended to have a more explicit employee-centred philosophy, there were signs of unionised organisations giving increased attention to 'direct communication'. In some cases, it appeared that the experience of implementing change itself had been an impetus to changing the 'industrial relations wisdom' whereby managing directors and personnel managers stress the importance of communication. And a study by Annette Davies (1984) suggests why, in part, this may be occurring.

Davies shows a tendency for trade union representatives who

had been involved with managements in joint 'problem-solving' over introducing new technology to be markedly more positive in their attitudes to information technology than those who had been less involved. Yet, it is very important to note that this study shows that the unions were consistently failing to achieve the kinds of substantive demands they were making for such things as increased holidays, shorter working hours, earlier retirement and job-sharing. Neither did they appear to be effective at preventing job losses. Generally, as Davies concludes, 'the design and choice of technology are still unquestionably managerial prerogatives'.

The trend towards somewhat more employee-oriented employment strategies and the reluctance overtly to attack organised labour, we can conclude, has nothing to do with any surrender of managerial control. It is quite the opposite. It is a reflection of a reasoned managerial strategy: one of coping with change and a challenging environment by achieving flexibility in the supply and cost of labour, on the one hand, and flexibility in the attitudes and willingness to cooperate of certain employees on the other. And a key part of this is likely to be a managerial attempt to abolish the traditional concept of 'industrial relations'. This is something which 'belongs to the '50s and must be consigned to the dustbin' according to the Institute of Personnel Management's Vice-President for Employee Relations (IPM Digest, 1985). Bill Mitchell goes on to argue that the old pattern of 'IR' being about containing the unions and 'ER' about looking after communications has to be replaced by a completely integrated approach to employee relations. This would involve a stress on consultation and communications within an 'enabling framework of agreements'.

And in the end...

The social scientific observer – however great their conceptual sophistication and knowledge of research findings – can only talk of what might occur. Like any other informed commentator who does their best to examine theories and practice in a spirit of critical commonsense and constructive scepticism, they may still get it wrong. Whatever we may predict, the politicians, managers, employees, unions, owners and consumers may act to make things turn out otherwise.

Nevertheless, to end on a positive and optimistic note, I will return to one new direction which, I trust, will continue to be followed: a trend towards a more sensible and healthy relationship between theory and practice in the sphere of management, organisation and employment policy. I would like to think that the social or 'behavioural' scientists are embracing what I dare to call a 'new realism'. This is not a matter of these academic analysts abandoning their traditional preferences for open, participative managerial approaches, job redesign, integrative organisational styles and sophisticated personnel policies. And it is not a matter of their turning to comfort and assist those engaged in crude manipulation of organisational employees. It is, rather, a recognition that if they are going to continue the traditional association of the applied social sciences with progressive employment policies then they are going to have to demonstrate to practitioners that such policies make sense in terms of the long-term effectiveness of organisations struggling to cope with a rapidly changing world.

To be at all influential, social scientists will need better theories and more rigorously conducted research studies than those upon which they have often depended. This is occurring, as I hope I have shown in this book. And this thinking will have to continue to be communicated in a more measured and less fervent or evangelical manner than it has often been previously. In the end, it will not be evidence from dubious research projects like the Hawthorne experiments or Herzberg's motivational researches that will convince managers. Nor will it be grandiose and suspect theories of human nature like those of Maslow that will make managers think hard about how they treat employees.

In the end, managers will discover for themselves what works. But the social scientific researchers, writers and teachers can greatly help in this by systematically observing, reviewing, appraising and reflecting back to practitioners a conceptually coherent account of what leads to managerial and organisational effectiveness. What is needed is a dialogue. And the key to achieving this is the following of those two principles which are followed by effective managers and effective scientists alike: the application to problems of critical commonsense thinking and the adoption of an attitude of constructive scepticism towards existing ideas and practices.

Bibliography

Adair, J. (1968) *Training for Leadership*, London: Macdonald.

Adams, J. S. (1963), 'Towards an understanding of inequity', *Journal of Abnormal and Social Psychology*, 67: 422–36.

Adams, J. S. (1965), 'Inequality in social exchange', in Berkovitz, L. ed., *Advances in Experimental Social Psychology*, vol. 2, New York: Academic Press.

Akinmayowa, J. T. (1980), 'Relationship of personnel managers to others', *Personnel Review*, 9: 4, 33–6.

Alderfer, C. P. (1972) *Existence, Relatedness and Growth*, New York: Free Press.

Aldrich, H. E. (1979), *Organisations and Environment*, Englewood Cliffs, N. J.: Prentice-Hall.

Aldrich, H. E. and Pfeffer, J. (1976), 'Environments and organisations', in Inkeles, Colman & Smelser, eds, *Annual Review of Sociology*, 2.

Anthony, P.D. (1977) *The Ideology of Work*, London: Tavistock.

Anthony, P. and Crichton, A. (1969) *Industrial Relations and the Personnel Specialists*, London: Batsford.

Armstrong, M. (1984), *A Handbook of Personnel Management Practice* (2nd ed), London: Kogan Page.

Babbage, C. (1832), *On the Economy of Machinery and Manufacture*, London: Charles Knight.

Bailey, J. (1983), *Job Design and Work Organisation*, Englewood Cliffs, N. J.: Prentice-Hall.

Bain, G. S., ed. (1983) *Industrial Relations in Britain*, Oxford: Blackwell.

Baldamus, W. (1961) *Efficiency and Effort*, London: Tavistock.

Baritz, L. (1960), *The Servants of Power*, New York: Wiley.

Barnard, C. I. (1938), *The Functions of the Executive*, Cambridge, Mass: Harvard University Press.

Barron, I. and Curnow, R. (1979), *The Future with Microelectronics*, London: Pinter.

Batstone, E. (1980), 'What have personnel managers done for industrial relations?', *Personnel Management*, June.

Batstone, E. (1984), *Working Order: Workplace industrial relations over two decades*, Oxford: Blackwell.

Batstone, E., Ferner, A. and Terry, M. (1983), *Consent and Efficiency*, Oxford: Blackwell.

Beaumont, P. and Deaton, D. (1980), 'Personnel management in the management hierarchy', *Management Decision*, Winter.

Bendix, R. (1963), *Work and Authority in Industry*, New York: Harper & Row.

Bennett, R. (1981), *Managing Personnel and Performance*, London: Hutchinson.

Benson, I. and Lloyd, J. (1983), *New Technology and Industrial Change*, London: Kogan Page.

Berger, P. L. and Luckman, T. (1971), *The Social Construction of Reality*, Harmondsworth: Penguin.

Bettelheim, B. (1976), *On the Uses of Enchantment: The Meaning and Importance of Fairy Tales*, New York: Knopf.

Bjorn-Anderson, N., Earl, M., Holst, O. and Munford, G. eds (1982), *Information Society: for richer for poorer*, Dordrecht: North Holland Publishing Company.

Blackler, F. and Shimmin, S. (1984), *Applying Psychology in Organisations*, London: Methuen.

Blau, P. M. (1970), 'A formal theory of differentiation in organisations', *American Sociological Review*, 35: 201–18.

Blau, P. M. and Schoenherr, R. A. (1971), *The Structure of Organisations*, New York: Basic Books.

Blauner, R. (1964), *Alienation and Freedom*, Chicago: University of Chicago Press.

Boddy, D. and Buchanan, D. (1985), 'New Technology with a human face', *Personnel Management*, April.

Bowey, A. *et al.* (1982), *Effects of Incentive Payment Systems in the U.K. 1977–80*, London: Department of Employment, Research Paper 36.

Bradford, D. L. and Cohen, A. R. (1984), *Managing for Excellence*, New York: Wiley.

Braverman, H. (1974), *Labor and Monopoly Capitalism*, New York: Monthly Review Press.

Brayfield, A. H. and Crockett, J. M. (1955), 'Employee attitudes and employee performance', *Psychological Bulletin*, 52: 284–90.

Broms, H. and Gahmberg, H. (1982), *Mythology in Management Culture*, Helsinki School of Economics.

Brown, J. A. C. (1954) *The Social Psychology of Industry*, Harmondsworth: Penguin.

Brown, W. ed. (1981), *The Changing Contours of British Industrial Relations*, Oxford: Blackwell.

Brown, W. and Sisson, K. (1984), 'Current trends and future possibilities', in Poole *et al.*

Buchanan, D. and Boddy, D. (1982) *Organisations and the Computer Age*, Farnborough, Hants: Gower.

Buchanan, D. A. and Huczynski, A. A. (1985), *Organisational Behaviour: an introductory text*, Englewood Cliffs, N.J.: Prentice-Hall.

Burns, A. (1984), *New Information Technology*, London: Wiley.

Burns, T. (1961), 'Micropolitics', *Administrative Science Quarterly*, 6.

Burns, T. and Stalker, G. M. (1961), *The Management of Innovation*, Oxford: Pergamon.

Burns, T. (1977), *The BBC: public institution and private world*, London: Macmillan.

Burowoy, M. (1979), *Manufacturing Consent*, Chicago: University of Chicago Press.

Campanis, P. (1970), 'Normlessness in management', in Douglas, J. ed., *Deviance and Respectability*, New York: Basic Books.

Carey, A. (1967), 'The Hawthorne Studies: a radical criticism', *American Sociological Review*, 32.

Carlson, S. (1951), *Executive Behaviour: A study of the workload and the working methods of managing directors*, Stockholm: Strombergs.

Chandler, A. D. (1962), *Strategy and Structure*, Cambridge, Mass.: M.I.T. Press.

Chandler, A. D. (1977), *The Visible Hand*, Cambridge Mass.: Harvard University Press.

Channon, D. (1973), *The Strategy & Structure of British Enterprise*, Cambridge, Mass.: Harvard University Press.

Cherns, A. B. (1972), 'Personnel management and the social sciences', *Personnel Review*, 1: 4–11.

Child, J. (1969), *British Management Thought*, London: Allen & Unwin.

Child, J. (1972), 'Organisational structure, environment and performance', *Sociology*, 6: 2–22.

Child, J. ed. (1973), *Man and Organisation*, London: Allen & Unwin.

Child, J. (1984), *Organisation* (2nd edition), London: Harper & Row.

Child, J., Fores, M., Glover, I. and Lawrence, P., (1983), 'A price to pay? Professionalism & work organisation in Britain and W. Germany', *Sociology*, 17, 1.

Child, J. & Mansfield, R. (1972), 'Technology, size & organisational structure', *Sociology*, 6: 369–93.

Child, J., Loveridge, R., Harvey, J. and Spencer, A. (1984), 'Microelectronics and the quality of employment in services', in Marstrand, P., ed. (1984).

Clegg, S. and Dunkerley, D. (1980), *Organisation, Class and Control*, London: Routledge & Kegan Paul.

Cleverley, G. (1971), *Managers and Magic*, London: Longman.

Clutterbuck, D. and Hill, R. (1981), *The Re-making of Work*, London: Grant McIntyre.

Coch, L. and French, J. R. P. (1948), 'Overcoming resistance to change', *Human Relations*, 1: 512–32.

Cohen, M. D., March, J. G. and Olsen, J. P. (1972), 'A garbage can model of organisational choice', *Administrative Science Quarterly*, 17, 1: 1–25.

Cotgrove, S., Dunham, J. and Vamplew, C. (1971), *The Nylon Spinners*, London: Allen & Unwin.

Crouch, C. (1979), 'The State, capital and liberal democracy', in Crouch, C., ed., *State and Economy in Contemporary Capitalism*, London: Croom Helm.

Crozier, M. (1964), *The Bureaucratic Phenomenon*, London: Tavistock.

Cummings, L. L. and Staw, B. M. (1981), *Research in Organisational Behaviour*, Vol. 3, Greenwich, Conn.: JAI Press.

Cyert, R. M. & March, J. G. (1963), *A Behavioural Theory of the Firm*, Englewood Cliffs, N. J.: Prentice-Hall.

Daito, E. (1979), 'Management & labour: the evolution of employer-employee relations in the course of industrial development', in Nakagawa (1979).

Daniel, W. W. (1973), 'Understanding employee behaviour in its context', in Child, J., ed. (1973).

Daniel, W. W. (1983), 'Who handles personnel issues in British industry?', *Personnel Management*, December: 25-7.

Daniel, W. W. and Milward, N. (1983), *Workplace Industrial Relations in Britain*, London: Heinemann.

Davies, A. (1984), 'Management–union participation during microtechnological change', in Warner, M., ed. (1984).

Davis, L. and Taylor, J. (1979), *The Design of Jobs* (2nd ed.), Santa Monica, California: Goodyear.

Davis, L. E., Canter, R. R. and Hoffman, J. (1955), 'Current job design criteria', *Journal of Industrial Engineering*, 6, 2: 5-11.

Deal, T. E. and Kennedy, A. A. (1982), *Corporate Cultures: the rites and rituals of corporate life*, Reading, Mass.: Addison-Wesley.

Doeringer, P. B. and Piore, M. J. (1971), *Internal Labor Markets and Manpower Analysis*, Lexington, Mass.: D. C. Heath.

Drucker, P. (1961), *The Practice of Management*, London: Mercury Books.

Dubin, R. (1956), 'Industrial workers' worlds', *Social Problems*, 3: 131-42.

Dubin, R., Champoux, J. E. and Porter, L. W. (1975), 'Central life interests and organisational commitment of blue-collar and clerical workers', *Administrative Science Quarterly*, 20: 411-21.

Dunn, S. and Gennard, J. (1984), *The Closed Shop in British Industry*, London: Macmillan.

Earl, M. J. (1983), *Perspectives on Management*, Oxford University Press.

Edwards, R. (1979), *Contested Terrain*, London: Heinemann.

Edwards, P. and Scullion, H. (1982), *The Social Organisation of Industrial Conflict*, Oxford: Blackwell.

Edwards, P. (1985), 'Myth of the Macho manager', *Personnel Management*, April.

Ellis, T. and Child, J. (1973), 'Placing stereotypes of the manager into perspective', *Journal of Management Studies*, 10.

Emery, F. E. and Thorsud, E. (1969), *Form & Content in Industrial Democracy*, London: Tavistock.

Etzioni, A. (1961), *A Comparative Analysis of Complex Organisations*, New York: Free Press.

Evans, A. and Cowling, A. (1985), 'Personnel's part in organisation restructuring', *Personnel Management*, January.

Fayol, H. (1949, orig. 1916), *General and Industrial Management*, London: Pitman.

Festinger, L. (1957), *A Theory of Cognitive Dissonance*, Evanston, Ill.: Row, Peterson.

Fidler, J. (1981), *The British Business Elite*, London: Routledge & Kegan Paul.

Fiedler, F. E. (1967), *A Theory of Leadership Effectiveness*, New York: McGraw-Hill.

Fiedler, F. E. (1977), 'Validation and extension of the contingency model of leadership effectiveness', *Psychological Bulletin*, 26: 128–48.

Flanders, A. (1964), *The Fawley Productivity Agreements*, London: Faber.

Fores, M. and Glover, I. (1978), 'The British Disease: professionalism', *The Times Higher Education Supplement*, 24 February.

Forester, T. (1980), *The Microelectronic Revolution*, Oxford: Blackwell.

Foulkes, F. K. (1975), 'The expanding role of the personnel function', *Harvard Business Review*, 53, 2.

Fox, A. (1966), 'From welfare to organisation', *New Society*, 17: 14–16.

Fox, A. (1974), *Beyond Contract: work, power and trust relations*, London: Faber.

Fox, A. (1979), 'Labour in a new era of law', *New Society*, 1 March.

Fox, A. (1985), *History and Heritage: the social origins of the British industrial relations system*, London: Allen & Unwin.

Freeman, R. E. (1984), *Strategic Management*, Boston: Pitman.

Friedman, A. L. (1977), *Industry and Labour*, London: Macmillan.

Friedman, H. and Meredeen, S. (1980), *The Dynamics of Industrial Conflict*, London: Croom Helm.

Gambling, T. (1977), 'Magic, accounting and morale', *Accounting, Organisations and Society*, 2, 2.

Gellerman, S. (1974), *Behavioural Science in Management*, Harmondsworth: Penguin.

Giddens, A. and Mackenzie, G. (eds) (1982), *Social Class and the Division of Labour*, Cambridge University Press.

Goldman, P. and Van Houten, D. R. (1981), 'Bureaucracy and domination: managerial strategy in turn-of-the century American industry', in Dunkerley, D. and Salaman, C. eds, *International Yearbook of Organisation Studies*, London: Routledge & Kegan Paul.

Goldner, F. H. (1970), 'The division of labor: process and power', in Zald, M. N., ed. (1970).

Goldsmith, W. and Clutterbuck, D. (1984), *The Winning Streak*, London: Weidenfeld & Nicolson.

Goldthorpe, J. H., Lockwood, D., Bechhofer, F. and Platt, J. (1968), *The Affluent Worker: industrial attitudes and behaviour*, Cambridge University Press.

Goodman, P. S., Pennings, J. M. *et al.* (1977), *New Perspectives on Organisational Effectiveness*, San Francisco: Jossey Bass.

Gouldner, A. W. (1964), *Patterns of Industrial Bureaucracy*, New York: Free Press.

Gruneberg, M. and Wall, T. (1984), *Social Psychology and Organisational Behaviour*, Chichester: Wiley.

Guest, D. and Horwood, R. (1980), *The Role and Effectiveness of Personnel Managers*, London: LSE.

Guest, D. and Horwood, R. (1981), 'Characteristics of the successful personnel manager', *Personnel Management*, May.

Guest, D. and Kenny, T. (1983), *A Textbook of Techniques and Strategies in Personnel Management*, London: IPM.

Gulik, L. and Urwick, L. (1937), *Papers on the Science of Administration*, New York: Columbia University Press.

Hackman, J., Oldham, G., Janson, R. and Purdy, K. (1975), 'A new strategy for job enrichment', *California Management Review*, 17: 57–71.

Hackman, J. R. and Oldham, G. R. (1976), 'Motivation through the design of work', *Organisational Behaviour & Human Performance*, 16: 250–79.

Hackman, J. R. and Oldham, G. R. (1980), *Work Redesign*, Reading, Mass.: Addison-Wesley.

Handy, C. (1976), *Understanding Organisations*, Harmondsworth: Penguin.

Handy, C. (1978), *Gods of Management*, London: Pan.

Hannan, M. T. and Freeman, J. H. (1977), 'The population ecology of organisations', *American Journal of Sociology*, 82: 929–64.

Harvey-Jones, J. (1982), 'How I see the personnel management function', *Personnel Management*, September.

Henstridge, J. (1975), 'Personnel Management – a framework for analysis', *Personnel Review*, 4.

Herzberg, F. (1966), *Work and the Nature of Man*, Cleveland, Ohio: World Publishing Company.

Herzberg, F. (1976), *The Managerial Choice: to be Effective and to be Human*, Homewood, Ill.: Dow-Jones-Irwin.

Herzberg, F., Mausner, B. and Snyderman, B. S. (1959), *The Motivation to Work*, New York: Wiley.

Hickson, D. J. (1966), 'A convergence in organisation theory', *Administrative Science Quarterly*, 11: 224–37.

Hickson, D. J. *et al.* (1971) 'A strategic contingencies theory of inter-organisational power', *Administrative Science Quarterly*, 16: 216–29.

HMSO (1968), *Report of the Royal Commission on Trade Unions and Employers' Associations*, London: HMSO.

Hollier, P. (1979), 'Top men and workers: the growing barrier', *Chief Executive*, September.

Hulin, C. L. and Blood, M. R. (1968), 'Job enlargement, individual differences, and worker responses', *Psychological Bulletin*, 69: 41–55.

Hunt, J. W. (1984), 'The shifting focus of personnel management', *Personnel Management*, February.

IPM (1963), 'Statement on personnel management and personnel policies', *Personnel Management*, March.

IPM Digest (1985), 'Personnel profile 9', *IPM Digest*, 236, March.

Institute of Manpower Studies (1984), *Flexible Manning – the way ahead*, London: IMS.

Jaques, E. (1951), *The Changing Culture of a Factory*, London: Tavistock.

Jaques, E. (1956), *Measurement of Responsibility*, London: Tavistock.

Jarrett, D. (1982), *The Electronic Office*, Farnborough, Hants: Gower.

Jenkins, C. (1973), 'Is personnel still underpowered?' *Personnel Management*, 5.

Jones, B. (1982), 'Destruction or redistribution of engineering skills?' in Wood, S. ed. (1982).

Joyce, P. (1980), *Work, Society and Politics; the culture of the factory in late Victorian England*, Brighton: Harvester Press.

Kanter, R. M. (1983), *The Change Masters: corporate entrepreneurs at work*, London: Allen & Unwin.

Koontz, H., O'Donnell, C. and Weihrich, H. (1980), *Management*, 7th ed., Tokyo Kogakusha/McGraw-Hill.

Kotter, J. P. (1982) *The General Manager*, New York: Free Press.

Kotter, J. P. and Lawrence, P. C. (1974), *Mayors in Action*, New York: Wiley.

Kudla, R. J. and McInish, T. H. (1984), *Corporate Spin-offs: strategy for the 1980's*, Westport, Conn: Quorum Books.

Lawler, E. E. (1971), *Pay and Organisational Effectiveness*, New York: McGraw-Hill.

Lawrence, P. (1980), *Managers and Management in West Germany*, London: Croom Helm.

Lawrence, P. R. and Lorsch, J. W. (1967), *Organisation and Environment*, Cambridge, Mass.: Harvard University Press.

Legge, K. (1978) *Power, Innovation and Problem-solving in Personnel Management*, London: McGraw-Hill.

Likert, R. (1961), *New Patterns of Management*, New York: McGraw-Hill.

Littler, C. (1982), *The Development of the Labour Process in Capitalist Societies*, London: Heinemann.

Littler, C. R. and Salaman, G. (1982), 'Bravermania and beyond: recent theories of the labour process', *Sociology*, 16, 2.

Littler, C. R. and Salaman, G. (1984), *Class at Work*, London: Batsford.

Locke, E. A. (1976), 'The nature and causes of job satisfaction', in Dunnette, M. D. (ed.), *Handbook of Industrial and Organisational Psychology*, Chicago: Rand McNally.

Lupton, T. (1964), *Industrial Behaviour and Personnel Management*, London: IPM.

McCall, M. W. Jr. and Lombardo, M. M., eds (1978), *Leadership: where else can we go?*, Durham N.C.: Duke University Press.

Maccoby, M. (1978), *The Gamesman*, London: Secker & Warburg.

Macfarlane, A. (1978), *The Origins of English Individualism*, Oxford: Blackwell.

McGregor, D. C. (1957), 'The human side of enterprise', *Management Development*, 46: 11, 22–8, 88–92.

McGregor, D. C. (1960), *The Human Side of Enterprise*, New York: McGraw-Hill.

Macpherson, C. B. (1962), *The Political Theory of Possessive Individualism*, Oxford: Clarendon.

Mangham, I. (1979), *The Politics of Organizational Change*, London: Associated Business Press.

Manning, K. (1983), 'The rise and fall of personnel', *Management Today*, March.

Mant, A. (1979), *The Rise and Fall of the British Manager*, London: Pan.

March, J. G. and Simon, H. A. (1958), *Organisations*, New York: Wiley.

March, J. G. and Romelaer, P. J. (1976), 'Position and presence in the drift of decisions' in March and Olsen (1976b).

March, J. G. and Olsen, J. P. (1976), *Ambiguity and Choice in Organisation*, Oslo: Universitetsforlagt.

Marks, W. (1978), *Politics and Personnel Management*, London: IPM.

Marsh, A. (1982), *Employee Relations Policy and Decision-making*, Aldershot: Gower.

Marstrand, P. ed. (1984), *New Technology and the Future of Work Skills*, London: Pinter.

Maslow, A. (1943), 'A theory of human motivation', *Psychological Development*, 50: 370–96.

Maslow, A. (1954, 1970), *Motivation and Personality*, New York: Harper & Row.

Maslow, A. (1965), *Eupsychian Management*, Homewood, Ill.: Irwin.

Mayo, E. (1933), *The Human Problems of an Industrial Civilisation*, New York: Macmillan.

Mayo, E. (1949), *The Social Problems of an Industrial Civilisation*, London: Routledge & Kegan Paul.

Merton, R. K. (1940), 'Bureaucratic structure and personality', *Social Forces*, 18: 560–8.

Meyer, M. W. (1978), *Environments and Organisation*, San Francisco: Jossey Bass.

Michels, R. (1949), *Political Parties*, Chicago: Free Press.

Middlemas, K. (1979), *Politics in Industrial Society*, London: Andre Deutsch.

Miles, R. E. and Snow, C. C. (1978), *Organisational Strategy, Structure and Process*, New York: McGraw-Hill.

Miles, R. H. (1980), *Macro Organisational Behaviour*, Santa Monica, California: Goodyear.

Miller, E. J. and Rice, A. K. (1967), *Systems of Organisation*, London: Tavistock.

Milton, C. R. (1970), *Ethics & Expediency in Personnel Management: a critical history of personnel philosophy*, Columbia, S. Carolina: University of S. Carolina Press.

Miner, J. B. (1976), 'Levels of motivation to manage among personnel & industrial relations managers,' *Journal of Applied Psychology*, 61: 419-27.

Miner, J. B. (1980), *Theories of Organisational Behaviour*, Hinsdale, Illinois: The Dryden Press.

Mintzberg, H. (1973), *The Nature of Managerial Work*, New York: Harper & Row.

Mintzberg, H. (1975), 'The Manager's Job', *Harvard Business Review*, July–August.

Mintzberg, H. (1978), 'Patterns in strategy formation', *Management Science*, 14: 9.

Mooney, J. D. and Reiley, A. C. (1931), *Onward Industry*, New York: Harper.

Mooney, J. (1947), *Principles of Organisation*, New York: Harper.

Mowday, R. T. (1979), 'Equity theory: predictions of behaviour in organisations' in Steers, R. M. and Porter, L. W. eds., *Motivation and Work Behaviour*, New York: McGraw-Hill.

Mowday, R. T., Porter, L. W. & Steers, R. M. (1982), *Employee-Organisation Linkages: the psychology of commitment, absenteeism and turnover*, New York: Academic Press.

Myers, C. S. (1920), *The Psychological Factor in Industry and Commerce*, University of London Press.

Nakagawa, K. ed. (1979), *Labour and Management*, University of Tokyo Press.

Niven, M. M. (1961), *Personnel Management 1913-1963*, London: IPM.

Northcott, J. and Rogers, P. (1982), *Microelectronics in Industry*, London: Policy Studies Institute.

Otway, H. & Pelton, M. eds (1983), *New Office Technology: Human and Organisational Aspects*, London: Pinter.

Ouchi, W. G. and Jaeger, A. M. (1978), 'Type Z organisation: stability in the midst of mobility', *Academy of Management Review*, 3: 305-14.

Ouchi, W. G. (1981), *Theory Z*, Reading, M.A.: Addison-Wesley.

Parkinson, C. N. (1957), *Parkinson's Law, and other studies in administration*, Boston: Houghton Mifflin.

Pascale, R. T. and Athos, A. G. (1982), *The Art of Japanese Management*, Harmondsworth: Penguin.

Perrow, C. (1970), 'Departmental power', in Zald, ed. (1970).

Perrow, C. (1977), 'Three types of effectiveness studies', in Goodman, Pennings *et al.* (1977).

Personnel Management (1984), 'News and Notes', *Personnel Management*, July.

Peter, L. J. and Hull, R. (1969), *The Peter Principle*, New York: Morrow.

Peters, T. J. (1978), 'Symbols, patterns and settings', *Organisational Dynamics*, 7: 3-23.

Peters, T. J. and Waterman, R. H. Jnr. (1982), *In Search of Excellence*, New York: Harper & Row.

Peterson, R. B. and Tracey, L. (1979), *Systematic Management of Human Resources*, Reading Mass.: Addison-Wesley.

Pettigrew, A. (1973) *The Politics of Organisational Decision-making*, London: Tavistock.

Pettigrew, A. (1979), 'On studying organisational cultures', *Administrative Science Quarterly*, 24: 570–81.

Pfeffer, J. (1978), 'The Micropolitics of Organisations' in Meyer (1978).

Pfeffer, J. (1981), 'Management as Symbolic Action', in Cummings and Staw (1981).

Pfeffer, J. and Salancik, G. R. (1978) *The External Control of Organisations: a resource dependence approach*, New York: Harper & Row.

Pfeffer, J. (1982), *Organisations & Organisation theory*, Boston: Pitman.

Pigors, P. and Myers, C. A. (1969), *Personnel Administration*, New York: McGraw-Hill.

Pitfield, M. and Palmer, R. (1981), 'The personnel student and the first job problem', *Personnel Management*, March.

Pollard, S. (1979), 'Two approaches to labour-management in Britain during the period of industrialisation', in Nakagawa, K., ed.

Pondy, L. R. (1978), 'Leadership as a language game', in McCall & Lombardo, eds (1978).

Poole, M., Mansfield, R., Blyton, P. and Frost, P. (1981), *Managers in Focus*, Farnborough, Hants: Gower.

Poole, M. (1973), 'A back seat for personnel', *Personnel Management*, 5.

Poole, M. *et al.* (1984), *Industrial Relations in the Future*, London: Routledge & Kegan Paul.

Prior, P. (1981), 'Toll the knell for leadership, the personnel man cometh', *Personnel Management*, October.

Pugh, D. S. and Hickson, C. D. (1976), *Organisational Structure: Extensions and Replications*, Farnborough, Hants: Saxon House.

Pugh, D. S. and Hinings, C. R., eds (1976), *Organisation Structure: extensions and replications, the Aston Studies II*, Farnborough, Hants: Gower.

Pugh, D. S. and Payne, R. L. (1977), *Organisational Behaviour in its Context: The Aston programme III*, London: Saxon House.

Purcell, J. (1981), *Good Industrial Relations*, London: Macmillan.

Quinn, J. B. (1980) *Strategies for Change: logical incrementalism*, Homewood, Ill.: Irwin.

Rauschenberger, J., Schmitt, N. and Hunter, T. E. (1980), 'A test of the need hierarchy concept', *Administrative Science Quarterly*, 25, 4: 654–70.

Rice, A. K. (1958), *Productivity and Social Organisation*, London: Tavistock.

Ritzer, G. and Trice, H. M. (1969), *An Occupation in Conflict*, Ithaca: Cornell University Press.

Robbins, S. P. (1983), *Organisation Theory*, Englewood Cliffs, N. J.: Prentice-Hall.

Robbins, S. P. (1983), *Organisational Behaviour: Concepts. Controversies and Applications*, Englewood Cliffs, N. J.: Prentice-Hall.

Roethlisberger, F. J. and Dickson, W. J. (1939), *Management and the Worker*, Cambridge, Mass.: Harvard University Press.

Rosenbrock, H. (1982), 'Technology and policy options', in Bjorn-Anderson *et al.*, eds (1982).

Rothwell, S. and Davidson, D. (1984), *Technological Change, Company Personnel Policies and Skill Deployment*, London: MSC.

Rothwell, S. (1984a), 'Integrating the elements of a company employment policy', *Personnel Management*, November: 31-3.

Rothwell, S. (1948b), 'Company employment policies and new technology in manufacturing and service sectors', in Warner, M. ed. (1984).

Salaman, G. (1982), 'Managing the frontier of control', in Giddens and Mackenzie, eds (1982).

Salancik, G. R. (1977), 'Commitment & control of organisational behaviour and belief', in Staw and Salancik (1977).

Schein, E. H. (1980), *Organisational Psychology*, 3rd edition, Englewood Cliffs, N. J.: Prentice-Hall.

Selznick, P. (1948), 'Foundations of the Theory of Organisation', *American Sociological Review*, 25-35.

Selznick, P. (1949, 1966), *TVA and the Grassroots*, Berkeley: University of California Press.

Selznick, P. (1957), *Leadership in Administration*, New York: Harper & Row.

Sethi, S. P., Namiki, N. and Swanson, C. L. (1984), *The False Promise of the Japanese Miracle*, London: Pitman.

Silverman, D. (1970), *The Theory of Organisations*, London: Heinemann.

Simon, H. A. (1948), *Administrative Behaviour*, New York: Macmillan.

Sloan, A. P., Jnr (1964), *My Years with General Motors*, New York: Doubleday.

Smith, M. *et al.* (1982), *Introducing Organisational Behaviour*, London: Macmillan.

Staw, B. M. and Salancik, G. R. (1977), *New Directions in Organisational Behaviour*, Chicago: St Clair Press.

Steers, R. M. (1975), 'Problems in the measurement of organisational effectiveness', *Administrative Science Quarterly*, 20: 546-58.

Stewart, R. (1963), *The Reality of Management*, London: Heinemann.

Stewart, R. (1976), *Contrasts in Management*, Maidenhead, Berks: McGraw-Hill.

Stewart, R. (1982), *Choices for the Manager*, Maidenhead, Berks: McGraw-Hill.

Stewart, R. (1983), 'Managerial Behaviour: how research has changed the traditional picture', in Earl, M. (1983).

Stogdill, R. M. (1974), *Handbook of Leadership*, New York: Free Press.

Storey, J. (1983), *Managerial Prerogative and the Question of Control*, London: Routledge & Kegan Paul.

Stouffer, S. A. *et al.* (1949), *The American Soldier vols I and II*, Princeton, N. J.: Princeton University Press.

Strauss, G. and Sayles, L. R. (1980), *Personnel: human problems of management (4th edition)*, Englewood Cliffs, N. J.: Prentice-Hall.

Taylor, F. W. (1911a), *Shop Management*, New York: Harper.

Taylor, F. W. (1911b), *The Principles of Scientific Management*, New York: Harper.

Terry, M. (1983), 'Shop steward development and managerial strategies', in Bain, ed. (1983).

Thomason, G. F. (1981), *A Textbook of Personnel Management*, London: IPM.

Thompson, J. D. (1976), *Organisation in Action*, New York: McGraw-Hill.

Thompson, P. (1983), *The Nature of Work*, London: Macmillan.

Thurley, K. (1981), 'Personnel management in the UK: a case for urgent treatment?' *Personnel Management*, August: 24–29.

Thurley, K. E., Reitsberger, W., Trevor, M. and Worm, P. (1980), *The Development of Personnel Management in Japanese Enterprises*, London: ICERD/LSE.

Torrington, D. and Chapman, J. (1979), *Personnel Management*, London: Prentice-Hall.

Townsend, R. (1970), *Up the Organisation*, London: Michael Joseph.

Trist, E. L. *et al.* (1963), *Organisational Choice*, London: Tavistock.

Tugwell, J. (1984), 'News and Notes', *Personnel Management*, September.

Turner, A. N. and Lawrence, P. R. (1965), *Industrial Jobs and the Worker*, Cambridge, Mass.: Harvard University Press.

Tyson, S. (1980), 'Taking advantage of ambiguity', *Personnel Management*, February.

Tyson, S. (1985), 'Is this the model of a modern personnel manager?', *Personnel Management*, May.

Urwick, L. (1944), *The Elements of Administration*, London: Pitman.

Vancil, R. F. (1979), *Decentralization: managerial ambiguity by design*, Homewood, Ill.: Dow Jones-Irwin.

Vroom, V. H. (1964), *Work and Motivation*, New York: Wiley.

Vroom, V. H. and Yetton, P. W. (1973), *Leadership and Decision Making*, Pittsburgh: University of Pittsburgh Press.

Wahba, M. A. and Bridwell, L. G. (1976), 'Maslow Reconsidered: a review of research on the need-hierarchy theory', *Organisational Behaviour and Human Performance*, 15: 212–40.

Warner, M., ed. (1984), *Microprocessors, Manpower and Society*, Aldershot: Gower.

Watson, T. J. (1976), 'The professionalisation process: a critical note', *Sociological Review*, 24.

Watson, T. J. (1977), *The Personnel Managers*, London: Routledge & Kegan Paul.

Watson, T. J. (1980a), *Sociology, Work and Industry*, London: Routledge & Kegan Paul.

Watson, T. J. (1980b), 'Understanding Organisations', in *International Yearbook of Organisation Studies*, Dunkerley, D. & Salaman, G., eds, London: Routledge & Kegan Paul.

Watson T. J. (1982), 'Group ideologies and organisational change', *Journal of Management Studies*, 19, 3: 259–75.

Watson, T. J. (1983), 'Towards a general theory of personnel & industrial relations management', *Trent Business School Occasional Paper 2*, Nottingham: Trent Polytechnic.

Weber, M. (1968), *Economy and Society*, New York: Bedminster Press.

Weick, K. E. (1979), *The Social Psychology of Organising*, Reading, Mass.: Addison-Wesley.

Wilkinson, B. (1983), *The Shopfloor Politics of New Technology*, London: Heinemann.

Williams, R. (1976), *Keywords*, London: Fontana.

Williamson, O. E. (1975), *Markets and Hierarchies*, New York: Free Press.

Winch, G., ed. (1983), *Information Technology in Manufacturing Processes*, London: Rossendale.

Winkler, J. (1974), 'The ghost at the bargaining table: directors and industrial relations', *British Journal of Industrial Relations*, 12.

Wood, S., ed. (1982), *The Degradation of Work?* London: Hutchinson.

Woodward, J. (1958), *Management and Technology*, London: HMSO.

Woodward, J. (1965), *Industrial Organisation*, Oxford University Press.

Woodward, J., ed. (1970), *Industrial Organisation: behaviour and control*, Oxford University Press.

Worcester, R. (1984), 'Keeping the tabs on public opinion'. *Personnel Management*, October.

Wright, M. and Coyne, J. (1985), *Management Buyouts*, London: Croom Helm.

Zald, M., ed. (1970), *Power in Organisations*, Vanderbilt University Press.

Index

For Product Safety Concerns and Information please contact our EU
representative GPSR@taylorandfrancis.com
Taylor & Francis Verlag GmbH, Kaufingerstraße 24, 80331 München, Germany